CORE

KU-558-781 ▶

‖‖‖ ‖‖ ‖ ‖‖‖‖‖‖‖‖‖‖‖ ‖‖ ‖‖‖‖ ‖‖‖‖‖‖‖‖ ‖‖ ‖‖‖

Dr. P.N. Chopra, Chief Editor of the *Collected
Works of Sardar Patel* was the Chief Editor, *Indian
Gazetteers* and *Who's Who of Indian Martyrs* of the
Ministry of Education, Government of India. He
is also the Chief Editor, *Towards Freedom* project
. the Indian Council of Historical Research. In
addition, he has written and edited more than forty
authoritative works on Indian history and culture.
These include *History of South India, Quit India
Movement of 1942, India — An Encyclopaedic
Survey, A Century of Indian National Congress,*
biographies of Maulana Azad and Sardar Patel and
A Nation Flawed: Lessons from Indian History,
published by Vision Books in 1997.

‖‖‖‖‖‖ ‖‖‖‖ ‖‖‖‖‖‖ ‖‖‖‖ ‖‖‖‖‖ ‖‖‖‖‖ ‖‖‖‖‖‖‖ ‖‖‖‖‖
8170 942969 0175 D9

CORE
STOCK

RELIGIONS
AND
COMMUNITIES
OF INDIA

Edited by
P. N. CHOPRA

Vision Books

(Incorporating Orient Paperbacks)
New Delhi ● Bombay ● Hyderabad

CORE
STOCK

WOLVERHAMPTON LIBRARIES	
1 2 NOV 2005	
81709429690175D9	
H J	341698
200.954 CHO	£9.99
ALL	✓

First Published 1998
Reprinted 2001

ISBN 81-7094-296-9

© P.N. Chopra, 1998, 2001

Published by
Vision Books Pvt. Ltd.
(Incorporating Orient Paperbacks & CARING Imprints)
24 Feroze Gandhi Road, Lajpat Nagar-III
New Delhi 110024 (India).
Phone: (+91-11) 6836470/80
Fax: (+91-11) 6836490
E-mail: visionbk@vsnl.com

Printed at
Rashtra Rachna Printers
C-88, Ganesh Nagar, Pandav Nagar Complex,
Delhi-110092 (India).

CONTENTS

PREFACE

NDIA IS A MULTILINGUAL COUNTRY, with different communities, castes and subcastes professing different religions, traditions and customs. This apparent diversity among its people makes India one of the most fascinating countries in the world.

Religion has played an important part in the lives of Indians from the earliest times, as in the case of many other ancient nations of the world. From the pre- and proto-historical periods up to the recent times, it assumed numerous forms with manifold designations in relation to different groups of people associated with them. Religious ideas, thoughts and practices differed among these groups, and transformations and developments took place in them in course of time. These changes were very often brought about by the ideas and actions of intellectual thinkers, while environment and association also played a major part in the process. Religion in India was never static in character. An inherent dynamic strength was indeed at the root of various religious movements that marked this country's history and culture.

With a population of more than 850 million*, India is the second most populous country in the world exceeded only by its northern neighbour, communist China.

---

* All population figures as per 1991 census.

Although over 687.6 million, i.e. 82 per cent of the people are Hindus, there are close to 101.6 million Muslims in India, more than anywhere else in the world except Indonesia. In addition, there are followers in substantial numbers of almost all the faiths in the world. Christians of various denominations (19.6 million), Sikhs (16.3 million), Buddhists (6.4 million), Jains (3.3 million), besides Parsis and Jews and those of animistic tribal religions (3.7 million).

Although the actual partition of the subcontinent in 1947 between India and Pakistan was determined largely on the basis of Hindu-Muslim distinction, India has given herself a secular constitution which guarantees every citizen the right to freedom of worship. In spite of this, however, religion is a pervasive influence that permeates all aspects of the society. A deep concern with life in relation to the supernatural is shared by all Indians. As rightly pointed out by Arnold Toynbee in *A Study of History*, the Indian civilisation shows a definite tendency towards a predominantly religious outlook. In the words of Mahatma Gandhi "religion covers the whole gamut of life in this country".

No wonder there has been a tremendous interest, the world over, in the religions of India — their sects and subsects, castes and subcastes which influences their style of living. The Hindu caste system, it is interesting to know, has greatly influenced the adherents of other faiths in India. Although Islam, Buddhism, Christianity, Sikhism and other religions profess the equality and brotherhood of man, in India they have developed some form of a modified caste social structure. It is not Hinduism alone which has been divided into various sects and subsects such as Chitpavans, Ayyangars, Khatris, etc., other religions consist of similar divisions and this is a unique feature of Indian society. Besides two principal branches of Islam, i.e. Shia and Sunni, there are many other subsects such as Moplahs, Bohras, etc. Similar is the case with the Sikhs, the Christians, the Jews and the Parsis.

We are living in an age of conflict and confusion. Man cannot recognise man. In order to break the barriers of communication between us it has become imperative to gain an understanding of the people around us; their identity, traditions,

culture, religious creeds, historical and socio-economic background — an understanding that is a precondition for the
establishment of a rapport between groups of people and which
in turn is a must for the development of human understanding,
mutual co-operation and harmonious living. *Religions and
Communities of India* attempts to provide this "understanding"
of the various Indian communities and religions, placing their
various groups in a proper perspective.

For centuries, Hindus and Muslims — the two largest communities in India — lived in peace and harmony, with respect
for each other. The recent past, however, has seen the development of misapprehensions and distortions about each other or a
lack of clear perspectives of each other. *Religions and Communities of India* has been compiled with the aim to provide the
readers with the best and most informative material on Hindus,
Muslims, Christians, Sikhs, Buddhists, Zoroastrians and so
forth. There are also separate articles on: Chitpavans, Ayyangars,
Nayars, Khatris, Kayasthas, Coorgis, Harijans, Ayyars, Banias,
Nagars, Reddis, Bunts, Kashmiri Pandits, Bhotias, Ahirs,
Ezhavas, Lingayats, Moplahs, Bohras, Khojas, Ahmadiyyas and
various other communities.

Although there are a number of works on the major religions
of India, there is hardly any comprehensive study of all the
castes and subcastes, groups and subgroups, their beliefs, rituals
and manners, customs and ceremonies, etc. together — a study
so very important for an understanding of the religions of India
in their proper historical perspective. This book intends to fill in
this lacuna and will serve as a source of reference for all those
interested in Indian society, culture and religions. Distinguished
scholars who have specialised in their respective fields have lent
to this work the benefit of their scholarship and have written the
various chapters, sections and subsections which have been made
use of by the editor in presenting a coherent and objective study
of Indian society.

I am obliged to Shri Khushwant Singh, formerly editor of the
Illustrated Weekly of India, who very kindly permitted me to
compile these articles in the form of a book. I would like to
mention that the articles have been edited thoroughly so as to
present an integrated account of the various castes and

communities which inhabit this land, and this sometimes involved additions and some alterations in their original form.

The first edition of this book which was brought out in 1982 was widely welcomed by the press and the public and its copies were sold out in a short time. There has been a persistent demand for second and, if possible, an abridged edition for the general public in India and abroad. Keeping this in view a revised edition which omits cumbersome details of the religions and communities, their castes and subcastes but at the same time retains their salient and important features is now being published in paperback so that it could be within the reach of all those interested in this multilingual country which is inhabited by almost all the religions of the world.

I am grateful to my wife Dr. Prabha Chopra, a scholar in her own right, for the meticulous care with which she read the various sections of the book and her suggestions for its improvement. I would also like to thank Dr. P.K.V. Kaimal for carefully reading the proofs. I am also thankful to Kapil Malhotra of Vision Books for undertaking the publication of this book.

New Delhi   P.N. CHOPRA
January 1998

1

HINDUISM

THE RELIGION PROFESSED BY THE ARYANS (the ancient Indians) came to be known as Hinduism. The four Vedas were their first sacred books, the earliest literature extant in the world, dating back to c. 3000-1500 BC, and were written in archaic Sanskrit. The earliest, the *Rig Veda,* contains the hymns and invocations to be recited at Vedic rites and sacrifices. The *Sama Veda* is a collection of verses from the same hymns with some later additions. The *Yajur Veda* is a book of mystical formulae and prayers while the *Atharva Veda* is composed mostly of incantations, spells and medical recipes and is an ancient book on magic conserving some of the most primitive traditions of the Indo-Aryan people. But it was not till about 800 BC when the Upanishads came to be written, that the emphasis shifted to what one might term 'religion' or spiritual knowledge and the Vedic gods began to be merged in the idea of an eternal, impersonal principal, neither male nor female, called Brahman or Atman.

Hinduism has neither a single founder nor a scripture; nor, too, does it have a clearly defined creed to which allegiance must be owed. It is, in fact, a way of life. A Hindu may be a monotheist monist or idolator, and a vegetarian, cow-worshipper or beef eater.

It subscribes to the doctrines of karma, reincarnation and transmigration of souls and salvation (*moksha*). Opinions differ on whether salvation means the preservation of the individual soul (*jivatma*) as a separate entity enjoying eternal bliss or its extinction (*nirvana*) or loss of identity in the oversoul or Brahman. Hinduism does not subscribe to the concepts of original sin or eternal damnation. Its doctrines vouchsafe repeated opportunities for self-perfection.

The question of the origin of Hinduism is complex because it involves language, race and beliefs. During the Vedic period, Rudra was the important god and Vishnu occupied only a minor place. Gradually, the great Vedic gods like Indra, Agni, Pushan, the Aswins, Varuna and the Visvedevas began to decline and their place was taken by other deities. The ancient gods are no longer a part of popular Hinduism and are invoked only during Vedic rituals. Goddesses like Kali and Sitaladevi (Mariamman in the South) must have been local deities which were absorbed into an all-embracing Hinduism.

Hindus, as a people, are the product of the intermingling of many races such as the Huns, Scythians, Mongols, Dravidians, Australoids and Mediterraneans. The Rigvedic Aryans probably formed an important part of the Indus Valley Civilisation (2500 BC) and contributed their share to its evolution.

Castes and Communities

Caste is a distinctive feature of the Hindus, although the division of society into four classes was also known to ancient Iran (Atharvas, Rathestas, Vestria, Fahouyanta and Huiti).

The Brahmana is said to have sprung from Purusha's face, the Kshatriya from his arms, the Vaisya from his thighs and the Sudra from his feet. According to the *Mahabharata*, the four castes are distinguished by their colour: white for the Brahmanas; red for the Kshatriyas; yellow for the Vaisyas; and black for the Sudras, a theory difficult to accept because it signifies an arbitrary division. The division must have evolved over some centuries and it is more reasonable to presume that it was based on functions performed: priesthood and the pursuit of knowledge indicating the Brahmanas; wars and governance, the Kshatriyas; trade and agriculture, the Vaisyas; and menial work and crafts, the Sudras.

This division gave Hindu society stability, cohesiveness and self-sufficiency but it also led to the exploitation of large sections of the population, the denial of many rights to them and produced a static community which became fragmented with the emergence of subcastes too numerous to be kept count of.

The 687.6 million Hindus (Census of India, 1991) are also split into sects on the basis of faith or region. Two sects of Brahmanas may belong to the same tradition but they do not usually have a sense of identity. Traditionally, the Brahmanas have a six-fold function: learning the Vedas and imparting their knowledge; performing sacrifices and officiating at them; giving gifts and receiving them. In some parts of India only one section is qualified to perform the first-mentioned in each of the three functional groups. A Vaisya is not entitled to participate in any of these functions but can only hear the Vedas and give gifts and a Sudra can only give gifts.

The caste system was probably not very rigid in ancient times and Brahmanas sometimes chose vocations other than priest-hood. Dronacharya, the great Brahmana teacher of the *Mahab-harata*, taught archery. Visvamitra, a Kshatriya, is said to have attained Brahmanahood. Rivalries between Brahmanas and Kshatriyas were not uncommon. Inter-caste marriages were also known; in the *Mahabharata*, King Santanu married a fishergirl and his son by her, Chitrangada, succeeded him as ruler.

The Kshatriyas today are members of most of the erstwhile Hindu ruling families and belong to the warrior caste but other communities whose caste position is not clear are also regarded as Kshatriyas, such as the Coorgis and Nayars, though they do not wear the sacred thread, the Khatris of North India, the Marathas, and the Nayudus of Andhra Pradesh and Tamil Nadu.

The Kayasthas are said to be those who lost their true Ksha-triya status when they became the clerical class. They are to be met with in Uttar Pradesh, Bihar and Bengal. In Maharashtra they are known as Chandraseniya Kayastha Prabhus. Vaisyas are more easily identified such as the Bania of Gujarat, the Chetti (derived from the Sanskrit *sreshthi*) of the South; and the Agarwal of the North.

Many castes or communities take their names from their professions or occupations: the Baidyas of Bengal (who enjoy the status of Brahmanas) were originally *vaidyas* or physicians.

Occupational labels are more common among the lower social orders such as Chamar (cobbler), Chakkiliyan (oil-monger), Ambattan (barber), Chaliyan (weaver), Lohar (smith), Barhai and Asari (carpenter), Dhobi and Vannan (washerman), etc.

There are many communities in India whose caste status is not determined and intermarriages have also resulted in inter-mediate castes. In Kerala, there are the Ambalavasis (literally temple-dwellers) who take such names as Pisharoti, Warrier (Variyar) and Kurup who are regarded as a step above the Sudras though their exact caste position is not known.

According to the anthropologist, Risley, there are 2,378 main castes among the Hindus. Although the occupational basis of caste has lost much of its meaning, caste prejudice exists even among various sections of the so-called lower orders and has been a major obstacle to Hindu integration and Indian unity.

The original Brahmana law-givers thought in terms of establishing only an intellectual and moral aristocracy and not a class of exploiters. In course of time, however, the Brahmanas departed from these high standards and began treating the other castes with contempt. In the latter part of the twentieth century, the tide began to turn and in many states of India the Brahmana is discriminated against in several ways such as admission to colleges and job recruitment. In addition, affirmative action leading to reservations in jobs and higher education for back-ward castes became a feature of India's political landscape after independence.

Customs and Rituals

Many a misconception about Hinduism abounds even today. For instance, one cannot say definitely if marriage is a sacrament among all castes. Contrary to belief, widow remarriage was originally allowed among Hindus, particularly among the scheduled castes and other backward classes and even divorce was not unknown, for instance among the Nayar community.

Polygamy was allowed but was not common and was confined to the ruling sections and big landowners. The idea of one wife only at a time was glorified in Rama's *ekapatni* in the *Ramayana*. Childlessness, however, was often a reason for a man to take a second wife. A classic case of polyandry was that of Draupadi, the wife of the five Pandava brothers in the *Mahabharata*. It was practised by the Nayars and Ezhavas until a few decades ago and is still practised in some sub-Himalayan regions.

Marriage and morals have not been the same throughout Hindu history. The institution of marriage is attributed to Svetaketu. In Vedic times, adultery was not looked upon as a moral sin. In the Upanishads there is the story of Jabaia who admitted he did not know who his father was. The system of *niyoga* allowed a woman, for the sake of her illegitimate child, to resort to a man other than her husband. Even illustrious sages are believed to have conferred on childless women the benefit of their seed. The custom of a widow marrying her husband's brother was also probably prevalent.

In succeeding centuries the rules of marital conduct became stricter and chastity, especially for women, was held up as the highest ideal.

Both endogamy and *sapinda* exogamy were observed. *Sagotra* marriages are traditionally not permitted among the twice-born castes.

Today, marriage taboos differ from community to community. In the South, marriages between cousins are common but are frowned upon in the North. The Hindu Marriage Act of 1955 bars marriage within five generations on the father's and three on the mother's side, permits the marriage of cousins where this is customary and also *sagotra* marriages.

Whatever the law, for most Hindus, marriage is still an inviolable sacrament which must be performed by priests. For Brahmanas, the rite of *panigrahanam* (the bridegroom holding the right hand of the bride) and *saptapadii* (taking seven steps round the holy fire) are the supreme rites that unite the couple. For most southern Hindus, the *tali* or *mangalasutra* (gold beads or pieces of gold strung on a cord) is a symbol of matrimony. The dowry system and the custom of matching of horoscopes of the bride and groom still prevail.

Except for matrilineal communities like the Nayars, Hindus are traditionally governed by two main schools of law in matters of succession and inheritance. Under the *mitakshara*, more commonly followed, the son has a vested interest in his father's ancestral property, the women relatives having a share only in the deceased's share of the ancestral property. Under the *dayabhaga*, applicable in Bengal and Assam, the father is the absolute owner. Although women had no right to property, they received recompense in the form of *stridhana* (woman's wealth) which was passed on from mother to daughter and they had certain natal and conjugal rights. According to the Hindu Marriage Act of 1955, all women are heirs.

The position of Hindu women has been a subject of controversy. Manu said, "The father takes care of her in childhood, the husband in youth, the son during old age. A woman does not deserve freedom". But it was this same lawgiver who also said that the gods would abandon a place where women were not honoured or that "the gods reside where women are honoured".

Sakti (feminine power) is a unique Indian concept. The Saiva manifestation of *Arddhanarisvara* (half woman, half man) integrates the female and male principles of life.

Though women were held in high esteem in ancient times, some Vedic hymns being attributed to women seers (like Gargi who figured in philosophical disputes), later tradition debarred women from learning the Vedas. Hindu custom also propagated the concept of woman being man's *sahadharmini* (both acting together, living together in pursuit of *dharma* and being together at the performance of most rituals). Vedic marriage rites proclaim that the bride is the mistress of the bridegroom's household and that she must rule over it.

The epics and the Puranas glorified chastity. A *pativrata* (woman who was devoted to her husband) was credited with superhuman powers and could even ignore the gods with impunity and from this concept, perhaps developed the later practice of sati and the ban on the marriage of widows in some castes. Even in the matter of marriage, care was taken not to lower their status — hypergamy (*anuloma*) was allowed but not hypogamy (*pratiloma*).

Hindus preferred sons to daughters not only because of the belief that it qualified them for the next world but also because daughters proved a burden when it came to getting them married.

Contrary to the general belief, vegetarianism was not extolled in ancient Hindu times and even Brahmanas ate meat as do the Brahmanas of Kashmir and the central Himalayan region today, while those of Bengal and the Gaud Saraswats eat fish.

There is evidence in the Vedas and the epics of the wide prevalence of drinking and meat-eating. Rama, a Kshatriya, was a meat eater. Nala, the legendary king, also excelled in making meat dishes. In the *Uttararamacharitam*, Bhavabhuti mentions that an animal was specially slaughtered for that greatest of Brahmana preceptors, Vasishtha.

It is doubtful that vegetarianism was due to the influence of Buddhism (Buddha himself is reported to have died of eating pork). It is possible that Jainism and ahimsa (the concept of non-violence) contributed to the vegetarian cult in some areas, notably Gujarat. Most Hindus, however, have been and are meat-eaters, the only prohibited item being beef. The majority of Buddhists today are non-vegetarians.

In its later development, Hinduism viewed all creation as one and developed the attitude of what Schweitzer calls "reverence for life" — an attitude reinforced by the doctrine of the transmigration of souls and ahimsa that is embedded as an ideal in the Hindu mind as deeply as the belief in karma. Nevertheless, it is full of contradictions and *ahimsa* (non-violence) and *himsa* (violence) go together.

Some orthodox Hindus do not eat root and bulb vegetables. For ceremonies (like *sraddha*) it is customary to use only indigenous vegetables. The Upanishads even equate food with the *Brahman* and consider food or *annam* as being one of the several coverings of the *Atman*.

Before he takes his food the Brahmana is enjoined to sprinkle water on and around it, reciting the names of the three worlds (*Bhuh, Bhuvah* and *Suvah*). The rice must be mixed with clarified butter. He starts his meal by first invoking the *Brahman* and the winds or vital airs (*prana, apana, vyana* and *samana*) which have different functions in the human body and are associated with important nerve centres.

In the *Bhagavad Gita* Krishna says, "Leaf, flower, fruit, water — I accept whatever is offered to me with devotion". The food is placed before the deity and the devotee invokes the vital airs and makes a pretence with his right hand of carrying the offering (*naivedya*) to his *devata*. In Vedic ritual, food is conveyed to the gods through the agency of fire, who are sustained by what is offered to them by mortals by the performance of *homa* or *havan* (a form of sacrifice).

Water plays an important part in Hindu ceremonies. There is nothing more auspicious than a *kumbha* (water-pot) with a coconut and mango leaves. It also represents Varuna and all the sacred rivers — the Ganga, Yamuna, Godavari, Saraswati, Narmada, Sindhu and Kaveri.

Hindu life and rituals are governed by various *sutras* (Sanskrit sayings or collections of sayings as texts) or aphorisms, chief among the authors of which being Apastamba, Baudhayana and Asvalayana. These *sutras* are the *srautasutras* (defining Vedic ritual), *grihyasutras* (laws for the householder), and *dharmasutras* (the general law of human conduct).

The *smritis* (what is remembered or the compilation of an oral tradition) deal with *achara* (rules of conduct and practice); *vyavahara* (judicature); and *prayaschitta* (penance). Among the authors of the *smritis* are Manu, Yajnavalkya, Parasara, Katyayana, Apastamba and Vasishtha.

The general basis of the sutras is constituted by *varnasrama* (or caste); the four stages of life: those of the student, householder, forest dweller and *sanyasin* — though it is doubtful if any Hindu today "dwells in the forest", the percentage of those who have become *sanyasins* being very small; and *purusharthas* or the objectives of man, which are the pursuit of duty (*dharma*), wealth (*artha*), desire (*kama*) and salvation (*moksha*).

The *dharmasastras* are based on the concept of *svadharma* (one's own *dharma* or one into which one is born) and the prime duty of a man is to perform it to perfection to earn merit and even qualify for release from the cycle of births and deaths.

An entire philosophy is based on this concept. The *Bhagavad Gita* says: "Better is one's own *dharma*, though imperfectly performed, than the *dharma* of another well performed".

Caste, *dharma*, *svadharma* — all knit society together as a fabric, give every individual a role and fit all the varying roles together so as to enact smoothly the *dharma* of life. *Dharma*, which defines and seeks to enforce these roles, is an expression of the cosmic order or the pivot on which the entire social mechanism turns.

Aparigraha (non-possession) is expected to be a Brahmana's ideal and he is expected to set an example in truthfulness, kindness and self-sacrifice.

One's *svadharma* is inexorable as it is determined by birth, by the fruits of one's karma and not by choice and in every caste there is the opportunity to attain the highest ideal of *moksha* and merit and rebirth into a higher class. The supreme virtue is to become assimilated with the timeless, immemorial, absolute role which one has acquired by birth, a process not of self-dissolution but of self-discovery.

The *dharmasastras* lay down rules for ritual, regulation of caste life and the expiation of offences against *dharma* in general. There are sixteen main samskaras which are prescribed and which apply mostly to the higher castes.

The first is *garbhadhanam* the consecration of the procreative act. The mantra (incantation) recited on the occasion says: "May Prajapati be the impregnator, may the Creator give the embryo."

Jatakarma is performed at birth. The child is fed with honey and ghee as the following hymn is chanted: "May thou live a hundred years, protected by the gods. May Indra bestow on thee his best treasures. May Savitri, may the Asvins grant thee wisdom." The naming ceremony or *namakaranam* is performed on the eleventh day. *Annaprasanam* (feeding the child with rice for the first time) and *chaulam* (tonsure) are the childhood *samskaras*.

Upanayanam (bringing near to a preceptor and initiation by wearing the sacred thread) is to be performed in the fifth or eighth year, though nowadays no age limit is observed. Samavaratanam, which formally signified the conclusion of pupilship, is observed before marriage which is one of the most important *samskaras*.

The Hindu death ceremony, called Aparakriya, is elaborate. The eldest son performs the obsequies. For ten days he offers *til* (sesame) and water to appease the hunger and thirst of the spirit caused by *dahana* (destruction by fire). The purpose is to ensure the passage of the deceased to a desirable state as, for a whole year after death, the spirit is a *preta* and is elevated to the world of the ancestors only by the performance on the first death anniversary, of which the most important is *Sapindikaran* (uniting the departed spirit with its ancestors by joining together balls of cooked rice). The *Sraddha* ceremony, performed on the death anniversary, signifies remembering one's forefathers.

A day in a Hindu's life is governed by the caste or sect to which he belongs. A Brahmana must perform the *sandhyavan-danam* (twilight prayer) at dawn and dusk, make oblations to the sun god and recite the Gayatri mantra (the greatest of the mantras). At midday he must do the Gayatri *japa*. His other devotions may include the reading of portions of the sacred books, the recitation of the thousand names of Vishnu, Lalita or Devi and the worship and praise of his *ishtadevata* (deity of one's choice) or a number of deities.

Special initiation into certain mantras which are believed to have esoteric meanings is done by gurus. There is an entire science of mantras dealing with the significance of formulae for repeated utterance, the hidden meaning behind their phonetic structure and the time and method of their use.

Though the Vedas extol co-operative endeavour, (a famous hymn says: Let us act together, let us be of one mind) congrega-tional prayer is not common except during certain festivals but there is group participation in singing hymns (*bhajans*). Many of the *bhajan mandalis* are of a sectarian character or are dedicated to preceptors of Hinduism who have emerged in recent times.

Hindu Sacred Places

For Hindus, India is a sacred land. Its rivers and mountains are deemed worthy of worship and journeys to religious centres or certain special temples, a sacred obligation. The *Mahabharata* and the Puranas have numerous passages relating to holy places. Kashi (Varanasi), the most celebrated (which acquired importance in later Vedic times), is primarily a Saiva centre and has been the religious and intellectual capital of Hindu India for at least two millennia. To die there and be cremated on the banks of the Ganga is for the Hindu a means of attaining *moksha*.

Rameswaram is another Saiva centre, the popular belief being that Kashi must be visited first and after water has been procured from the Ganga, the pilgrimage made to Rameswaram to wash the lingam there with that water. According to the Saiva tradition, there are many kinds of *lingams* among which are those representing the five elements. Some of the important centres which are associated with these *lingams* are Srisailam, Kalahasti and Chidambaram.

The confluence of rivers are specially sacred, the most famous being Prayag (Allahabad), the meeting place of the Ganga, the Yamuna and the mythical Saraswati. Great gatherings are held here periodically (particularly on the Makar Sankranti day in the month of Magha) as Hindus believe that much merit accrues if a bath is taken at the confluence on these occasions. Hardwar, another ancient place of pilgrimage, is associated with Daksha (one of the primeval progenitors). Gaya and Nasik are among the sacred places preferred for performing the rites for departed relatives and at Gaya one may perform a *sraddha* for oneself; Kurukshetra, Mathura and Vrindavan are associated with the life of Krishna; Puri is famous for the car festival of the god Jagannath; Kamakhya is a one-time Shakta centre; Kanchipuram, Gokarna, Dwaraka and Sringeri are other important centres of pilgrimage.

The temple of Venkateswara in Tirupati (in Andhra Pradesh) attracts more pilgrims than any other shrine in India. Pandharpur (in Maharashtra), Bhadrachalam (Andhra Pradesh), Tiruchendur and Pazhani (in Tamil Nadu) and Guruvayur and Sabarimala (in Kerala) are popular centres of worship.

Festivals

Festivals are observed according to the lunar and solar calendars. The new year's day of those who follow the solar calendar, falls on the vernal equinox (*Vishu*) in mid-April. There is no common new year's day for those (mostly in the North) who observe the lunar calendar. In Gujarat, the first day of the year is the one following Diwali and for some communities it is the first day of the month of *Vaisakha* in the Hindu calendar.

The birthdays of the deities are celebrated according to the lunar calendar. Janmashtami is on the eighth day of the waning moon of Sravana, when scenes of joy on the birth of Krishna are re-enacted, particularly in Gokul; Ramanavami, on the ninth day of the bright half of Phalguna celebrates the birthday of Rama; and Ganesh Chaturthi, on the fourth day of the waxing moon in Bhadrapada, when clay images of Ganesha, the remover of obstacles and the god of beginnings, are made and he is worshipped with certain herbs, a festival which has a special importance in Maharashtra.

Navaratri (the first nine days of Asvina) has a different significance in different parts of India. The tenth day, Dussehra, is Vijayadasami, the day of victory, when people in the North burn effigies of Ravana and and his younger brother, Kumbhakarna, symbolising their slaying by Rama. Navaratri is the most important festival for Bengalis and is associated with Durga. In the South the accent is on Saraswati and Navaratri is celebrated in South Indian households with a display of dolls.

Diwali or Dipavali (garland of lamps) falls in Kartika when every Hindu house is illuminated with myriads of small *divas* (oil lamps) as are many buildings, etc. Many who are not Hindus also illuminate their houses and Diwali is regarded as India's common festival being celebrated alike by Sikhs, Jains, Buddhists and others. It is not observed in Kerala where Onam (derived from the name of the asterism, Sravana) is the most important festival. Onam is associated with Vamana, an *avatar* of Vishnu, who banished the *asura* (demon) emperor, Bali, to the nether world.

Basant Panchami is the festival that ushers in the spring. Holi is the spring festival. It symbolises the destruction by fire of evil personified by Holika, the demon sister of Hiranyakasipu. On the day after Holi people throw coloured water and coloured powder on one another with great abandon and meet friends and relatives in a spirit of affection and comradeship. This festival is not popular in the South, except in parts of Andhra Pradesh, Karnataka and Tamil Nadu.

Sivaratri (in the month of Magha) is more a day of piety than of festivity. It is observed in honour of Siva. Upakarma (coconut day) is celebrated in Maharashtra and falls on the full moon day of Sravana.

Beliefs and Philosophy

Many Hindus worship trees and snakes and certain animals. They adore thousands of gods and goddesses and their progeny. According to them there is a creator, a preserver and a destroyer — Brahma, Vishnu and Siva respectively.

Hinduism holds that there is only one Reality and that the multiplicity of divine personalities represents various aspects of one God. Hinduism also stresses that this Reality has no attributes, that it cannot be described, and that it is beyond time and space. The Hindu who bows before a thousand gods also says, *Aham Brahmasmi* ("I am Brahman").

A characteristic feature of Hinduism is its universalism, catholicity of outlook and its readiness to see the truth in other faiths.

Hinduism is comparatively free from dogmas and its doctrines of karma and *samsara* welcome rational investigation. Karma is not a matter of blind belief. It means that one is responsible for one's actions and reaps their consequences, and that one's future will depend on what one has done. Thus it stands for a rational order in the realm of moral action. Nor does it mean resignation to fate. An important teaching of the *Bhagavad Gita* is that there should be determination, initiative and drive in the performance of one's duty.

Samsara means the empirical process from birth to death and from death to birth, a process every living being goes through, the particular manner of its existence in any given span of life depending on its past karma with the option of making its future better or worse.

Social institutions like caste, etc., which change from time to time, are not a part of the core of Hindu religion. Originally, caste was based on occupation and obligations and became hereditary only subsequently. The system was evolved to keep the social fabric in a harmonious condition but in later ages it became divisive, rigid and uncompromising with its labyrinth of castes and subcastes including the relegation of a large section (the Sudra caste) outside the pale of civilisation to be considered untouchables.

In the seventh, eighth and ninth centuries, there developed the great Bhakti cult in the Tamil country with the rise of the Vaishnava Alvars and the Saiva Nayannars. Men and women of high and low degree, walked from place to place singing devotional songs in Tamil in praise of Vishnu and Siva. Their message was that the path of *bhakti* (or devotion to a personal God) was open to all, the only pre-conditions being a desire for liberation from material bonds and a willing and loving self-surrender. In time the movement produced such great names as those of Mirabai (c. 1450-1547), Chaitanya (1469-1539), Tulasidas (1532-1623), Ramananda (c. 1360-1470), Kabir (1440-1518), Nanak (1469-1539) and Tukaram (1608-1649).

Hindus worship either one deity (of their choice) or more than one, among whom are Vishnu, Siva, the three most important Saiva deities — Ganesha (to some he is Vaishnava), Murugan and Ayyappa; also Rama, Krishna, Hanuman, Saraswati and Devi (the latter called by many names including Durga, Lakshmi, Parvati, Amba or Amman). The Mother Goddess has a special appeal for the Hindu mind. She symbolises fertility, prosperity and freedom from fear. Devi worship in the past was a part of the Sakti cult.

The various deities of Hinduism portray various aspects of nature and or the Supreme Power. With the deities removed, much of the beauty and poetry of Hinduism would vanish.

There is a curious belief among Hindus that religion is meant for old age. This is possibly the result of distortion of the concept of the four *asramas* or stages of life: *brahmacharya* (studentship and celibacy), *grahasthya* (householder's life), *vanaprastha* (forest dwelling) and *sanyasa* (renunciation).

The Upanishads, along with the *Brahma Sutra* of Badarayana and the *Bhagavad Gita,* constitute the basis of Hindu theistic philosophy. Sankara, Ramanuja and Madhava wrote epoch-making commentaries on these three texts.

Some of the great exponents of Hindu philosophy and the main points of their teaching are highlighted below.

Advaita or monism is an original concept of Hindu thought. Its basic idea is inherent in the Vedas but it was Shankara (AD 738-770) who developed it as one of the significant tenets of Indian philosophy. It seeks to establish the identity of the *Atman* with *Brahman.* It is not that the *Atman* is a part of the *Brahman,* which is the whole, but that the *Atman,* without the limitations placed on it, is the *Brahman.* The limitations and feeling of separateness are due to *avidya* (lack of enlightenment) or *adhyasa* (error)and *jnana* is the means of liberation.

A life-long celibate, Sankara interpreted the *Brahma Sutra* in a spirit of compromise between ascetics and householders. Life's journey could be undertaken meaningfully, without renouncing the world, provided one's duties were performed in the proper manner and with the religious values in mind. With four chosen disciples, he established four centres for the order of *sanyasins* and for religious learning: Dwaraka, Puri, Badrinath and Sringeri.

Ramanuja (1037-1137), who systematised Visishtadvaita (qualified monism), held that the supreme soul is not impersonal (as Sankara theorised) but an entity possessing the finest qualities. The individual soul is related to the absolute and has no separate existence. *Moksha* is to be obtained by surrender to a personal God *(prajapati).* For him, the phenomenal world is real, as is *jiva* or individual soul, with God dwelling in it. For Ramanuja karma and *jnana* are steps leading to *bhakti.*

Basava (twelfth century), the great Virasaiva (Lingayat) leader, revolted against the caste system as a negation of the doctrine of fundamental unity. He was the founder of the Lingayat sect.

Madhava (b. 1238) is the exponent of Dvaita or dualism. Madhava regarded the distinction between the *Brahman* and *jiva* as real and held that salvation can be achieved only through a mediator who imparts knowledge. The distinction between the phenomenal world and individual *jivas* is absolute but it is qualified in the sense that the *jivas* are one with the absolute.

Among other famous Hindu philosophers were Prabhakara and Kumarila, who upheld the supremacy of the Vedas: Vedantadesika (next in importance to Ramanuja in Visishtadvaita); Nimbarka (to whom the world was no illusion); Vallabha (who propounded the doctrine of Suddhadvaita or pure non-dualism); and Jnanesvar (who wrote a Marathi commentary on the *Bhagavad Gita*).

Hindu tradition has always recognised asceticism as a way of life. The earliest reference to the ascetic community is found in the *Rig Veda* which says 'Indra is a friend of the *munis*' and mentions *yatis,* or the self-controlled.

In the *Taittiriya Aranyaka* of the *Yajur Veda,* there is a passage narrating the emergence of three types of *rishis,* consequent to the penance of Prajapati: Arunas, Ketus and Vatarasenas.

Hindu sadhus belong to several distinct orders, each paying homage to the founder of his group and his living guru. In principle, a sadhu represents the highest values of the spiritual world, is accepted as a spiritual leader and is expected to set an example for the people of the world, in thought, word and deed.

Each type came to represent a particular trait of asceticism, the prime objectives being celibacy, austerity, concentration and ecstasy.

With asceticism developed the Yoga system and Brahma was identified with meditation and the powers of the mind.

Celibacy remains the prime trait of asceticism. The list of legendary life-long celibates ends with Svetaketu and Rishabha (c. ninth century BC). The former is known for his contribution to philosophy and the latter for laying the foundations of a school of thought that led the way to Jainism.

Asceticism came of age with Mahavira, the Jain Tirthankara, and the Buddha and later the Jain and Buddhist monastic orders institutionalised asceticism.

The Kapalins and Pasupatas are the two Saivite ascetic sects of the seventh century referred to in the Upanishads. Huien

Tsang, the famous Chinese (Buddhist) monk who visited many Buddhist sites in India, gives a description of the Pasupatas of North India. The Buddhists, Jains, Pasupatas and Kapalikas formed the ascetic world of India till the end of the eighth century. But there were non-denominational ascetics also and it was from this group that the renowned philosopher and celibate, Sankara, hailed.

Excluding the Jain *munis* and the Buddhist *bhikkus*, Indian sadhus fall into two broad groups: the Saivites and the Vaishnavites. The former are generally grouped as Dasanamis, Dandis, Paramahamsas or Brahmacharis.

The Dasanami school consists of ten orders: Aranya, Asrama, Bharati, Giri, Parvata, Puri, Saraswati, Sagara, Tiratha and Vana.

A Saivite sadhu wears ochre garments which are cut and stitched. He carries a panther skin on his shoulders and has a three-finger *vibhuti* mark (signifying the cult of Siva) on his forehead.

The Vaishnavite sadhus fall into different groups, according to their philosophical predilections. Ramanuja, Ramananda, Nimbarka, Vallabha, Madhava and Chaitanya are the main founders of the various sects.

Tulasi *malas* and a vertical caste mark of two white lines with a black dot in the centre are characteristic of all Vaishnava sadhus, except the followers of Ramanuja (who wear the Triphala caste mark) and the Chaitanyas.

The branches of certain groups are known as *Dwaras.*

The Kabirpanthis, followers of Kabir, set in motion a reformist movement by rejecting idol worship and caste system, and by not attaching any importance to pilgrimages. A Kabirpanthi ascetic wears a pyramidal cap of white material. A 108-bead tulasi *mala* is also worn at times.

Other reformist sects include those of Radhavallabhi, Rasika, Dhami, Dadupantha, Karunadasi, Ramansanehi, Garibadasi and Swaminarayana.

The naked (*nanga*) sadhus are to be found both in the Saivite and Vaishnavite groups.

Apart from sadhus and swamis, the yogis form a distinct section of the "holy men" community of India. The Nathapanthi and Aghorapanthi are the two broad divisions of the Yogi order. The Yogis claim to represent the earliest ascetics in respect of self-control and the power to rise above the world of ordinary beings. The ultimate spiritual strength gained by them is believed to give them the power to make all their wishes come true, to change their form, shape and size at will and to exercise full control over their senses and resist any temptation.

The Upanishadic yogis sought inner strength both on the physical and the mental plane for greater powers of concentration and self-realisation. In time, certain groups channelised this strength to realise ecstasy on the sensual plane.

The *Maitri Upanishad* laid down the six steps of the yoga system: *pranayama, pratyahara, dhyana, dharana, tarka* and *samadhi*. Patanjali's *Yoga Sutra* details eight *angas* or limbs of yoga, omitting *tarka* and adding three more to the earlier steps: *yama, niyama* and *asana*.

"By cleansing the *nadis,* the *prana* is restricted, the digestive fire is kindled, internal sound is heard and one becomes disease-less" — this, according to Gorakhanatha, is the final objective of the Hathayogis, the practitioners of physical yoga. Breath control is also practised by the yogi for acquiring occult powers. Siva, who is often depicted in temples in yogic postures, is considered to be a *mahayogi*.

In course of time certain cults and movements developed, usually because of the genius and zeal of an individual. Some were based on certain aspects of Hinduism, such as Bhakts, or were reformist and seceded from orthodoxy. Some of the important movements that developed particularly in the nineteenth century are briefly described in the next chapter.

2

HINDU RELIGIOUS ORDERS
AND MOVEMENTS

Brahmo Samaj

In the nineteenth century Bengal, corruption, judicial malpractices, polygamy, child marriage, persecution of widows, caste intolerance and domination by Brahmanas were a part of life and led to acute social injustice.

The person who first protested against this growing lack of humanism and social degradation was Raja Rammohun Roy. The Brahmo Samaj grew out of the weekly meetings held in 1828 by Raja Rammohan Roy for those who wished to worship one God without regard to caste, creed or nationality. In 1830, a specially constructed building in Calcutta was consecrated for its use (which is now used by the Adi Brahmo Samaj).

Rammohun Roy left for England in 1830. During his absence the work of the Samaj was carried on by Ramchandra Vidyavagish, the first minister or *acharya* who was appointed by Rammohun. Rammohun Roy died in England in 1833.

Devendranath (the eldest son of Dwarkanath Tagore) had studied the old Sanskrit scriptures and with the help of Vidyavagish started a society called the Tattva Bodhini Sabha (Truth-Teaching Society). He joined the Brahmo Samaj in 1843 in a formal public ceremony and brought new life into the movement. He started a monthly journal known as the *Tattva Bodhini Patrika* which contained discussions on faith and translations of the Vedas and Upanishads.

At first the Brahmos accepted the Vedas as infallible but later a group of believers broke away and Devendranath and the other leaders also gave up their belief in the infallibility of the Vedas and replaced it with belief in one God. He compiled the *Brahmo Dharma* containing texts from the Hindu scriptures illustrating the principles of natural theism and this major change in belief was announced at the anniversary festival of 1850.

He then began a series of visits to different parts of the country to spread the word of the Samaj and to start active groups. A band of dedicated missionaries and preachers was trained and sent to small towns and major villages.

In 1858, Keshab Chandra Sen (grandson of Ram Kamol Sen, and orthodox aristocrat) joined the Samaj. In 1864 he visited Madras and Bombay and aroused public interest and the Ved Samaj of Madras was established (now known as the Southern India Brahmo Samaj). The Bombay Prarthana Samaj came into existence in 1867.

For some years the Samaj attracted new members willing to usher in social and religious reforms. But a time came when Devendranath did not see eye to eye with Keshab Chandra and, being the sole surviving trustee of the Samaj, replaced the younger workers with the previous office bearers.

In 1866 Keshab and his followers started the Brahmo Samaj of India. Freed of restriction, this progressive group began a national campaign of visits by missionaries and distribution of books and leaflets. In Calcutta, Bengali replaced Sanskrit in Brahmo prayers and the movement gained universal appeal as Keshab introduced the reading and study of scriptures from almost every known religion. The prayer meetings of the Brahmo Samaj of India became imbued with great devotional fervour.

A progressive group now gained force in the Brahmo Samaj of India which wanted a constitutional type of church government with trustees to take care of the *mandirs* and a separate group to work and press for radical reforms.

The group formed its own Sadharan Brahmo Samaj in 1878 and through it was spread the theistic message of the Samaj. In 1880 a prayer hall was dedicated in central Calcutta. The Brahmo Samaj of India retained their prayer hall and all their previous resources. The old missionaries and many new followers remained faithful to Keshab Chandra Sen's Samaj which in 1880 he renamed the Navavidhan (new dispensation) and started publishing *The New Dispensation* with a symbol denoting the unity of the religions of the world on the cover.

The Navavidhan introduced many novel mystic forms of worship such as the placing of the family income on the family altar and mixed Hindu and Christian rituals when ordaining ministers. The philanthropic work of the Brahmo Samaj included the establishment of school for boys and girls, orphanages, homes for unmarried mothers, schools for girls and the deaf and dumb and famine relief centres.

Today the differences between the Sadharan, Navavidhan and Adi Brahmo Samaj occur only in certain observances and the old rivalries have more or less been forgotten.

The Brahmo Samaj is not a community but a brotherhood and its members can belong to any faith, caste or status. They believe in a God without form and there are no idols, images or symbols in their places of assembly. There are about ninety Samajs in the country. Nor does the Samaj believe in priesthood. Any member who is familiar with the tenets of the Brahmo Samaj may take the place of the person appointed to conduct the service.

Despite its service to educational and social progress, the Brahmo Samaj has succeeded in influencing mainly the educated middle class. It could not reach the masses because it did not compromise with idolatry and caste intolerance. The Brahmo Samaj functions today as a passive movement which has succeeded in contributing to certain basic rights and reforms for which it agitated throughout the past century, arousing the consciousness of thinking Indians.

Arya Samaj

The Arya Samaj was born in Bombay in 1875 but flourished at Lahore. Its founder, Mool Shankar Tiwari (1824-83) (who became famous as Dayanand Saraswati) sought to combat the influence of Christian missionaries by strengthening Hinduism and ridding it of antiquated and corrupt practices. He reinterpreted the Vedas, emphasising their universal application and propagated a rational religion based on monotheism, a caste system based on vocation, not birth, equality of the sexes and rejection of idol worship.

Though Dayanand came from Gujarat, he found his following mainly in the Punjab, Haryana and west Uttar Pradesh. The last seventeen years of his life were spent in preaching his message. Dying eight years after its birth, he did not get enough time to nourish it but the initial momentum imparted to it by him was so enduring that in a few years the Arya Samaj had spread all over northern India.

After fifteen years of wandering, which brought him face to face with the weaknesses of Hinduism, he arrived at Mathura and knocked at the door of a blind Punjabi *sanyasi* and a Sanskrit grammarian, Virjanand, after association with whom, Dayanand became a *sanyasi*. He was also responsible for Dayanand's etymological interpretation of the Vedas and his rejection of the Puranas, the backbone of popular Hinduism. Virjanand held that only the *arsha granthas* (original sacred books) revealed to the *rishis* were true and all others were false.

At this time the writings of Christian missionaries were filled with the hope that before long the whole of India would be won for Christianity and for the missionaries the most vulnerable feature of Hinduism was its idol worship. This was the situation when Dayanand came on the scene. Even in his childhood, Dayanand had been assailed by doubts on the validity of this mode of worship and when he went to the Vedas for light, he found no sanction there for idolatry.

Varanasi was the stronghold of Brahmanism and it was Dayanand's greatest desire to convert it to his views as this would help him in his life's task of extirpating idol worship and orthodoxy. Idolatry was also a lucrative source of income for Brahmana priests and at first they tried to win him over with tempting offers of *mahantship*. When they failed, they began plotting against him and about a dozen attempts were made against his life. But he remained steadfast to his convictions and rejected as un-vedic not only idolatry but also the related concepts of polytheism and god incarnation and substituted for these the concept of monotheism (but not Semitic monotheism). In the end his enemies had him poisoned and he died in 1883.

Christian mission schools were popular with Indians because they imparted knowledge of English (without which no good positions could be held in government service) and the study of science. But the thought of Indian students coming under the influence of Christian missionaries was not countenanced by Indians who nevertheless felt the need for schools where Western education could be imparted without the children's faith in their own religion being imparted.

In these circumstances the Arya Samaj started the Dayanand Anglo-Vedic College at Lahore in 1886, the first non-government and non-Christian college in the Punjab. Further, the spirit of reform did not remain confined to the sphere of religion; it invaded the social field also and customs like child marriage, forced widowhood, bigamy, untouchability and women's illiteracy were also militated against.

The concept of equality, which Western education emphasised and the new economic order which came in the wake of the advent of the British in India, demanded a reappraisal of the caste system. The Arya Samaj substituted the fourfold *varna vyavastha* for the caste system and based it on functions and occupations rather than on birth, and under its new dispensation, any person could practise any profession, none being considered derogatory though he would still be allotted one of the four *varnas* (Brahmana, Kshatriya, Vaishya or Sudra) according to his choice of profession. The first shoe shop opened in Lahore was by a high caste Hindu. The Aryas promoted many new lines of commerce and trade, such as the Punjab National Bank.

Though the regeneration of Hindu society remained his main preoccupation, Dayanand dreamed of a world order in which the Vedas would be accepted as the only revealed knowledge of God, the Arya (Hindu) nation would assume the leadership of all other nations and Aryavarta (India) would have suzerainty over all other countries.

Though he did not campaign actively for political independence and in a way felt grateful to the British government for being allowed freedom of expression, he was the herald of *swaraj* and *swadeshi.* He proclaimed in the *Satyarth Prakash,* the manifesto of the Arya Samaj, that "good government is no substitute for self-government".

The first to welcome the Indian National Congress to the Punjab were the Aryas and the first political agitation in the Punjab (which started in 1898 against the agrarian laws) was led by them. Lajpat Rai and Ajit Singh, the first deportees from the Punjab on sedition charges, had been brought up in the Arya Samaj fold. In 1909, a large number of Aryas were prosecuted at Patiala for their allegedly seditious activities. But as the leaders of the Arya Samaj were apprehensive that a direct clash with the government would impede the useful work the Samaj was doing for the Hindus, it was decided that it would remain a purely religious institution.

In spite of this, when Mahatma Gandhi launched his non-co-operation movement in 1920, the more radical elements in the Arya Samaj joined the Indian National Congress.

The Arya Samajists believe in the *shuddhi* movement (accepting into the fold of Hinduism after a ceremony of purification, converts from other religions). Their chief concern was the halting of the conversion of Hindus to Islam. Muslims denounced the Arya Samaj's *shuddhi* movement as an obstacle in the way of accord with the Hindus. Anyone who dared to induce such conversions or any Muslim who turned apostate, was in danger of his life. Twenty-four Aryas were killed as a result of this type of strife, one being Shraddhanand, founder of the Gurukula Kangri at Hardwar. A few years before his assassination in 1926, he had been given the unique honour of addressing a Friday prayer meeting from the pulpit of the Jama Masjid of Delhi, an honour never accorded to a Hindu before or since.

The social reform movement of the Arya Samaj also embraced cow protection, eradication of untouchability, advocacy of vege-tarianism and teetotalism and the recognition of a person according to his *guna* (qualities), karma and *svabhava* (temperament) and not lineage. It also endeavoured to convert Christians to Hinduism and organised philanthropic work.

Today the Arya Samaj is a force and has spread over the entire country and to East Africa, South Africa Mauritius, Guyana, Trinidad, Singapore, Bangkok and other places. There are thousands of Arya Samaj branches all over the world. Arya Samaj also runs hundreds of high schools and primary schools, *gurukulas*, Sanskrit schools, schools for Harijans, technical institutes, orphanages, gymnasiums and hostels, newspapers and periodicals and libraries.

Brahma Kumaris

Brahma Kumari is a sect of sadhu and non-sadhu men and women which has no prescribed scriptures and no guru, and professes that its belief teaches its members to worship Siva through Pita Shriji, who became the corporal medium of God in 1937 and has since then been called Prajapati Brahma.

There are more than two hundred Brahma Kumari centres in the world with the main centre at Mount Abu in Rajasthan. The organisation finances itself by voluntary donations from members and does not accept any money from outsiders. According to their belief, Sahaj Rajyoga (the yoga of the intellect) is the means of the realisation of God. Their principles include vegetarianism, celibacy and abstinence from liquor. — *Similar to christian Values.*

Bharat Sadhu Samaj

The Bharat Sadhu Samaj is an organisation of the sadhus of the country. Its basic aim is to raise the moral standard of the people and has over ten thousand members of all orders and sects. Its head office is at Delhi. It does volunteer work where and when necessary. Its membership is open only to those who have renounced the world. It is aided in its mission by private donations and public loans.

The Theosophical Society

Although not really a Hindu movement, the Theosophical Society was inspired by the philosophy and mysticism inherent in Hinduism and came into being through the efforts of the celebrated Russian-born occultist, H.P. Blavatsky, and her American colleagues, B.S. Olcott, W.Q. Judge and thirteen others who established the society in New York on 17 November 1875.

Their motivation was the "wisdom of the east" and their desire for the "spiritual regeneration of man". They declared themselves to be the disciples of an Indian *mahatma*, a *jivan-mukta* (liberated soul) dwelling in the Himalayas, himself a member of *samsara* (the ocean of births and deaths) but who remained "in incarnation to help the world on its upward path" and they turned to India for inspiration and strength and moved the headquarters of the society to India in 1879. In 1882 they chose a site on the banks of the Adyar (in Madras) for its permanent headquarters which is visited by hundreds of thousands of people every year and is a shrine of all religions. The main hall has bas-reliefs representing the founders of the world religions — Christ knocking at a closed door, signifying the call of the God without to the God within; the Buddha in meditation; Krishna, flute in hand, leaning on a cow; Zarathushtra; a verse from the *Koran* inscribed on the wall; symbolic representations of Jainism, Buddhism, Judaism, Sikhism, Confucianism and other faiths of the world, including those which have only a historical interest today such as the beliefs of ancient Egypt and Mexico and Mithraism.

The society has autonomous national branches in some sixty countries of the world with the international president being elected once in seven years by the vote of the world membership. One of the first five was Annie Besant who was British by birth but Indian by choice.

The objectives of the society are the forming of a nucleus of the universal brotherhood of humanity without distinction of race, creed, sex, culture, philosophy and science; and the investigation of the unexplained laws of nature and the powers latent in man. The real danger that had to be safeguarded against in the search to develop the powers latent in him, was man's laying far too much stress on the psychic rather than the spiritual. The true occult life is the renunciation of the self in the service of all life.

The interest in theosophy of A.P. Sinnett (editor at that time of the Allahabad newspaper, *The Pioneer*) and his compatriot, Alan Octavian Hume (a co-founder of the Indian National Congress) was first aroused by the material objects and other phenomena that Blavatsky produced (through her occult powers) "from the air" — a cup and saucer, in as good condition today as when materialised nearly a hundred years ago (and preserved in Adyar), the sound of temple bells and much else but only when there was a (high) purpose to be served and not for satisfying curiosity or producing a sensation.

By "spiritual means", Blavatsky carried on a correspondence between Sinnet on the one hand and with Koot Hoomi and Morya (her guru), the two *jivan-muktas* who are described as the real founders of the society. Sinnett used to forward his letters to her which she transmitted to them by "thought transference" and related occult methods. Replies were sent by them through similar occult means, "precipitated" in English on sheets of paper. The originals of these are now in the British Museum and the letters have been published in a 524-page volume, *The Mahatma Letters to A.P. Sinnett.*

In these letters the Mahatmas emphasised that they wanted "a brotherhood of humanity, a real universal fraternity to be started ... an institution which would make itself known throughout the world and arrest the attention of the highest minds". This became the real objective of the society which teaches the brotherhood of man and of all life, basing itself on the Vedantic, Gnostic, Hermetic, Platonic and Universal Truth of the unity of all life in God. The main doctrines of theosophy are that the soul is immortal; God is good and immanent in all life and matter; and as a man sows, so shall he reap.

Sri Lankan C. Jinarajadasa, the fourth international president of the Society (1946-53), described theosophists as the forerunners of the United Nations as they have encircled the world with the idea of brotherhood. He said that the conception of the undying, immortal nature of man had to be brought into all world policies by the Theosophical Society and that theosophists were "the red cross of mankind".

Theosophists have worked for the promotion of harmony, understanding and mutual respect among the religions. Much of theosophical lecturing and literature has concerned itself with the comparative study of religions, tracing their essential unity and reverentially analysing their teachings.

The society's Adyar library and research centre has books on indology and the promotion of oriental learning. Started in 1886 by Olcott, it has some 17,500 palm leaf and paper manuscripts from many countries and more than a hundred and fifty thousand books on the religions, philosophies and cultures of the world, and on occultism and the spiritual life, in most of the major languages. It has published some two hundred books on indological subjects and scholars from the West and the East use them for research.

Theosophists all over the world regard India as the home of true religion and as the spiritual teacher of the world. The Indian section is numerically the largest national section of the society and has influenced large numbers who are not professed theosophists.

There are several organisations somewhat parallel to the Theosophical Society at Adyar, which draw their inspiration and their teaching from Blavatsky but have a separate and independent existence. Some of them think that her teachings have undergone a transformation in certain aspects at the hands of some leaders of the Adyar Society and they prefer to revert to the original form in which it was originated by her.

There are many branches of the Society in the world — the Theosophical Society at Pasadena, California; the Theosophical Society with its headquarters at Unterlengenhardt, Germany; the United Lodge of Theosophists, with its main office at Los Angeles and branches in several countries including Holland, India, Canada, England, France and Australia; and the Anthroposophical Society, founded in 1912 in Germany, which is a section that broke away from the parent body at Adyar and is active in some countries.

There is a great deal of co-operation between these offshoots of the theosophical movement, which is given voice through the monthly journal, *Theosophists Reunite,* which is published in California

3

HINDU COMMUNITIES
THE BRAHMANA CASTE

TRADITIONALLY THERE ARE FOUR HINDU CASTES: Brahmana, Kshatriya, Vaisya and Sudra, an arrangement of hereditary groups in a hierarchy. In Vedic times a caste was associated with a hereditary occupation or profession. In course of time, however, every member of a particular caste did not necessarily continue to practise the occupation associated with it. Certain socio-economic changes that took place in India in the last few decades affected the caste system considerably. For instance, the impact of education and the consequent change in social institutions. A certain standardisation of the Indian society was also brought about with the broadening of contacts within it as well as with the outside world. Also, education and certain economic factors created the need for taking up employment outside the hereditary occupation. As a result the caste restrictions are not so meticulously observed now as they were some decades ago. A brief description of some of the various communities belonging to the four castes follows.

The Anavil Community

The origin of the Anavils is traced to the period of Rama. According to the *Skanda Purana,* when Rama was returning from Lanka with Sita after killing Ravana, he came to the hermitage of Agastya which was situated in a dense forest on the southern slopes of the Vindhya hills. At the great *rishi's* bidding, Rama decided to perform a solemn act of expiation at Anadisidha, for the slaying of Ravana. But as there were no Brahmanas (without whom he could not perform the *yajna*) some Ajachak Brahmanas were summoned from Gangakulgiri in the Himalayas. Rama offered them a handsome *dakshina* but they would not accept it and insisted that they had merely performed their duty. Displeased with their refusal, Rama deprived them of the privilege of teaching the Vedas and performing *yajnas*. Like the Vaisyas, their function in society became agricultural. It is said it was these Brahmanas who became the progenitors of the people of the Bhathela or the Anavil caste, the subdivisions of which are the Naik and the Vashi.

Another version of the story goes that after the performance of the sacrifice, Rama gave several villages as gifts to the Brahmanas, the names of the villages apparently being reminiscent of names connected with Rama — Sitapur, Hanumanbari, Lakshmanpur and Vanarvel. The Brahmanas were advised by Rama to settle down there and the place came to be known as Anaval, Rama himself establishing the deity of Anavils (Shukleshwer Mahadev) there. This place was also known as Anadipur, Anadipatan, Anaditirth and Anadikshetra. It is situated in the Bulsar district, eight miles from Mahuva near the Kala-Amba railway station and can be reached from the Bilimora station on the Western Railway.

Brahmanas, numbering 12 thousand belonging to twelve different *gotras,* came from the Himalayas and were married to daughters of the Sesha tribe.

Of the twelve clans, ten preferred to settle in Anavil or Anandipur, as it was then called. Two clans shifted to a place known as Kantarsvami, now called Katargaun (near Surat) and another to Varitapiya which came to be known as Vashis.

The Anavils claim that they are the descendants of the *rishis* of the *Yajur Veda* period, like Vasishtha, Atri, Kashyapa, Bharadwaja, Kanva and Gautama.

Anaval was once upon a time a flourishing city. There is a reference in Abul Fazal's *Ain-i-Akbari* which mentions that "Anaval had a stone fort".

Historical records show that Anavil Brahmanas were a ruling class and carried on administration from their city over an area of 1,280 square kilometres. The town had ninety temples dedicated to Siva.

Their administrative acumen can be gauged by the fact that during the Mughal period seven forts in south Gujarat were in their charge — Saler, Muller, Gambhirgadh, Suvarnagadh, Rupgadh and Anaval, those in charge being called Naiks.

On the eleventh day of Vaisakha of Vikram Samvat, 1152, that Anaval was destroyed following a surprise attack by a Bhil warrior, Vanshia, when it was celebrating the marriage of seven hundred girls. In the massacre that followed, hundreds perished and many brides committed *sati,* warning the people against settling in the town for another nine hundred years and no Anavil lives there now. Most of the survivors settled in the Surat district, twenty-eight families went to Abrikh Abram and the Anavil commander, Samdhar Vashi, settled in a village which he named Palsana, after his two sons, Pala and Sana.

With the help of Maharaja Siddharaj Solani, he succeeded in killing Vanshia but did not reoccupy Anaval because of the curse laid on it. He requested the maharaja to rule over the place and whenever a king was enthroned there, the Anavils from Palsana were invited to perform the coronation ceremony.

The Anavil Brahmanas are the earliest settlers in south Gujarat. Unlike other Brahmanas, all Anavils are laymen or *grahasthas* and it was under their management that south Gujarat was brought under tillage. Being land-owning farmers, the Anavils enjoyed a dominant position in south Gujarat but did not exercise any priestly function or accept any *dakshina.*

They are normally known as Desais. Under the Mughals and the British they were given the work of collecting the revenue but the Surat Desais were more than mere government servants appointed to superintend the collection of land revenue.

They were so firmly established in position that in many cases a large group of villages was distributed among the members of one family, each of whom styled himself 'Desai'. As manager of a village or group of villages, the Desai was also called *talukdar,* a position in which he exercised the function of a *patel* or village headman, collecting rent from different cultivators. The Anavils also played an important role in the development of Surat and many areas in the city were named after the Desais.

In the earlier part of the twentieth century, many joined the Railway and insurance companies. For years, what is now the Western Railway was called the Anavila Railway because most of the employees were Anavils.

The Anavils played a big part in India's freedom struggle. During Mahatma Gandhi's famous Dandi March, the Navsari district was the hub of the struggle when hundreds of people, young and old, laid down their lives.

There are several hundred thousand Anavils spread over hundreds of villages between the cities of Surat and Vapi in the state of Gujarat as also in cities like Bombay, Ahmedabad, Surat and Navsari. Hundreds had settled in Africa but because of the ill-treatment of Asians in that continent, many either returned to India or migrated to England.

The Andhra Brahmana Community

The Andhra Brahmanas can trace their origin to the time of the Brahmana Satavahana dynasty, one of the earliest recorded in their history (c. second century BC to AD second century) which was a period of prosperity for the region as well as a time of Brahmanical achievement.

Andhra Brahmanas, born to learning and nurtured in it, were often of invaluable help to their rulers who rewarded them suitably. Copper-plate charters of the Chalukya rulers (sixth to thirteenth century) record the extensive grants made to the members of this community. Their competence led to the rulers appointing them in secular posts.

This also created one of the main subdivisions of the community on the basis of pursuits, the religions being followed by the Vaidikis and the secular by the Niyogis (a word which comes from *niyogani,* meaning employment). The Vaidikis continued the traditional occupation of priesthood, observing Vedic rituals and vows; officiating at ceremonies; expounding the sacred books and the *Mahabharata* and the *Ramayana* to the royal family and the public; and serving as temple priests and astrologers. Since Brahmana tradition had to be perpetuated, some of their time was given to teaching. The Vaidikis were either looked after directly by their royal patrons or were settled in the *agraharams* (villages) given as gifts for their maintenance. Some lived on alms, which was devoid of stigma, being ordained by the scriptures. The Niyogis also followed Brahmana tradition in their personal lives.

During the Chalukya rule, a number of Brahmana families from Tamil Nadu and Karnataka settled in Andhra. They formed the nucleus of the Dravida sect of the Telugu Brahmana community. The Telugu kingdom under the Vijayanagar rulers (AD 1336-1646) extended its sphere of influence as more and more opportunities for important posts came the way of these people. This period also saw the burgeoning of Telugu culture all over south India. A number of Telugu Brahmanas migrated to and settled in Tamil Nadu and Karnataka and assimilated some of the customs of the Brahmanas there, both parties benefiting by the association. The Telugu Brahmanas, for their part, produced great musicians, Kshetrajna and Tyagaraja who was also a great saint poet as was Narayana Tirtha and more recently like Visvesvarayya and Radhakrishnan, who was a leading philosopher as well. The only cultural element that suffered in the process was Kannada as when the Telugu Brahmanas settled in Karnataka, its language lost its purity and lyrical quality.

Some of the subsects of the Vaidikis, which evolved long ago on a regional basis, are the Velanadu, Mulakanadu, Kasalnadu, Veginadu, Koneseema, Telaganyam, Karnakammulu, and Parthamasakis. The subsects of the Niyogis, which are based mostly on distinctions of employment, are Nandavarikulu, Kammalu, Desalavayulu and Pranganadu. In times past the distinctions of each sect were jealously maintained by it and intermarriage was not permitted but these distinctions and restrictions are slowly wearing away.

Apart from these divisions based on occupational or regional differences, there are the sects based on faith: the Madhavas, Saivas (numerically the largest group) comprising the Smartas who worship all the gods of the Hindu pantheon and the Lingayats or

Virsaivas who wear lingas on their persons and proclaim the supremacy of Siva. At one stage during the mediaeval period, the conflict between the Virasaivas and the Vaishnavas was so bitter that it threatened to split the community. This was in the twelfth century when the linga cult was popularised by Basava of Karnataka and his contemporary, Mallikarjuna, a Telugu Brahmana. Calling themselves Aradhyas, the followers of this cult tended to be extremists. A most unusual decree called for a woman to leave her husband if he did not follow the cult and to "sacrifice" herself to a practising Aradhya.

Vaishnavism was present among Telugu Brahmanas as far back as the second century. In the twelfth century the stirring lyrics of Jayadeva found their way into Andhra adding a poetic dimension to the Bhakti cult. This inspired a number of artistic works in Andhra which were suffused with devotion. Inspired by divine ecstasy, Potana, a Telugu Brahmana poet, wrote the *Bhagavata*. The love of Krishna and the need to seek redemption through divine grace found expression in the creation of two major classical dance styles — Kuchipudi and Bhagavata Mela.

It is believed that during the proselytising crusades of the Vaishnavas, some Smartas were converted but continued to dominate Telugu Brahmana society and Saivism continues to remain a pervasive force in the community.

As in the rest of India, the Andhra Brahmana's confrontation with the modern age has caused many a compromise with tradition and orthodoxy. Within the community there is a definite trend towards modernisation but this trend is not very marked. They still cling to certain attitudes, especially regarding women and though education for girls is acceptable, it is mostly meant to enhance their matrimonial projects. A woman's role is strictly limited to the home and the family and the dowry system exists in one subtle form or another though forbidden by the law.

The Telugu Brahmana shares many temperamental characteristics of the Andhras in general. He is excitable but amiable; quick to take offence at any attempt to belittle his honour or status; frank to the point of bluntness; and emotional, impulsive and gregarious; by and large he is nevertheless, a hearty person.

The Telugu flair for humour is seen in the *chatuvulu* (humorous verses) composed on the spot and based on contemporary events and characters. Srinatha, a colourful character of the fifteenth century, wrote a number of these, wittily exposing flaws in the social fabric.

The community has not been lacking in pioneers of social reform. The dowry evil, child marriage, the miserable condition of widows, *sati* — all have been targets of attack. Many Telugu Brahmanas rallied to the call for national independence.

Cultural Contribution

The development of Telugu literature owes much to the great Brahmana trio, Namnaya Bhatta, Tikkana and Yerapragada, who between them completed the monumental translation of the *Mahabharata*, created new styles and enriched the vocabulary of the language. Srinatha started the romantic movement by using the prabandha form of literary composition. Telugu literature received a great impetus under the Vijayanagar kings and their viceroys, the Nayakas, and to which the Brahmanas contributed one outstanding writer, Allasani Peddanna, the poet laureate of Krishnadevaraya. Even today many of the outstanding writers in Telugu are Brahmanas.

To the arts of dancing and music the community has contributed out of all proportion to its size. Siddhendra, a Brahmana, who was a scholar and mystic wrote, it is said, at the behest of Krishna, a great dance drama, *Bhama Kalapam*. Not happy with the *devadasi* system he gathered a few Brahmana boys and taught them a particular style of dancing but as they were ostracised by the community, he moved his troupe to another small village and settled there. As they were actors, the village came to be known as Kuseelapuram, later corrupted to Kuchipudi, from which this style of the dance came to take its name.

The Bhagavata Mela dance drama, another dance form, was also created by a Telugu Brahmana, Narayana Tirtha and twelve other dance dramas, which form the basis of mela repertoire today, were created by another Telugu Brahmana, Melatur Venkatarama Sastri.

In Andhra, from the earliest times, the *devadasis* (temple dancers) had Brahmana gurus. The Yakshagana, another form of the dance drama, now so popular in Kanara, owes its origin to the authorship of and performance by Telugu Brahmanas.

Born in Tiruvarur (near Tanjavur) in a Telugu Brahmana family, Tyagaraja (1767-1847) spent a life time expressing his ecstatic *bhakti* for Rama in hundreds of songs in Telugu. He built upon the Karnataka system of music giving it a form and supplying the living grammar of music that has survived to this day. He composed a few operas such as *Prahlad Bhakti Viayaur* and *Nauka Charitram* and over seven hundred *kritis,* each producing the image of a raga and how it should be elaborated. The *sangatis* form the architectonics of his music. The text, mostly in Telugu, is not burdened by being recondite and is poetic and full of feeling.

Other luminaries in the world of music are Kshetrayya (seventeenth century), the composer of about 4,200 padams (lyrical compositions sung in slow tempo), of which only a few hundreds are extent; Kancheria Gopanna (Ramdasa) who composed songs in devotion to Rama while languishing in prison; and Annamacharya (fifteenth century), the author of the monumental work, *Samkirtalakshana* and composer of nearly 32 thousand lyrics addressed to the deity of Tirupati and group songs for Yakshagana plays.

Muvvanallur Sabhapatyya (1767-1847), a contemporary of Tyagaraja, was also born in Tanjavur District. Inspired by Kshetrajna he composed *padams* which dextrously combine *bhakti* with *sringara.*

Melatur Venkatarama Sastri (1807-1860), also from the Tanjavur District, created twelve Yakshagna dramas based on the stories of Prahlada, Usha and Rukmini. These form part of the repertoire of the famous Bhagvata Mela dance dramas which are enacted in the village of Melatur.

Narayana Tirtha was a celebrated saint. His work, *Krishnalilaturagini,* is written in the form of a dance drama. Another work of his is *Haribhaktisudharnava.*

Pallavi Seshayyar (1842-1909) excelled in *pallavi* singing. He composed many songs in Telugu and his *tillanas* are particularly famous.

The Telugu Brahmana also traces his ancestry to one of the seven *rishis,* to whose gotram he is linked throughout his life.

Two eminent Telugu Brahmanas, Sarvepalli Radhakrishnan and V.V. Giri, rose to become President of India. Visvesvarayya, the famous administrator, and the modern spiritual teacher, Jiddu Krishnamurti, were also Telugu Brahmanas.

Philosophers and Religious Teachers

Nagarjuna, the celebrated Buddhist philosopher, was born in an Andhra Brahmana family in Vidarbha (first century). He was an exponent of the Madhyamika philosophy in Buddhism and was regarded as having a master mind. He wrote a commentary on *Panchavimsatisahasrika-Prajnaparamitra* which ·is extant in its Chinese translation. He expounded the doctrine of existence and non-existence and became the head of the Buddhist sangha at Nalanda.

The Ultimate, according to Nagarjuna is *sunyata* (the void) or *tatatha* (suchness) and cannot be categorised, being beyond the reach of mind and speech.

His name is perpetuated in history by a Buddhist university and, about the middle of the present century, a dam, Nagarjunasagar (in Andhra Pradesh), which has been named after him.

Nimbarka (eleventh century) was born in a Telugu Brahmana family in a village that bears his name (now in Karnataka). He wrote a commentary on the *Brahma Sutra* and spent most of his life in Brindavan. He propounded the theory of Advaitodvaita (dualistic non-dualism). According to him, the *jiva* is knowledge as well as the possessor of knowledge, just as the sun is light as well as the source of light. The universe cannot be dismissed as a mere illusion since it is a manifestation of what is contained subtly in the nature of God.

Vallabha (fourteenth century), a Brahmana of Andhra, lived mostly in North India. His doctrine is called Subhadvaita (pure non-dualism). According to him, the whole world is real and is subtly Brahman and individual souls and the inanimate world are in essence one with *Brahman.* God is *sachchidhananda* and has qualities; the Sruti passages that state that he has no qualities mean merely that he has not the ordinary qualities.

Vidyaranya (1296-1386), the guru of Harihara and Bukka Rayulu, the founders of the Vijayanagar empire, was a famous exponent of advaita. Among his works are *Jivanmuktiviveka* and *Panchandasi.* He became the Sankaracharya of the Sarada Pitham, Sringeri.

The Ayyangar Brahmana Community

The Ayyangars are members of a sect of South Indian Brahmanas as are Srivaishnavas (not to be confused with the Vaishnavas of south India, an equally distinctive community subscribing to the teachings of Madhava, who lived in the early fourteenth century). Ayyangars are the followers of Ramanuja (1037-1137) whose commentary on the *Brahma Sutra* gives an interpretation of the teachings of the Upanishads and the *Gita* which is different from others.

The philosophy of Ramanuja is Visishtadvaita (qualified monism) and his theology is Srivaishnavism, the original exponent of the Visishtadvaita philosophy being Alavandar (or Yamunacharya) an elder contemporary of his, whose monumental work he completed after the master's death. According to Ramanuja, the soul does not lose its identity in God when it attains salvation. It continues to retain its individuality and the highest spiritual duty of man is to so utilise the blessings of life that he may attain divine grace through service to God and His devotees (*kainkarya*) which alone is the highest form of bliss. A unique feature of Ramanuja's theology is the doctrine of *Prapatti* (unqualified self-surrender to God), a concept which is the philosophical culmination of the entire doctrine of *bhakti.*

Ramanuja, the great religious teacher, though a Tamilian Brahmana by birth was a liberal. He taught that God's grace comes to everyone, whether high or low born, whether of the highest caste or an untouchable, if he makes an honest effort to achieve it and believed that those treated as untouchables deserved special attention and called them Tirukkualattar (of the sacred caste), something like the term Harijan (people of God) coined by Mahatma Gandhi.

Tamil is considered to be a sacred language by the Ayyangars because the Alvars (the celebrated Vaishnava saints and mystics of the Tamil country who preceded Ramanuja) composed their four thousand hymns in Tamil, which are held to the Tamil Vedas but Sanskrit, the language of the Vedas and the scriptures, continues to occupy a place of pre-eminence and Tamil has only supplemented, not supplanted it.

To the Srivaishnavas, the lives and works of the ten Alvars (the last of whom preceded Ramanuja by at least two centuries) are as important as the works of Ramanuja himself.

The Tamil country was the cradle of the *bhakti* movement and some of the earliest saints, both Saiva and Vaishnava, belong to Tamil Nadu. Their hymns are among the most beautiful composi- tions in Tamil literature and they are as popular today as they were in the times of the composers.

The Alvars flourished from about AD 600 to 900. The majority was Brahmana by birth but men and women of high and low degree and of any caste, who had a deep mystical and intuitive knowledge of God and were immersed in His contemplation, joined the band of saints. The hymns composed by these Alvars, numbering four thousand (together called the Prabandha) are full of intense devotion and love for a personal god (Vishnu) and are still recited in the services held in the Vishnu temples of South India.

Andal (or Goda), one of the great Alvars spent her life in devo- tion to Krishna. As a mystic she produced poetry unrivalled for its beauty and emotional intensity.

The most prolific composer among the Alvars was Nammalvar who was born in a Sudra family at Kurukur (now Alvar Tirunagari in the Tirunelvelli district). Tirumangai Alvar, who was a devotee of the deity in the Srirangam temple, was a brigand and highway robber before divine wisdom came to him through the grace of God.

The literature produced by Srivaishnava scholars, composers and saints from the time of the Alvars to the end of the sixteenth century on philosophy, religious poetry, commentaries, etc., adds up to a stupendous total. Some of this is highly sectarian and argumentative and is designed to demolish the thesis of other protagonists like the Advaitins, Buddhists, Jains and Charvakas.

In the fourteenth century the community was split into the two schismatic schools; the Tengalai (southern sect) and the Vadagalai (northern sect) the members of which can be identified by the distinctive mark of each sect, which is worn on the forehead. In the course of time the two sects fell out and inter-marriage and other types of associations between them came to be frowned upon.

After the schism of the fourteenth century, dividing the follow-ers of Ramanuja into the Tengalai (led by Manavala Mahamuni) and the Vadagalai (led by Vedantadesika) several new works were written full of sophistry and philosophical hair-splitting. But most Srivaishnavas of today are ignorant of this schismatic literature and remember only the Alvars' hymns and Ramanuja's *Sribhashva* (commentary on the *Brahma Sutra*) as their common heritage. The separatism is now disappearing as far as the more liberal and enlightened members of the community are concerned.

The suffix "Ayyangar", like Ayyar, has a Sanskrit origin. Both are derived from "Arya", a form of respectful address reserved in ancient days for Brahmanas and Kshatriyas; "Arya" becoming "Ajja" in Prakrit and then "Ayya" in Dravidian (Tamil, Kannada and Telugu).

The name Srinivasan is very common and shows the popularity of the deity at Tirupati but has no regional or caste denotation like Ranganathan, Varadarajan, Sarangapani, etc., which are traceable to Srirangam, Kanjivaram, Kumbakonam, etc.

Of the Brahmana population of South India, which is roughly about 4 per cent of the total, Ayyangars account for about 10 per cent. But their contribution to philosophy, religious lore, literature, art, science, social reform and politics is far out of proportion to their numerical strength. Many Ayyangars have occupied leading positions in several walks of life. Outstanding are Chakravarti Rajagopalachari (1878-1979), the first and the last Indian gover-nor-general of India, at the time of independence; Vijayantimala and Hema Malini, the film actresses; Srinivasa Ramanujanm (1887-1920), one of the greatest mathematicians of modern times; "Poochi" Ayyangar, "Tiger" Varadachari and Ariyakudi Ramanuja

Iyenagar, who greatly enriched Carnatic music; C.V. Narasimhan (under secretary-general at the United Nations), famous administrators like N. Gopalaswami Ayyangar, T.T. Krishnamachari, G. Parthasarathy (former Indian representative at the United Nations) and former vice-chancellor of the Jawaharlal Nehru University, T.V. Sundaram Iyengar; Ananthasayanam Ayyangar (deputy Speaker and Speaker of the Lok Sabha and governor of Bihar), leaders in the national struggle like Salem Vijayaraghavachariar and S. Srinivasa Iyengar, Prativadi Bhayankaram, (author of *Craig's Paradise* describing the inhuman prison conditions in the Andamans), G. Subramanya Iyer and Veeraraghavachariar (who started the newspaper, *The Hindu,* later taken over by Kasturi Ranga Iyengar, and owned and managed by the Kasturi family), the Sanskrit scholars, Prativadi Bhayanakaram Annangarachariar and Agnihotram Thathachariar and K.S. Krishnan (physicist of international repute).

The orthodox Ayyangar of yore, branded with the symbols of the conch and discus on his shoulders, learned only in the religious lore of his community, painted all over with the marks of Vishnu, bigoted, exclusive, insular and indifferent to the spiritual or cultural attainments of others, is becoming a museum piece. But he can still be met with in remote centres in the countryside or well-known Vaishnava temple towns.

Today's orthodox Ayyangar wakes up with bird song and goes to the waterfront for a bath. He paints the *namam* prominently on his forehead and specified parts of his torso (twelve in all, as prescribed in the scriptures) after putting on fresh clothes, he performs his *japam* (Gayatri incantation). Coming back home, he reads portions of the *Ramayana* and select religious texts. Then he offers his midday prayers *(sandhya)* to the sun, after which he starts the worship of his family icons. All this takes him up to lunch time. The lunch, prepared at home, is presented to the family diet as an offering before it is partaken. After the meal he retires for a while. If he is well versed in the Vedas or the *Nalayiram,* he might spend some time giving lessons to young pupils. At dusk he does his evening ablutions and *sandhya* again, after which he recites the Vishnu *Sahasranamam* and other *stotras* (compositions in praise of God). This over, he is ready for supper.

Culturally, Srivaishnavas are principally Tamilians though thousands belong to Andhra with Telugu as their mother tongue. For the majority of Srivaishnavas, including those who have settled far beyond the confines of the Tamil country for unremembered generations, Tamil is still the mother tongue.

The Ayyar Community

The Ayyars belong to the largest Brahmana community of South India and Tamil Nadu is their home state though there is a large number in Kerala as well. They are mostly engaged in administration and in the professions. Slow to change the Ayyars still cherish their age-old Brahmanical customs and practices. This community has made a great contribution to the literary and cultural heritage of the South.

Ayyar is the plural form of 'Ayya' which as mentioned before evolved from 'Arya'. These days, however, the members of this sect have begun to give up the caste name of Ayyar. Earlier, a typical Ayyar name had four constituents: the name of the birth place or place of origin of the family; the initial letter of the father's name; the "given" name, and the caste name.

The Ayyars like other Brahmanas, may follow any of the three Vedas — *Rig, Yajur* or *Sama*. The followers of the three Vedas are regarded as equals and can intermarry, the wife adopting the Veda of the husband. There are a number of *gotras* into which all Brahmanas — hence the Ayyars also — are divided, such as those of Atri, Bhrigu, Rutsa, Vasishtha, Gautama, Kasyapa, Bharadwaja, Kaundinya and Angirasa. In their ceremonial rites they are guided either by the laws (*sutras*) laid down by Apastamba or Bodhayana.

When he performs his *sandhya* or salutes an elder, an Ayyar mentions his lineage or *gotra* and his law giver (Apastamba or Bodhayana) in addition to his name.

Ayyars are *Smratas* (followers of the *Smritis*), though they may appear to be Saivas (as they usually mark themselves with *vibhuti* or the sacred ashes). Most of them followers of Sankara (AD 732-770) and sixfold faith or 'Shanmata'. Another distinction is that the

Ayyars wear the leaves of both the *tulasi* plant, sacred to Vishnu and the *bilva* plant, sacred to Siva, in their hair.

Ayyars are further divided into various subsects, each subsect claiming to be superior to the rest. How the community came to be subdivided is not clear. Until recently marriage between one subsect and another was strictly forbidden but such restrictions are now disappearing.

Lifestyle

An Ayyar is enjoined to lead a disciplined life. He must rise at the *muhurta* or hour of Brahma (3 a.m.) make his ablutions and recite the Gayatri mantra at least 108 times. The *brahmachari* performs the *samidadhanam* and the *grahastha* (householder) the aupasana. In both these rites, offerings are made to the sacred fire. This is followed by what is called *Siva puja*, though all the deities are worshipped at this time. Along with a *Sivalinga* it is important to have a *saligram*, which is a Vaishnava symbol, in the household. The various images are washed with water and milk as the performer of the *puja* chants Vedic hymns, this *abhisheka* being followed by the offering of flowers.

The devout Ayyar makes it a point to read the *Ramayana* or the *Bhagavata*. He recites the thousand names of Vishnu at dusk, followed by *stotras* (praises) addressed to Ganapati his guru (or teacher who may be Dakshinamurti), Sarasvati, Lakshmi, Rama, Krishna, Hanuman, Subrahmanya and other gods and goddesses. He may also read the *Devi-Mahatmayan* (known in the north as *Durga Saptasati*). He performs the *sandhya* at dawn and dusk and the *madhayhnikam* at midday. The Gayatri *japa* is the most important part of these daily rites. An Ayyar who does not chant the *Gayatri* is not fit to perform any other ceremony.

Before the commencement of any rite, Ayyars invoke Ganapati, Vishnu and Paramesvara (Siva) but in their *sankalpa* (mental resolve) they declare that they are performing the rite to please Paramesvara (the Supreme God).

Initiation by a guru is necessary before certain deities can be worshipped. There is a *mulamantra* (root mantra) pertaining to Siva and to Vasudeva or Narayana into which Ayyars are usually initiated.

There is a Saiva flavour about Ayyar religion as the worship of Rudra is a part of their individual and community life. But the worship of Vishnu and Vaishnava deities (like Rama, Krishna and Hanuman) has a place of equal importance in their life. When an Ayyar performs his *sandhya*, he invokes the various names of Vishnu and touches various parts of his body when mentioning them.

Like members of other Brahmana communities, Ayyars must observe the sixteen *samskaras* (literally meaning refinement but in practice also connoting consecration or sanctification). Some of the important ones are briefly described below.

Garbhadhanam is performed at the time of the nuptial ceremony and sanctifies the procreative act; *pumsavanam* and *simantonnayanam* (parting of the hair) ceremonies protect the mother and the child she is carrying and are performed during the first pregnancy.

Jatakarma is performed at birth, the child being fed with gold, honey and *ghee; namakaranam* (name-giving ceremony) is gone through when the child is eleven days old; the rite of *annaprasanam* is the feeding of rice or solid food to the child for the first time; *upanayanam* ('bringing near' to a preceptor) must be conducted in the fifth or eighth year although the Ayyars are not strict about keeping this rule.

The boy is invested with the *yajnopavita* (sacred thread consisting of three strands knotted together) which implies that he has now had a second birth and has become *dvija* (twice-born) and can now qualify for studentship or *brahmacharya*, the scriptures enjoining on him the leading of a disciplined life, the strict observance of celibacy and bodily and mental cleanliness; *samavartanam* is the ceremony which concludes studentship.

It is doubtful if Ayyars today remember the meaning of this *samavartanam* as most of them go through it hurriedly on the day of their marriage.

An Ayyar marriage is mixture of Vedic ritual and Tamil custom. First, horoscopes are matched. When the amount of dowry (despite the law against it) is fixed and an understanding arrived at about the jewellery, vessels and other articles to be given to the bride by her father, an auspicious day is fixed by the priests for the marriage.

The bridegroom is taken in procession to the bride's place and is welcomed with music and the betrothal ceremony is then held. The *vratam* is conducted on the morning of the marriage day.

The bridegroom goes on a short symbolic "pilgrimage" as if to Kasi carrying umbrella, walking stick and a coconut. The bride's father goes to meet him and persuades him to return and marry his daughter. Some non-Brahmana communities also enact this prelude.

The couple sit before the holy fire and the priests chant Vedic hymns. The bride's father washes the bridegroom's feet with milk and water and affirms that he is giving away his daughter in marriage. Then follows the *panigrahanam* or the clasping of each other's hands by the couple, which is a most important rite. *Saptapadi* or taking seven steps together round the sacred fire, is of equal significance.

Among the non-Vedic rites observed is the tying of the *tali* by the bridegroom round the bride's neck, which is of the highest importance.

The festivals of the Ayyars are numerous, most of them being common to other Hindu communities. They are Upakarma, Dipavali (festival of lights), Bhogi Pandigal, Pongal, Taipusam, Mahasivaratri, Ramanavami, Janamashtami, Vinayaka Chaturthi and Navaratri.

Ayyars observe a number of *vratams* (vows). One is to propitiate Varalakshmi. Rishipanchami is observed by elderly women. Fasting is common with the devout.

For centuries the Ayyars preserved the Hindu way of life, orthodoxy and Brahmanic ritual and though they took to modern education, they did not become westernised. But in recent decades they have spearheaded social reform and played a great role in the struggle for freedom. Their contribution to music is immense. They have produced some of India's greatest lawyers, administrators, statesmen and scientists and others who have kept alive the religious and cultural heritage of India.

The Ayyar community has produced outstanding administrators and politicians, such as C.P. Ramaswami Aiyar (1879-1966); scholars such as U.V. Swaminatha Iyer (1855-1942) who brought to light many palm-leaf manuscripts to enrich Tamil literature, the famous scientist, C.V. Raman (1888-1976) who was the first Indian to win the Nobel Prize in a science subject (physics); many legal luminaries; outstanding poets like the revolutionary poet, Subrahmanya Bharati, who gave a new direction to Tamil literature by taking the language to the masses; famous dancers and musicians, two of whom, Muthuswami Dikshitar and Syama Sastri, were famous composers of music. The defence services have also attracted a large number of Ayyar young men.

Ayyars believe that they are descended from the ancient *rishis*. Each family belongs to a *gotra* named after a *rishi*. Traditionally they adopt one of the following appellations: Ayyar, Sastri, Sarma, Dikshitar, Ghanapathigal, Sroutigal and Rao. They are divided into subsects, each denoting either a particular origin, mode of worship or social practice, which are Vathima, Ashtasahasram, Dikshitar, Sholiar (or Chozhiar), Mukkani, Kaniyalar, Sankethi, Prathamasaki and Gurukkal.

The Chitpavan Community

The Chitpavan Brahmanas of Maharashtra, whose origin is obscure, were not heard of before AD 1700. According to the *Sahyadri Khand*, the legend goes that Parashurama was so defiled by the slaughter of the Kshatriyas that the Brahmanas refused to perform any ceremonies for him. At that time, the bodies of fourteen shipwrecked foreigners happened to be cast ashore by the sea that washed the foot of the Sahyadri hills. Parashurama purified their corpses by burning them on a funeral pyre and restored them to life, taught them Brahmana rites and made them perform ceremonies so as to free him from his blood guilt. As he wished to reward his new priests, the Deccan having already been given to the Brahmanas, he prayed to the sea to spare some of its domain and in response it retired as far west as Parasurama's arrow, shot from the crest of the Sahyadris could go. He thus reclaimed a belt of land about forty-eight kilometres broad and a tract on the banks of the Vashishthi, about sixty-four kilometres north of Ratnagiri, was set apart for these new Brahmanas. In memory of the process by which they had been purified, they were given the name of Chitpavans and their settlement that of Chitpolan.

The Chitpavans are a community whose impact long since outgrew its size; no community of its size having produced as many political and social leaders. They began to call themselves Konkanastha about AD 1715, when Peshwa Balaji Viswanath rose to eminence in the Maratha kingdom. They are light-complexioned, well made and handsome, often having blue or green eyes and hair that is not dark which suggests a foreign origin. Originally from the town of Chitpol in Ratnagiri, they are well placed in government service and had become prominent in the fields of scholarship, the arts, social reform and law by the nineteenth century. Of their two sect names, Konkanasth and Chitpavan, the first indicates the rocky, unyielding land in the Ratnagiri District of the Konkan, which they farmed traditionally, all Konkanasthas tracing their history as far as the Konkan. The name, Chitpavan, would seem to have originated in the name 'Chitpol', the Konkan town.

A historian of the Bene Israelis, who settled in the Kolaba District of the Konkan, claims the Chitpavans are fellow Jews who became separated from their shipmates and settled in India. Other accounts have guessed at a homeland anywhere from Iran to just north of Sholapur.

As long as they remained in the Konkan, the Chitpavans were simply an obscure Brahmana community of farmers and priests. The land that they tilled afforded only a poor living but money has rarely been their primary goal. They were neither the largest nor the purest in the Brahmana hierarchy but their common-sense and intelligence made them rise to power.

Balaji Vishwanath Bhat took up service with the Maratha government in the early 1700s. He had a talent for making himself indispensable so much so that within seven years Shivaji's grandson, Shadu, had appointed him his *peshwa* (prime minister). His son, Bajirao, succeeded him in 1720 and thus began a century of rule by the Chitpavan Peshwas. Lured by these examples of good fortune, the Chitpavans migrated in large numbers to the Deccan, especially to Pune (Poona) the seat of the Peshwas, where they quickly rose in stature and influence, claiming economic and other privileges.

The end of power and glory came in 1818, when the British subjugated the Maratha kingdom. They served the British for some time albeit unwillingly. Wasudeo Balwant Phadke, one of the more spirited among them, dreamed of restoring the office and power of the Peshwa. In 1879 he left his job of a government clerk and started raiding the countryside. Although he was captured his example inspired others to become restive.

Among the outstanding social reformers from this community were D.K. Karve, who established a home and school for young widows, and set an example by marrying a widow himself; M.G. Ranade, who wrote in favour of widow marriage and of raising the marriage age of consent; and G.K. Gokhale, who established the Servants of the India Society. D.K. Karve was, however, ostracised for breaking the orthodoxy rules and he had to make a visit for purification to Varanasi so as not to be excommunicated.

Among the great nationalists were B.G. Tilak and S.M. Paranjpe. Both were jailed several times. Vishnu Shastri Chiplunkar wrote *Our Country's Condition* to attack British rule on the one hand and Phule's non-Brahmana movement on the other.

From the time of Balaji's rise to power in the Maratha court, the Chitpavans have had a hand in government, a tradition perpetuated by men like Ranade and Gopal Krishna Gokhale. Both urged peaceful reforms in British policy. Ranade and another young Chitpavan intellectual, G.V. Joshi formed the Poona Sarvajanik Sabha in 1870 as a representative body to recommend changes to the government. Moderates like Gokhale and Ranade led the Indian National Congress in its early stages in political reform.

But the other side to the Chitpavans' political activity was terrorism. The Chapekar brothers formed the Society for the Removal of Obstacles to the Hindu Religion; one of the 'obstacles' being Rand of the Plague Commission who, on a June night in 1897, was 'removed'.

Other conspiracies were brewed, sometimes among students of the Ferguson College, which had been established by such eminent Chitpavans as Tilak, V.S. Apte and Gokhale. Another pair of young brothers, Vinayak and Ganesh Savarkar, planned ways of overthrowing the British government with their friends. When Ganesh was convicted of writing "inflammatory verse" in 1909, the district magistrate of Nasik was murdered in reprisal. Twenty-seven men were convicted as members of the conspiracy, most of them Chitpavans.

Nathuram Vinayak Godse was probably the last, and certainly the best-known, of the Chitpavan terrorists and the news of his assassination of Gandhi caused anti-Brahmana riots to break out in Maharashtra.

Bal Gangadhar Tilak, a revered public figure, both orthodox and revolutionary, tried to reconcile the opposing elements in the community. Though not against all social change, he opposed British social legislation, insisting that it should come from the people. In an attempt to realise this he drew the masses into meaningful political movements. He revived the Ganapati celebrations and renewed people's interest in Shivaji, making both these subjects the vehicles of political action.

During the 1930s and 1940s, discontented Maharashtrian Brahmanas began to leave the Congress and non-Brahmanas took their places. Though they were among the leaders in certain other parties, they found that democracy in India did not do justice to minorities. The Brahmanas being only about 2 per cent of the population, could not hope to carry much weight politically.

Like those from other communities, many Chitpavans now opt for employment in the professions instead of the government service they once preferred. Especially popular are engineering and other technical vocations.

Today the young Chitpavan is not much concerned about the community's reduced political role and the anti-Brahmana sentiment that still lingers. In a society frequently tied up in its traditions and restrictions, the Chitpavans have been adaptable enough to change with the times.

The Deshastha Community

The valleys of the Krishna and the Godavari and the plateau of the Sahyadri Hills are known as Desha and the Brahmanas from this region are called Deshastha Brahmanas. Vedic literature describes people closely resembling the Deshastha Brahmanas and so it may be said that this community is as old as the Vedas.

The Deshasthas are spread all over the Deccan, especially in the states of Maharashtra, Karnataka and Andhra. They are intensely religious, steeped in rituals, trustworthy and hardworking. They have produced saints, politicians and men of learning.

There are two major groups in the community. The people of one follow the *Rig Veda* and are called Rigvedis and those of the other the *Yajur Veda* and are known as Yajurvedis. There is not much difference in the rites and rituals of these two groups but among the Yajurvedis a boy is not allowed to marry the daughter of his maternal uncle. No such restriction, however, exists among the Rigvedis.

Deshastha Brahmanas generally have a sturdy physique, high forehead and a dark complexion. They are usually intelligent, courteous, honest and hospitable. Their love for religion and God gives them a love for morality. Most of the well-known saints from Maharashtra, Karnataka and Andhra were Deshastha Brahmanas. They are also peace-loving, just, conscientious and reliable.

The surnames of Deshasthas are peculiar. Some surnames indicate traditionally held administrative offices, for example, Kulkarni, Deshpande, Patil and Deshmukh. Others indicate physical and mental characteristics such as Hirve and Buddhisagar. Most are derived from the name of the native place of origin. In Karnataka and Andhra are found place names such as Gokak, Anikhindi and Bewur, while in Maharashtra the suffix *kar* is attached to the name of the place to make it a surname as in Mangalvedhekar, Gajendragadkar and Junnarkar.

Each family has its own deity which is the *kuladevata* and it is strongly believed that if this deity is not properly propitiated by rites and rituals, the well-being of the family will be threatened. Every village also has its own deity (*gramadevata*) and it is presumed that the wrath of this deity brings on epidemics, natural calamities and invasions. The deities commonly worshipped are Narasimha, Siva, Vishnu, Vyankatesa, Rama and Hanuman. The major goddesses worshipped are Bhavani of Tuljapur, Ambabai of Kolhapur and Yamai of Aundha. Khandoba of Jejuri and Pali are also worshipped. In Karnataka, Krishna at Udipi, Vyankatesa at

Tirupati, Yallamma at Sundatti and Banashankari are some of the other prominent deities.

Navaratri, during the first nine days of the month of Ashvina, is the most popular festival of the Deshasthas. Fasting during this time and keeping a *til*-oil lamp (*samai*) burning continuously before the household deities, is obligatory. Every day hymns from the Durga *Saptashati,* which describe the noble and heroic deeds of the mother goddesses, are recited. Towards the end of the festival, offerings of bangles, rice balls, coconuts, etc. are made to *agni* (fire). A virgin and a married woman are invited to the festive meals. Other Navaratris like Champashashthi and Narasimha are also observed by certain groups.

In the old days, a Deshastha marriage used to last five to six days. In Maharashtra, the bride's party is supposed to offer *karhi bhat* (rice and curd curry) to the bridegroom's party on the eve of the marriage but in Karnataka a variety of food and sweets are served. Though customs vary from place to place, fondness for good food is a notable characteristic of this community. Other Hindu rituals like *kanyadan, lajahoma, saptapadi* are meticulously performed at the marriage ceremony.

The community has produced a number of *acharyas* who have presided over various *maths.* These seats of religion and learning spread the teachings of the Vedas, Smritis, Puranas and especially the Advaita philosophy all over India which points to the fact that the community has Smartas as well as Madhavas. Among other prominent cults started by them is the Mahanubhava, which has a special significance in Maharashtra since it produced the first written literary work in Marathi, the *Leela Charitra* by Chakradhar.

The Bhagavat cult (*Varkari Sampradaya*) was started by the great saint of Maharashtra, Dhyanesvara, who was one of the greatest mystics of India. Vithal worship was accepted and made popular by this cult.

Eknath was another great saint who developed these teachings further by his learning and devotion. *Dhyaneshwari* and *Eknathi Bhagavat* are two great works written by these two religious teachers through whom the teachings of the Vedas reached the common man.

The Ramdasi cult was started by the great saint, Ramdasa, who preached the harmony of spiritual, material and political value in life. This cult emphasises asceticism and devotion to duty. *Dasabodha* is its main contribution. The Dasa cult was the mainstream of spiritual life and teaching in Karnataka. It mainly preached the philosophy of Bhakti and produced great saints like Purandaradas, Vijayadasa and others.

Deshasthas have contributed to mathematics and literature as well as to the cultural and religious heritage of India. Bhaskar II (twelfth century) was one of the greatest mathematicians of medieval India. Eminent pundits and philosophers like Yajnavalkya, Vasishtha and Bharadvaja are said to have belonged to this community. In Sanskrit literature, Bhavabhuti (eighth century), the great dramatist, is held by many to be second in dramatic genius only next to Kalidasa. *Malati Madhava* is his best play. The philosophic works of Dhyaneshvar, Ramdasa and Eknath have enriched Marathi literature and Purandaradasa's devotional lyrics are unsurpassed in Kannada. Two of the devoted and dedicated Sanskrit research scholars of the present day are Rajeshwarshastri Dravid of Varanasi and M.M. Siddeshwarashastri Chitdao of Pune.

The Karhada Community

This small Maharashtra community has played a very influential role in the country's political and industrial development. Generations of intermarriage in this small community has connected all the families of this community.

These Brahmanas are divided on the basis of their belief in one of the Vedas. There are the Rigvedis, Samavedis and Atharvavedis. One more division, on the basis of specialisation in the *shakhas* (branches — the Shakala, Kanvashakha, etc.) also exists, one group of Brahmanas becoming known as Rigvedi Shakalahakhiya Brahmanas, etc. The Rigvedi Brahmanas have lived in Maharashtra for a long time but were concentrated in the southern part, the region called the Karhatak province, extending over the modern Satara, Sangli and Kolhapur Districts. The capital was Karhatak (modern Karad). The earliest reference to the Karhatak province is

in the *Mahabharata* when Sahadeva had conquered it for Yud-
hishthira's *rajasuya yajna*. It was also called Karhakat, Karhakad
and Karhat in the Briharrut and Yadav edicts. According to the
Kalyani edict, it extended from the Sahyadris in the west, Tardu-
wadi (about 220 kilometres north of Bijapur) in the east to the
River Krishna in the south and to Pratyandak (modern Phaltan) in
the north. At that time the town of Karhatak was a flourishing
commercial centre as it was situated on the road between Konkan
and Desh. There are only five *shakhas* in the *Rig Veda* and so the
number of Rigvedi Brahmanas is small and from among them
those who specialised in the *Ashyalayana Sutra* and *Shakal Shakha*
came and settled in Karhatak. It is said that they are the descendants of foreign invaders like the Shakhas, the Pallavas or the
Hunas.

The earliest reference in literature to those Shakal Shakhiya and
Ashvalayana Sutra Brahmanas is in *Mitakshari Teeka* by Vik-
ramaditya (1076-1126).

The Karhatak province was ruled by the Shilahars, who enjoyed
some autonomy even when they were vassals of the Chalukyas.
When the Shilahars annexed Konkan in the eleventh century, they
took with them their Ashvalayana Sutra Shakal Shakhiya Brahmana
priests and settled down there. The people of Konkan called these
newcomers Karhads as they came from Karhat, which was the
capital of the Shilahars.

Another version of the migration is that Desh, where these
Brahmanas stayed, was always threatened by famines and when a
terrible famine, lasting for about twelve years, occurred about the
end of the fourteenth century, the Brahmanas migrated to the
Konkan where the land was fertile and there was plenty of water.
As they came through Karad, they were called Karhads by the
Konkanis.

The Karhade are worshippers of Devi. The Goddess Mahalakshmi is not worshipped for five years after marriage. In the Navra-
tra festival, Lalita Panchami and Durgashtami (the fifth and the
eighth days of the first fortnight of the month of *Ashvina*) are two
important days. The day of Anant Chaturdashi (the fourteenth day
in the first fortnight of *Bhadrapada*) is also important as on that
day Anant worship is carried out, a practice that supposedly

originated with this community that was later adopted by the Chitpavans. Some other festivals, common to Hindus, like Ganesh Chaturthi, Dussehra and Diwali are also celebrated.

The Shilahars, who were the original lords of Karnataka worshipped the Goddess Metruka (or mother). This practice the Karhade began to follow. But when the community started spreading out, different families began to worship the goddesses of the locality in which they settled. For those staying near Kolhapur, Ambabai and for those staying in or near Goa, Mhalsa or Shantadurga or Vijayadurga became important. Those in Konkan worshipped whichever Goddess was closest. For those Karhade who were originally from the Godavari valley, Ambejogai in the Bhir district of Maharashtra became important. Near Kolhapur, the gods that are worshipped along with these *devis* are Adinath, Prayagmadhav or Jyotiba.

The Karhada community, unlike the other sects of Maharashtra, is not subdivided into many sects. All Karhade, with the exception of a very few Vaishnavites, are Rigvedis of the Smarta sect. The highest authority on religious and social matters, is that of Sankara.

Karhada marriages are like those of other Brahmana communities and follow the usual Hindu rituals of *kanyadan, lajahoma* and *saptapadi*. Normally marriages do not take place across community borders though there are exceptions. The rules of exogamy prevent marriages in the same *gotras* or *pravaras*.

Though not very rich, the average Karhada is financially on a sound footing. The Karhade of Desh are well-off compared to those in Konkan and the Padhya Brahmanas of Goa. They are good cooks, well known for their vegetarian dishes.

In appearance they tend to be of slight build and are generally dark in complexion though there are some who are fair-skinned. Perhaps, the most admirable qualities of these people are adaptability and a love for neatness.

The Kashmiri Brahmana Community

The Brahmanas of Kashmir are handsome and gifted people. Based in their Vedic Aryan background, they have retained their ancient traditions but have also assimilated other cultures that flourish in the country. As poets, scholars, statesmen and diplomats they continue to make their impact on the national and international scenes.

Kashmir or Kashir, the homeland of the Kashmiri Pandits, has been for centuries a great centre of art and culture. In area the state of Jammu and Kashmir covers about 135,150 square kilometres and is a little smaller than Great Britain. For centuries Kashmir has been the homeland of different groups of people such as Brahmanas, Buddhists, Huns, Muslims (Mughals and Pathans), Sikhs and Dogras. More than half a dozen languages and dialects are spoken by them; Dogri, Pahari, Ladakhi and Dardi being the principal ones. Linguistically, Kashmir was for long the home of Sanskrit and Persian and it is a mixture of these two languages.

It is said that originally the Valley of Kashmir was a mountain lake called Satisar (or the lake of the virtuous women). The etymology of the word, Kashmir is ambiguous. According to a legend the plateaux (*karevas*) of Kashmir were inundated and remained submerged for centuries in a vast and deep lake which the sage Kashyapa drained. The reclaimed land was called Kashyappur or Kashyapmar which later became Kashmir.

In the Puranas, Kashmir bears the name Gerek (hill). Kashmir also implies "land desiccated from water", from the Sanskrit *ka* (water) and *shimira* (to desiccate). The Hellenes have given it the name of Kaspeiria. Herodotus mentions it as Kaspatyros and Hekataois as Kaspalyros. Hiuen Tsang, the Chinese monk who came to India about AD 631, refers to it as Kia-shi-milo. The people of Kashmir call it Kashir, the Tibetans Khachal and the Dards, Kash-rat.

The history of the Kashmiri Brahmanas (who are often referred to as Kashmiri Pandits) is aeons old. The Kashmiris form a branch of the race which brought the language of the Indo-Aryan type into India as evinced by their language and physical appearance but the period of their immigration and the route they came by are still moot points.

They are a distinct class and are probably the purest specimen of the ancient Aryan settlers in India.

Between the eighth and ninth centuries several of them wrote many scholarly works. The *wak* (sayings) of the mystic, Lalla Arifa (popularly known as Lalla Didi) are greatly revered by them. She was a fifteenth century Saiva poetess and a disciple of the famous Muslim Sufi, Mir Syed Ali Hamadani. In his *Rajatarangini,* Kalhana (twelfth century) has portrayed writers, poets, priests and educationists. They have also enriched Indian philosophical thought with the Saiva philosophy which is known as Kashmir Saivism, Trika-Sastra (or simply Trika) and Rahasya Sampradaya or Trambaka Sampradaya.

Before 1930, they were all-powerful in Kashmir, economically, socially and politically. But after the partition of the country their population started diminishing and is now almost on the verge of extinction. Meanwhile, Muslim dominance, both political and economic, grew considerably in Kashmir.

About a thousand years ago, Kashmir came under Arab and Persian influence and, later, under Muslim rule. Persian became the official language. The Kashmiri Brahmanas who had become well-versed in Persian, got good posts under the Muslims as Persian was also the court language at Delhi. Particularly because of their good knowledge of Persian, some of the Kashmiri Pandits who migrated to Bengal, Rajasthan and Central India, became *diwans* of the princely States.

They are a charming, highly cultured people. Fair-complexioned, intelligent and hardworking, they are endowed with an extraordinarily artistic temperament. Most of them have a handsome physique with long or aquiline nose and beautiful eyes and Aryan features. Their women, with their lovely eyes and chiselled features, are among the most beautiful in the world.

Having a great sense of adaptability, those who migrated to the plains adapted themselves to Muslim culture and their knowledge of Persian helped them to occupy high positions, as ministers in the courts of maharajas, administrators in various princely states and other posts of prestige and responsibility.

When Urdu came into being, they made it their language and produced monumental works, some becoming great Urdu writers and poets. The Kashmiri Brahmanas of Delhi, Lucknow and

Allahabad speak fluent Urdu but many of those who left Kashmir can not speak Kashmiri.

They were also otherwise influenced by the Muslim way of life and showed preference for Muslim dress and food.

The customary dress, the *Phiran,* worn by most Kashmiris (men and women) is a loose smock coming down below the knees. However, in Delhi, Bombay, Uttar Pradesh and other parts of India, they dress in the Indian or European manner; the women wear saris and the younger people wear whatever is in vogue.

They have a rich musical tradition that developed from the chanting of Hindu scriptures and the singing of devotional songs in Kashmiri at the time of the sacred thread and marriage ceremonies.

Some of the well-known surnames are: Wanchoo, Bhan, Kao, Gunju, Muttu, Razdan, Takru, Manwati, Panju, Gurtu, Walli, Kak, Shingloo (or Shinhlu), Thresal, Jhalan, Yan, Malla, Sapru, Kitchlu, Drulu, Dar (or Dhar), Haksar (or Hak), Bangru, Langar, Gadi, Thalssor, Kalpush, Warikim, Tikku, Lala, Minshi, Zitshi (or Zutshi), Amdarzan, Kaul (or Koul), Raina, Pulairu, Madan, Bakaya, Rawal, Kachru and Shivpuri.

The Kashmiri Pandits are scattered throughout India, particularly in the northern regions and many occupy high governmental and private posts. But the majority lives in Kashmir. As a community, over the past three decades, they became more liberal in their outlook. Inter-caste marriages now take place, chiefly among the upper classes. The dowry system continues to prevail. This group of Brahmanas does not have any subcastes. Several rituals and ceremonies are observed. On the sixth day after a child's birth, the mother and child have a ritual bath (*shran sunder*). On the eleventh day, a purification ceremony (*kahnethar*) takes place when the mother leaves her room. Then a *havan* is performed and the child is given its name.

When a boy is five years old, a hair-cutting ceremony (*zara kasai* or *moodan*) is performed. The head is shaved, only a tuft of hair being left on the top as is the practice among Brahmanas. When the boy is twelve years old, the sacred thread is put round his neck by his guru and he becomes a *dvija* (twice-born) Brahmana. In accordance with Brahmanical rites, he then begs alms for his guru from all those present, to whom the money collected is given. The bath and anointing ceremony (*deragon*) include the colouring of the boy's hands with henna.

Marriages are mostly arranged by the parents. The horoscopes of the boy and the girl are studied by astrologers to see if they tally. On the wedding day, the bridegroom (who wears traditional Indian dress and a coloured turban) is made to stand on the *vyug* (a design made on the floor of his house, for the purpose). The oldest woman relative brings a tray of lighted lamps and releases a couple of pigeons over his head. The guests sing songs and shower coins and sugar on him. Then he goes to the bride's house in procession where the *vyug* ceremonies are again performed outside her house. The nuptial rites (*lagan*) are conducted by the family priests near the sacrificial fire. The couple partakes of curds and sweetmeats from the same plate. Then hand in hand they go round the sacred fire seven times, to the chanting of Vedic mantras by the priests, a rite that is common to all caste-Hindu marriages.

Till the end of the nineteenth century, the dowry system of this community was different from what it is today. Along with the bridegroom, his parents also received gifts from the bride's parents and in their turn, they also gave a dowry to the bride. Now the bride's parents send the bridegroom a kilo of cream (in a silver vessel), seven *thals* (large trays) of sweets, a few flowers (an odd number), cloth for suits and an amount of five hundred rupees or more. In return his parents send the bride clothes, jewellery, seven or more *thals* of sweets, five or seven flowers, one kilo of cream and cash.

The orthodox Brahmanas (and there are many) do not eat anything touched by a Muslim or anything cooked in the daughter's new home. They are bitterly opposed to inter-caste marriages.

Sivaratri is an important Kashmiri festival. It begins on the first day of the dark fortnight of Phalguna (February-March). The house is cleaned, etc., from the 5th to the 9th day and cash presents are sent to the daughters on the 10th day. On the 11th day, fish and bread are specially included in the menu. On the 13th day, the head of the family undertakes a fast and worships Siva at night. On the 14th day, a feast is held. The elder relatives receive presents from the younger. Cooked rice and meat are customarily sent to the daughters. On the 15th day, walnuts are distributed among relatives and friends.

The spring festival, called Sont, is celebrated on 15 March. Unhusked and cooked rice, a mirror, a cup of curd, a pen case, a few walnuts, a basket of unhusked rice and sweets are kept together overnight and have to be seen the first thing the next morning. Each person then picks up a walnut or two and then drops them into the nearest river in which a bath has then to be taken. Nav Warih (New Year's Day) falls on the first day of the bright fortnight of Chaitra (March-April).

Other festivals celebrated by the Kashmiri Brahmanas are Baisakhi, Jeth Ashtami, Har Navami, Punn, Kambari Pach, Dussehra and Krishna Ashtami.

The Madhava Community

The Madhavas, who are Vaishnava Brahmanas and followers of the philosopher, Madhava (1238-1317) who propounded the dualistic principle, are spread over Karnataka, Tamil Nadu, Andhra and parts of Maharashtra. Essentially peace loving, they are intellectually minded and scholarly. The Tuluva and Tamil Nadu Madhavas (Madhava himself was a Tuluva Brahmana) are light complexioned and well built.

Most Madhavas are comfortably off and many of them are well educated. They rarely intermarry with other sects. Madhava men (especially the orthodox) can be recognised by their distinctive Vaishnava caste marks, the *akshata* (round dark mark) and the *angara* (a vertical central charcoal-black line drawn on the forehead), the additional sandal paste caste marks on the arms, chest and abdomen representing the *sankha* (conch), *padma* (lotus) and the like. Women and girls worship the *tulasi* plant daily. But in custom, tradition and dress the Madhavas can hardly be distinguished from Maharashtra Brahmanas. The mother tongue of many Madhava families of Madras and Tanjavur is Marathi, though a corrupt form of that language.

The Dvaita philosophy is essentially rooted in the Bhakti cult of a supreme God which emerged with the advent of the Alvar and the Nayanamar saints, who lived from the sixth to the tenth century in the Tamil country. Ramanuja (1037-1137) who preached Vasisht advaita (qualified monism) established the Vaishnava Bhakti cult as a faith but it was Madhava's intellect, learning and inspiration that led him to propound a system which defied the concepts of *maya* (illusion) and *jivabrahmaikya* (the oneness of God and the individual soul). Later another great mind, Jayatirtha (Tika) interpreted the sayings of Madhava in detail to consolidate the Dvaita belief.

Madhava established a temple dedicated to Krishna at Udipi (in Karnataka) and initiated eight *balabrahmacharis* to continue the worship of the Lord and to propagate the Dvaita philosophy. Each *swami* had to serve the temple for two years in turn without leaving it. In course of time each of the eight *swamis* attracted their own followers and eight *maths* became established. Three important *maths* have also played a significant part in upholding and spreading the message of Dvaita: the Uttaradi (in Bangalore) the Raghavendraswami (in Nanjangud) and the Vyasaraya (in the South). A great Madhava guru, Satyadhanatirtha of the Uttaradi *math,* also made an outstanding contribution to this faith.

The catholicity of Madhavas and their tolerance and admiration for other faiths can be gauged from the fact that even now Anantasvara's *ratha* (chariot) precedes that of Krishna in all major festivals at Udipi in spite of the fact that the Madhavas are staunch Vaishnavas.

Some of the best devotional hymns inspired by Madhava's philosophy are those of Purandaradasa but out of over four lakh *bhajans* in praise of the Lord, only about nine hundred are extant. With him, Vijaya-Vithala, Jagannathadas, Mohandas, Seshadas and Kankadasa (a Kuruba shepherd) form the *dasakuta.*

Together with Sankara's Advaita and Ramanuja's Vashista dvaita, Madhava's Dvaita principle forms a comprehensive philosophy of the Vedantic tradition.

Madhava is one of the world's greatest theistic philosophers. His theism stands for the recognition of God or *Brahman* as the one and only independent being to which all else is subordinated.

According to his philosophy, matter and soul, time and space are all dependent realities which exist by the will of God. The

Upanishads express this truth by saying that *Brahman* is the real of the "reals" (*sarvasya satyam*) and that everything here is *aitadatmyam* — has the supreme being for its source and sustaining principle. The object of philosophy is not merely to enable him to realise the distinction between the real and the unreal (*satya* and *anrita*) but to make him realise the profound significance of the distinction between what is *svatantra* and what is *paratantra*, which is the knowledge that can put an end to bondage and suffering.

Other philosophers have tried to classify reality in other ways, such as positive and negative (*bhava* and *abhava*), sentient and insentient (*chetana* and *achetana*), living and non-living (*jiva* and *ajiva*), matter and mind, real and unreal, but they miss the point which is to enable man to realise *moksha*.

The second important point of Madhava's teaching is that the supreme being (God, Brahman, Paramatman or Bhagavan) cannot be a mere abstraction but is a perfect personality of infinite and auspicious attributes of perfection.

The attributes of God are one with this personality and are not separable from it. To speak of God and His divine nature and attributes is only a distinction of reference and not of essence.

His teaching is that humanity should work hard for its salvation and that work should be treated as the worship of God and offered to him in prayerful dedication and is based on the teachings of the *Gita* and that *karmayoga* is the path for mortals.

The Maithil Community

Mithila, situated in North Bihar, has an area of 40 thousand square kilometres with a population of more than five million. It has a rich cultural heritage but its Brahmana community is, perhaps, the most backward in the country.

The name 'Mithila' goes back to Pauranic times. It occurs in the *Mahabharata* and in Pali literature and, according to the Pauranic tradition, is derived from that of Mithi (son of Nimi) King of Ayodhya and grandson of Manu who founded a kingdom which was called Mithila after him. It is associated with Valmiki, Ashtavakra, Yajnavalkya, Udayana, Mahavira, Gautama, Kanada,

Jaimini and Kapila as well as the women philosophers Gargi, Maitreyi, Bharati and Katyayani.

After the age of the *Ramayana,* it is said that the three seats of Vedic culture — Kosala, Kasi and Videha — merged to form the Vajjian confederacy and the centre of political gravity shifted from Mithila to Vaisali.

The emperor of Magadha, Ajatasatru, annexed the states of the confederation the fifth century BC. After the Mauryas, a number of rulers captured Mithila and it was only fifteen hundred years after the fall of the Vajjian confederacy that the glory of Mithila was restored, in AD 1097, with the establishment of the kingdom of Karnatas by Nanyadeva, who came from the Deccan. From the Karnatas Mithila passed to the Tughluqs in the fifteenth century under whom the Thakkuras ruled the land as their vassals, the most reputed being Sivasimha under whom flourished the great philosopher, Ayachi Misra and the poet Vidyapati. The Thakkura dynasty ruled over Mithila till the middle of the sixteenth century and, revolting against the Delhi Sultanate, Sivasimha issued his own gold coins but not after he was defeated by the troops of Ibrahim Shah.

Akbar handed over Mithila to Maharaja Mahesa Thakkura, the founder of the Darbhanga Raj which continues to be a dominant force and represents the highest class of Brahmanas who are known as Srotriyas. It produced three illustrious maharajas in the last century : Lakshmishvar Singh, Rameshvar Singh and Kameshvar Singh. Rameshvar Singh was a great Tantrik and a Sanskrit scholar as was his son, Kameshvar Singh. All of them promoted learning, culture and Sanskrit and English education as did Banaili Raj (in District Purnea, Bihar).

Mithila saw its resurgence in the world of thought between 700-1500 and since the time of Gautama it has been a centre of philosophy.

. Gangesa Upadhya, an outstanding *mimamsakar,* piloted the Navyanyaya school of philosophy. He lived during the time of the Karnata king, Bhava Simha. His *Nyayatattvachintamani* is an outstanding work on Nyaya (logic), one of the six orthodox systems of Indian philosophy.

After Gangesa, the most glorious name is that of Paksadhar Mishra (c. 1450) who was a great dialectician and gave impetus to the study of Navyanyaya by writing a commentary on *Tattya-chintamani.*

The three main deities who have inspired the Maithils are Siva, Sakti and Vishnu, in whose honour threefold marks are worn on the forehead by the Maithils, the horizontal lines made with ash representing devotion to Siva, the white vertical lines in sandal-wood paste faith in Vishnu and the dot of wood paste in red or vermilion signifying Sakti.

In the past excessive orthodoxy and conservatism characterised Maithil life but after the thirteenth century there was a significant change. King Harisimha Deva introduced Kulinism by which the Maithil Brahmanas were divided into four subclasses: Srotriya, Yogya, Panjbadh and Jaibar, and the kayasthas. The latter was further divided into two, Kulina and Grahastha. Around this time the system of *Panjiprabandh* came into use according to which a collection of the genealogical data of each individual was maintained and these *panjis* were collected and consolidated by 1313. It is said that the system was introduced to protect the "purity of blood" by making people record their ancestry which would help in avoiding the forbidden degrees of relationship in contracting marriage. No marriage could be contracted without the authorised marriage clearance certificate issued by the Panjikaras, a custom which still holds good. It caused considerable rigidity in society as polygamy was widely practised by the Kulins. A new group known as the Baikaus or vendors group that had come into being, could marry as many as fifty or sixty wives at a time. The condition of women worsened and often they were sold by their parents for a few coins. It was only in the early part of the twentieth century that polygamy was banned and the status of women improved somewhat.

The first available piece of literature in Mithila (written in Maithili by Jyotirishwar Thakur during the age of the Karnata kings), *Varna Ratnakar,* contains a description of the daily life of the kings.

The most profound literary influence was that of Vidyapati (eighteenth century) who enjoyed the patronage of King Sivasimha.

He wrote in three languages — Abhatta (Apabhramsa), Sanskrit and Maithili. In Abhatta he wrote two books, *Kirtilata* and *Kirtipataka.* Among his many Sanskrit works are *Purusha Pariksha,* and *Vibhaga-Sara.* His *Padavali* songs and lyrics stirred all of eastern India. He was a warrior, minister, historian and commentator on religion and Rabindranath Tagore was influenced by him.

Mithila still maintains age-old traditions in the sphere of the folk arts which the women practise as an ordinary, domestic affair. Even the poorest decorate the home and compound with beautiful designs, geometrical patterns and representations of gods and human figures. Among the arts practised today, many of which show the impress of Tantra, are *sikki, sujani, kashida,* the famous Madhubani wall paintings and *alpana.* Women make use of indigenous materials such as vegetable colours and gum and in place of a brush use thread, match sticks or thin bamboo sticks wrapped in cotton for these paintings. Mithila arts and crafts are alive because of the vital relationship between them and the festivals observed. Special *pujas* like Chhinavasta, Kali, Kameshwari, Matangi, Teru and Vaneshwari keep alive the tradition of these colourful arts and crafts.

Almost every month has its special *puja* or festival. A few large fairs are held in different parts of Mithila on many occasions. Rajnagar, Banaili, Singheshwarsthan, Raghopur, Kapileshwar and Janakpur are some of the sites where *melas* and many other festivals are held on Vijayadashmi, Sivaratri and Ramanavami.

The Maithils believe in early marriage and even today, in the villages, a girl is usually married by the time she is fourteen or fifteen. Marriages are arranged through the 'marriage market'. The dowry paid, the bride's father and the bridegroom go to her home where the marriage ceremony takes place. Marriages take place any time of the year on an auspicious *tithi.* The *barat* does not eat any salt in the bride's house till the marriage rituals are completed when the guests are served with rice and salt and other food.

The marriage over, the *baratis* are given *vidayee* — a gift consisting of a pair of coloured *dhotis,* a sacred thread, a handful of betel nut and double the amount of cash that each member of the party had earlier given the bride. The money is not accepted but the other things are. The bridegroom remains at the bride's place. Next come the Chaturthi rites, during which the bridegroom observes *brahmacharya*, does not eat salt and does not oil his hair. He then leaves for home but the bride goes to his home only after the "second marriage" (*dwiragaman*) is celebrated, which may be two or three years later. Maithils rarely marry outside their community.

Darbhanga, the centre of Mithila, has a Sanskrit university and an institute devoted to historical and cultural research on Mithila. The All-India Maithili Mahasabha looks after the interests of Maithils. In Patna, the Chetna Samiti, a leading organisation of Maithils, promotes the cultural life of Mithila and the Maithili Sahitya Sansthan promotes literary activities.

The Mohyal Community

The Mohyals are originally a branch of the Sarasvat Brahmanas but they have renounced their priestly calling to become clerks, soldiers and farmers. They have produced eminent soldiers, doctors, educationists and artists. Mainly a Punjabi-speaking community, they number less than five lakh. They live mostly in the states of Punjab, Haryana, Delhi and Uttar Pradesh.

Different connotations of the name 'Mohyal' have been suggested. The most commonly accepted is that it is derived from the word 'Muhins', meaning the seven classes into which the community is divided : Dutt, Chibbar, Vaid, Mohan, Bali, Lau and Bhimwal. Another explanation is that Mohyal is a corrupt form of Mahiwal, meaning owner of land. Another name applied to the Mohyals in the North-West Frontier Province was Pathan Brahmanas because they had fought many battles shoulder to shoulder .ith the Pathans.

Mohyals claim to be the descendants of six *'raj' rishis* : Bharadwaj (Datt and Vaid), Bhargava (Chhibbar), Parashara (Bali), Kashyappa (Mohan), Vasishtha (Lau) and Koshal (Bhimwal). They have a prominent place in the annals of India and have also figured in the affairs of Arabia, Central Asia, Afghanistan, Persia and China.

In Arabia they were not forced to embrace Islam and fraternal bonds evolved between the Datt chief, Sultan Rahab and the descendants of the prophet Mohammed, Hassan and Hussain, whose allies they became in the war of Karbala and whose defeat they later avenged. Consequently, the Sayyids, the descendants of the Prophet, continued to show great reverence for the Mohyals as dauntless defenders of humanity.

After avenging this defeat and extending their influence in Iran and Afghanistan, they returned to India and spread out in Punjab, Sind, Kashmir, Uttar Pradesh, Bihar, Bengal and Central India.

Before they could consolidate their position and unite, they came into conflict with the invaders from the countries they had left. Their martial instincts and traditions made them countenance love of discipline so that though they opposed each wave of invasion, they adapted themselves to a loyal observance of the order which succeeded.

On their way home from Arabia, they established a Brahmana dynasty in Kabul where they reigned from about AD 860 to 950 and even today the Mohyals residing in Kabul are called *dewans* (ministers). The Chhibbars claim to have ruled Bhera, known as *Chhibbaran-di-Rajdhani* (capital of the Chhibbars). It is claimed that all the Brahmana dynasties encountered by the Chinese pilgrims in the seventh century were Mohyals, a claim which rests on the assumption that other Brahmanas in arrogating to themselves the priestly functions, gave up all claims to royalty and reigning.

Before the partition of India, most Mohyals were settled in the Jhelum District. With partition, the vast majority was rendered homeless. They came and settled down in Punjab and Haryana in the districts of Gurdaspur, Amritsar, Jullundur, Ambala and Karnal. Many also came to Delhi, Meerut, Agra, Jabalpur and other cities.

They have produced a number of heroes who have fought determinedly against fanaticism, social and religious intolerance and other forms of injustice. Bhai Mati Dass was sawed alive because he challenged Aurangzeb and refused to embrace Islam. Banda Bairagi gave up his mendicancy to mould the destinies of Sikhs and Hindus.

The Datts of Gandhia Paniara fought to the last man to defend the honour of a Hindu girl. Lekh Ram Arya (Musafir), an Arya Samajist, was done to death by a Qadiani fanatic.

Among the other Mohyals, it was Bhai Parmanand who organised the Ghadr Party in America and later waged a constant battle against the British *raj* and died as a soldier in the cause of Hinduism. His cousin, Bhai Balmukund, was decapitated for taking part in the Delhi Conspiracy Case; Ram Bhaj Dutt was the first person to invite Mahatma Gandhi to stay in his house in Lahore; Bakshi Lachhman Das Chhibbar founded the first opposition newspaper, *Rajputana Malwa Time,* in India; Kaviraj Om Prakash Datt was a companion of the great martyr Bhagat Singh. Today many Mohyals occupy notable positions in many walks of life, especially in government service, in the police and particularly the civil administration.

Some of the contemporary Mohyals who are well-known are: Bhai Mahavir, Subhadra Joshi, Kapil Mohan and Sunil Dutt. Most of the educational institutions run by the Arya Samaj in Punjab are manned by Mohyals.

The birth of a boy in a Mohyal family is an occasion for rejoicing. At one time, female infanticide was practised among them for three reasons: the system of dowry, the difficulty in protecting a large number of girls, the men of the community being liable to be called out at any time for active military service, and the problem of arranging suitable marriages within the sect which was narrowed by sectarian and customary laws.

After birth the child is given a name (*namakaran*). When a boy attains the age of twelve, he undergoes the ceremony of *yajnopavit* (wearing the sacred thread). This thread is renewed every six months on the Nauratra Ashtami.

The *mundan* (shaving of the head) ceremony is another event in a Mohyal's life which generally takes place on his fifth birthday. Today the ceremony has been shorn of many ritualistic details.

On most festive days a sweet dish (*mitteran da halwa* — friends' sweet) is prepared and distributed only among people of the community, to celebrate the occasion.

Mohyals generally confine their matrimonial alliances to their own seven groups. Earlier they used to take girls in marriage from other Brahmana communities but they never gave their daughters to them in marriage. However, of late, many leading Mohyals have married girls from and given their daughters in marriage to not only other Brahmanas but other castes as well. Mohyals may marry in the mother's *gotra* but never in the father's.

Mohyals reprobate three things : the taking of charity, the handling of grocer's scales and living a life of indolence. They use titles in reminiscence of their close association with rulers, like Mehta, Raizada, Dewan, Bhai, Bakshi and Choudhari.

The Nagar Community of Gujarat

Gujarat is the home of the Nagars but many Nagar families are settled in Uttar Pradesh, West Bengal and Punjab. They have a history going back to Puranic times. Though Brahmanas follow orthodox practices, they have a martial tradition. They also became *dewans* in princely states and have been outstanding administrators, diplomats, poets and musicians.

Their's is recognised as one of the oldest groups of Brahmanas occupying a special place in the social, educational, cultural and religious life of Gujarat. There are more than fifteen thousand Nagar families in India, the majority being settled in the towns of Gujarat and quite a number in Uttar Pradesh and West Bengal.

Some historians say that the Nagars are of the purely Aryan stock belonging originally to Southern Europe or Central Asia. According to one theory, they journeyed from the Hindu Kush to Trivishtapa or Tibet and then through Kashmir into India and settled down around Kurukshetra. They have also been regarded to be of Graeco-Scythian or Dravido-Scythian origin.

The earliest reference to the Nagar is in the *Skanda Purana*. Siva, who created them in celebration of his marriage to Uma, is said to have granted them the land of Hatheshwar. The *Saunka Smriti* also mentions them. According to one opinion, they are of Scythian-Turkish descent, perhaps the descendants of a class of priests in the invading armies, who were purified at a historic fire sacrifice in Mount Abu and were received as a new set of Brahmanas.

Recent research points to their Aryan origin from Hatak (modern Ladakh). The presiding deity is the lord of Hatak, Katkesh or Hatkeshwar.

According to legend, while on a hunt King Chamatkar of Anarta killed a deer suckling her young. The deer cursed him and as a result he developed leukoderma. The Brahmanas who lived in those parts cured him with herbs and he rewarded them with gifts of money and land which they refused, being men of high principles. But the queen persuaded sixty-eight of the seventy-two wives to accept the gift. The four families who refused the reward went away to the Himalayas but the other sixty-eight Brahmanas stayed on and are believed to be the founders of the sixty-eight *gotras* of the Nagars. According to another version, the king showed his gratitude by renovating an old city for them and consecrating a temple to Hatkeshwar, the new city there being named Chamatkarpur. With the passage of time it came to be known by various names such as Madanpur, Skandapur, Anartapur, Anandpur, Nagar, Vrudha Nagar and lastly Vadnagar. The Brahmanas who lived here came to be known as Nagars.

Around 1043, King Vishaldev of Ajmer conquered Gujarat and established a city known as Vishalnagar (later as Visnagar) and presented it to the officiating priests who were an offshoot of the Nagars from Vadnagar. The king also established and gifted the cities of Chitrakupati or Chitrod, Prashnipur, Krashnor and Shatpad or Sathod to the various branches of the original Nagars from Vadnagar.

The Nagars from Vadnagar are known as Vadnagars. In the same manner there are Visnagars, Chitrodas, Prashnoras and Sathodras; the Nagars belong to one or another of these branches. There are some characteristics peculiar to each of these groups and their rites and rituals also differ slightly.

Nagar women have enjoyed a privileged status since ancient times. In the home, they participate equally with men in religious and family affairs and monogamy is practised strictly. The birth of a girl is greeted with the same joy as that of a boy. A widow can be sure of a secure and respectable place in the family.

To preserve their identity, the Nagars formulated a certain code of conduct in AD 347 which is recorded in the *Nagar Khand* of the

Skanda Purana. It admonishes Nagars to preserve their religion (the worship of Siva and Sakti) and to practise good conduct and justice. It forbids inter-caste marriages and eating with those outside one's caste and prescribes forty-eight rituals or *samskaras.* Vadnagar was sacked twice or three times by invaders and the Nagars sought shelter in other places in Saurashtra and Rajasthan but always observed their religious code strictly. Some of them became Buddhists and Jains and a number of Jain religious texts are the works of Nagars. The Chinese monk, Hiuen Tsang, has referred to them in his account of his Indian pilgrimage. They also departed from their brahmanical calling and took a leading part in politics and even in wars. Nagar warriors and generals became well-known for their statesmanship and diplomacy.

Nagars have great adaptability. During the Mughal era they dominated nearly every field of activity -- diplomacy, statesmanship and war. They helped the rulers to administer the state and won their confidence. In recognition of their services, they received big *jagirs* (estates). They learnt Persian and Arabic and also excelled as writers.

Nagars are said to have once come into conflict with Akbar. On a visit to Vadnagar, Akbar was so charmed with the singing of the Raag Malhar by the Nagar sisters, Tana and Riri, that he invited them to Delhi to become his court musicians. But the Nagars took offence at this invitation which led to a serious rift between the rulers and the proud Nagars. Many thousands were killed in the encounter that followed and the sisters immolated themselves. A monument (*deri*) still stands to their memory in the Mahakaleshwar cremation ground of Vadnagar. It is in the memory of those sisters that Tansen named his own *raag* 'Tanariti'.

After the struggle with the Mughals, the Nagars gradually left Vadnagar and settled down in various towns of Gujarat and in other places in north India. From Uttar Pradesh about two hundred families went to the Punjab and Kashmir.

The Nagars played a leading part during the rise and fall of the Maratha empire and maintained their reputation for statesmanship, learning and courage in battle. After the 1857 upsurge, when peace was established, they bade farewell to arms and devoted themselves to scholarly pursuits.

The Sarasvat Community

A small, highly urbanised community, the Sarasvats are divided into three main groups: the Vaishnavite Goud, the Smarta Chitrapur and the Shenvis. Although their home is in the Kanaras and the region around them, more than 90 per cent of the erstwhile Sarasvat landowners have migrated to cities like Bombay, Bangalore and Dharwar in search of education or employment.

The name 'Sarasvat' suggests the legendary origin of the community which is Aryan, a people who originally inhabited the valley of the river Saraswati in Kashmir. One theory proclaims that the Aryans left the Sarasvat country and travelled further northwest, to settle down in Iran and to establish the Zoroastrian religion there. Another is that the Sarasvats are the descendants of a *rishi* whose name was Sarasvat and who preserved Vedic texts during a calamity in the region which is now Kashmir. Yet another theory suggests that being Kashmiri Brahmanas who venerated Saraswati (the goddess of learning) they came to be called after her.

Quite possibly they migrated from Kashmir to Goud (Bengal) and from there to the Konkan coast and Gomantak about the twelfth century. The legend of their arrival in Western India relates that Parasurama invited ten of his learned relatives from the northern regions to preside over a *yajna* at Pande in Goa and it was these scholars who settled down in the ninety-six villages Parasurama gifted to them and from which they came to be known as Shahnavi or Shenvi. Their *gotras* are said to have originated from the names of some of those settlers such as Bhardvaja, Vasta, Kaundinya and Kasyapa.

During their sojourn in Goa the Sarasvats made a significant contribution to cultural life and built some of the many beautiful temples in the western region (dedicated to their deities, particularly Mangesh, Mahalakshmi, Shantadurga and Ramnath). One of the customs followed by the community is that a Sarasvat couple visiting the *Kuladevta* (family deity) for the first time after their marriage, are 'remarried' in the deity's presence.

When Goa became Portuguese, the Sarasvat families began migrating south to the Kanaras for fear of being forced to accept

Christianity. The Goud Sarasvats went as far as Cochin and Travancore (now Kerala).

Some Sarasvat families remained in their original homes so that there still are Sarasvats in Kashmir, Goa, Bengal, and Kanara. Later, under the influence of the teachings of Madhava, many became Vaishnavites. In an age when the means of communication were very limited, these sub-communities tended to lose track of each other and only three emerged: Shenvis, Goud Sarasvats (Vaishnavites) and Chitrapur Sarasvats, each owing allegiance to a different *math*. The chief *maths* of the Goud Sarasvats are in Pertagali and Kasi and that of the Chitrapur Sarasvats in Shirali. All the *maths* have their own guru *paramparas* and are centres of Sanskrit learning.

At the beginning of the twentieth century the Sarasvats began to migrate from the Kanaras to the cities, chiefly Bombay and now only a few Sarasvat families are to be met within the villages. Their ancestral homes are set in mango, jack fruit and cashew groves. The local people still refer to them as Shambhagru, Shenoy or Patel.

Since independence, the Sarasvats have become an urban phe-nomenon. Almost every Sarasvat is literate, those who are well educated become civil servants, teachers, writers or journalists (almost every newspaper in India with a national outlook had at some time or other at least one Sarasvat in a position of editorial responsibility). Young Sarasvat men and women have in recent years done well in engineering, medicine, law, industry, publishing and research. They have written and produced Konkani, Kannada and Marathi plays, contributed to music and received national acclaim. There have been well-known painters, film directors, actors and dancers.

The first people in India, many say in Asia, to plan and execute a scheme for a co-operative housing project, the Sarasvats have successfully operated many types of co-operative activities such as holiday homes, schools, housing projects, banks, libraries, buying and selling co-operatives, religious shrines and social welfare or self-help units.

As the community is fully literate, social progress had made great strides. Sarasvat women (reputed for their beauty and accomplishments) have more freedom, receive more education and have been exposed to the world outside their homes for decades, working in their own community development projects but doing laudable work as devoted social workers in nation-wide organisations. Thousands of Sarasvats have travelled abroad, bringing a certain amount of Westernisation into their homes and ways of life.

The winds of change that education has brought have more or less blown away the cobwebs of social taboos and outdated customs, resulting in a voluntary acceptance of widow marriage, equal status for women, restrictions on the amount of the dowry and on other unwholesome practices. There has been a keen awareness of family planning.

A number of young Sarasvats have married outside the community. There are many examples of Sarasvats marrying Jews, Christians, Muslims, Parsis, foreigners, as well as Hindus of different castes and from different States.

4

HINDU COMMUNITIES
THE KSHATRIYA CASTE

The Baidya Community

Traditionally Baidyas are physicians and there are legends associating them with the gods of medicine, Dhanvantari and the Asvin. Though small in number, they have also made a notable contribution to other aspects of life in India, particularly in Bengal. They do not believe in amassing wealth and enjoy life as long as health and means permit.

A Panini *Sutra* says that *vaidya* or *baidya* means one who has studied the Vedas. There are references to Brahmanas who, after becoming conversant with the Vedas, studied *Ayurveda* and became *Baidyas* or physicians.

Legend has it that Dhanvantari was born when the *devas* and *asuras* churned the ocean. He is considered to be an incarnation of Vishnu and has four hands — in one he holds medicinal herbs and in one the text of *Ayurveda*. He was the first Baidya. Another legend about his birth is that when the *muni* Galava was on a pilgrimage and dying of thirst, he accepted water from a Vaidya girl named Virbhadra. He blessed her and said she would have a son. But as she was unmarried, Galava chanted a Vedic mantra and a boy arose out of a wisp of grass and it was this child who was

Dhanvantari, Amritacharya or Ambastha. He was a Baidya because he owed his birth to a Vedic hymn and he was an Ambastha because he had no father and was brought up by the mother (*amba*) and her family. So Baidyas are also called Ambasthas. But Baidyas say that Ambastha is the name of a place on the banks of the river Indus from where one branch of Baidyas went to South India and another to Bengal (Goud).

There is still another legend which describes Baidyas as begotten of a Brahmana woman by the Ashvins, the gods of healing. Their union being *pratiloma* in which the father is inferior in caste to the mother (even the gods were inferior to a Brahmana) the offspring were not Brahmana. Originally the practice of medicine all over India was mostly in the hands of Brahmanas.

Medicine was the original profession of the Baidyas, but from the time of the Sena kings, they began to adopt other pursuits as well. A Baidya by caste no longer had to be a physician.

The Sena kings themselves were probably Baidyas. The evidence of inscriptions shows that a dynasty of Baidya kings ruled over at least a part of Bengal from AD 1010 to 1200, the most famous being Ballal Sena. He separated the Baidyas into divisions: one, allowed the sacred thread and fifteen days observance of mourning, and the other, an option to adopt the thread and to observe the mourning for a month. He is also said to have made three classes — the Rarhi, Barendra and Bangaja, according to the place of residence and introduced three hypergamous divisions — the Kulin, Bangsaj and Maulik.

He is also supposed to have instituted three other rigid divisions of purity of lineage—the Siddha, Sadhya, and Kashta. The nomenclature is interesting because, according to a legend, Amritacharya or Dhanvantari married the Ashvin's three daughters—Siddha Vidya, Sadhya Vidya and Kashta Vidya. Even in recent times, the Baidyas of these *sthanas* consider themselves higher than others. Those who went farther east to places like Tripura, Sylhet and Chittagong were looked down upon still further. They intermarried with the Kayasthas probably because in those distant parts they could not always get a suitable match within their own clan.

Centuries later, Raja Raj Ballav Sena was not only the undisputed leader of the Baidya community but a great Indian whose name will always find a place in history. He was appointed collector general of the province of Dacca and given the title of Raja by the Nawab of Murshidabad. Shah Alam, the Mughal emperor of Delhi, made him a maharaja with the title Rai Raiyan Salar Jung Bahadur and presented him with a sword of honour. He played an important role in political history and court intrigues during a chequered period. When Mir Jaffar succeeded Sirajuddaula (the nawab vizier of Avadh) with the help of the British, he made Raj Ballav his minister. He (with Miran) tried to get rid of the British but Mir Qasim's men drowned him and his son (Krishnadas Sena) in the Ganga when he was the Subedar of Monghyr.

He persuaded some Brahmanas to invest his son with the sacred thread after which many Baidyas wore this badge of distinction. For several generations, the leadership of the Baidyas has been vested in his family which had its seat at Rajnagar on the south bank of the River Padma (called Kirtinasha for destroying the glory that was Rajnagar).

The Baidyas retained among their group not only rajas and maharajas and powerful zamindars but also scholars of great distinction such as the five gems at the court of Lakshman Sena, two of whom were Jayadeva, the famous composer of the *Gita Govinda;* and Dhoyee Kaviraj.

With some exceptions, *Kaviraji* or Ayurveda was the main profession of the Baidyas throughout the ages and in time, each *kaviraj* came to have a particular master or developed a system of treatment.

Dhanvantari was worshipped by all *kavirajas* who invoked him. Divodasa, the Kasiraja and the two Ashvins, the twin sons of Surya (the sun god), when they prescribed medicines for patients. The first three are often identified as one person.

The Baidya *kavirajas* were often skilled practitioners of medicine and some of their medicines anticipated modern medicines such as cobra venom (called *vish bari*). *Pachan* or mixtures were prepared using from nine to ninety ingredients. The examination of the pulse (*nadi*) was most important in diagnosis.

In 1567, Bharat Mullick, in his book *Chandraprabha,* and in 1575 Rama Kanta Das, in *Baidya Kula Panjika,* wrote in detail about the surnames and *gotras* of Baidyas: Gupta, Sen, Gupta, Datta, Kar, Rakshit, Chaudhuri, Roy, Sarcar, Khan, Mullick, Mazumdar, etc. Some surnames such as Barat, Sen, Das, Datta, Kar and Rakshit, are common among Kayasthas as well. Rakshit, Chaudhuri, Roy, Sarcar are Hindu titles of honour common among the rich in every caste, while Khan, Mullick and Mazumdar are Muslim titles of honour.

While on the one hand there have been Baidya claims even on Kalidasa because his name was Matri Gupta, on the other there was a demand for discarding the name 'Gupta' as being a Vaishya surname. There was perhaps not a single Baidya among traders and shopkeepers, which shows that the Vaishya occupations were not pursued by them. Even as landholders, they never held the plough and always got the work done by hired labour even if they were not zamindars as such.

Talented, cultured and intelligent as a class, the percentage of literacy and education of the Baidyas is much higher than that of any other community in Bengal. The women are treated as equals and even in the days of Kulinism, when polygamy was practised, a Baidya hardly ever had two wives at a time.

Baidyas form a small percentage of caste Hindus, being only about 10 per cent or so of the Brahmanas or Kayasthas. They are sometimes clannish and are like a single family, guarding their interests jealously.

Although they have shed much of their rigidity they have retained their identity. By and large, being of the intellectual middle class and always ready to accept radical changes, they have been liberal in outlook. Even in the early days, well-known Baidya *kavirajas* distributed gifts among Brahmanas on *puja* days as well as to the *maulvis* of *maktabs* where they might have studied Arabic or Persian. The Baidyas were greatly influenced by Buddhism which was powerful in eastern India at one time. Buddhists gave them a place of high esteem in society because healing and relieving suffering of any kind were considered the highest virtue by the Buddhists.

In recent times, many Baidyas have joined the Brahmo Samaj, including some of the leaders. Some well-known Baidyas (men and women) have achieved distinction as political and social workers, historians, authors, music directors, film directors, film stars, actors, dancers and singers.

There have been famous Baidya ministers in the state and central cabinets, administrators, doctors, physicians and surgeons, at the head of the Bengal chamber of commerce and banking, eminent lawyers, *dewans*, educationists and revolutionary leaders.

The Bhatia Community

Originally a warrior race, the Bhatias are now mostly in trade and commerce. The Bhatias (called Bhattis in the past) claim descent from Kshatriyas or Rajputs, a militant people of exemplary fortitude and resourcefulness.

Some time in the sixth century, there reigned Raja Bhoopat in Lahore who acquired fame for his valour, courage and administrative shrewdness. His dynasty came to be known as Bhatti or Bhati dynasty from which the word Bhatia is derived. They successively founded Tannot, Deraval and Jaisalmer in 1156.

During the reign of Raja Mulraj, 1316 was a crucial year for the Bhatias as they were threatened with extinction. It was at this time that Allauddin Khilji invaded Jaisalmer and besieged it for a year. With their resources of arms, ammunition and food dwindling, Mulraj sent the aged and the very young away from the fortress through a secret exit. With his soldiers he launched a do-or-die offensive but his people met their end fighting valiantly and thousands of widowed women committed *sati.*

The two thousand families who had escaped from Jaisalmer settled in Punjab and made their mark in trade and commerce. Within a few years the question whether endogamous marriages might be permitted was dealt with in Multan where the pundits ordained that boys and girls whose blood relationship was beyond seven generations could marry, a decision that marked the beginning of the formation of *nockhs* (groups or clans). The Bhatias now spread out in Rajasthan, Madhya Pradesh, Khandesh, Halar and Kutch. Those who settled in Kutch came to be known as Kutchins and those in Halar as Halars. In different regions the Bhatias acquired different styles of dress. As far as religion was concerned, they accepted the Pushti Marg or Vaishnavism (founded by Vallabha in the sixteenth century), and as Vaishnavites they wear a U-shaped caste mark on the forehead and their tutelary deity is Krishna (enshrined at Nathdwara in Mewar).

They follow the customary sixteen *samskaras*, the important ones being described briefly below: *simanta* is performed during the seventh month of pregnancy. The woman goes through a purificatory *puja* in which mantras are recited to bless and protect her and the unborn child.

Upanayana is the initiation ceremony of a young boy (*batuk*) who is invested with a sacred thread, *yajnopavita*, symbolising a promise made to fulfil his debt to the Creditor, his preceptor and his father. The guru initiates the boy, giving him the Gayatri mantra. He is given a staff which symbolically imposes on him the responsibility of protecting his country and the people and working for their welfare through control over his mind, speech and body.

Vivah is the marriage ceremony, prior to which there is another rite, the *chhakki*. On the day previous to the marriage, the bride goes to the house of her future husband to pay her respects to his relatives, accompanied with her brother who walks alongside with a drawn sword. Then the bridegroom comes to the home of the bride and, hand in hand, they walk round the sacred fire four times which completes the wedding ceremony.

Uthamna is a funeral rite when the friends and relatives of a dead person come at an appointed time to condole with the bereaved family.

The Bhatias were and still are an inherently enterprising people and successfully entered many spheres of commerce and industry such as the textiles, cotton, iron and steel, mining and shipping industries and some have become millionaires as a result.

In recent years the Bhatias have felt the need for higher specialised foreign education and a number of boys and girls have gone to the United States of America and Germany for advanced studies. A large number of them have settled down abroad.

Inter-caste marriages are regarded as corrosive by orthodox Bhatias and strongly discouraged but now their incidence appears to be on the increase at all social levels.

The Rajput Community

There are over 200 million Rajputs in India. Rajasthan is their original home but they are to be met with in Jammu and Kashmir, Himachal Pradesh, Haryana, Madhya Pradesh, Uttar Pradesh, Bihar, Orissa, Saurashtra, Maharashtra and Andhra Pradesh. Some people of Bengal and Assam also claim Rajput descent. The members of nearly all the Hindu ruling families have been Rajputs of the Sisodia clan, originating from Udaipur.

The word 'rajput' means king's son or the prince. Rajputs claim to be the descendants of the Kshatriyas who were the original Aryans. They are considered *dvija* (twice-born) and are entitled to wear the sacred thread.

There are thirty-six Rajput clans tracing their (mythical) descent from the sun, the moon and the sacred fire, known as the Suryavansi, Chandravansi and Agnivansi respectively.

Bravery, chivalry, loyalty, beauty, feuds, assassinations, wars — all these abound in the history of the Rajputs.

The Rajputs considered war and governance as the highest arts of all, but among them have been poets, scientists, musicians and architects. The Rajput noble's court was a centre for the cultivation of the fine arts and even some sciences. The Jantar Mantar observatory at New Delhi was the creation of a Rajput prince, Maharaja Jai Singh II (1699-1744), who was a great astronomer, who also built similar observatories at Varanasi, Ujjain, Udaipur and Mathura.

Beautiful paintings, which are acclaimed as exquisite pieces of art, have been produced by Rajput artists in certain distinctive styles.

Hakim Khan Sur, Pathan, was one of the prominent generals in Maharana Pratap Singh's army, who fought the battle of Haldi Ghati. A Rajput prince gave shelter to Prince Khurram (later Shahjahan). There was a tradition in many Rajput States, of having at least one Muslim amongst their social chiefs.

Amongst themselves Rajputs are egalitarian in their social norms and behaviour. Within the clan or the sub-clan, the richest and the poorest share the same hookah, eat out of the same *thali* and expect the same treatment from their priests. The Rajput values honour more than anything else in life but is somewhat vain and extravagant in money matters. In most Rajput families the men and not the women eat meat.

Many Rajputs are engaged in agriculture today and serve in the armed forces and the police as well. A minority is engaged as clerks and in the professions though some have occupied senior positions in the services. Of late some have been attracted to the field of politics.

5

HINDU COMMUNITIES
THE VAISH CASTE

The Agrawal Community

The Agrawals who belong to the large Vaish community, are found in almost every part of the country. They are also known as *Banias* (traders) from their occupation. They number about a crore. The term Vaish is very comprehensive and covers several business communities such as the Agrawal, Maheshwari, Khandelwal, Oswal, Jaiswal, Poswal, Dasse and Mahajan. Of these, the Agrawal is by far the largest and has about a crore members in India.

The name Agrawal or Aggarwal, is derived from the Agragan state said to be founded by Maharaja Agrasen some five thousand years ago. Agra (not Aggar) was the name of the state and *wal* or *wala,* a suffix denoting possession. So Agrawal or Aggarwal (a corruption) means an inhabitant of the Agragan state.

In those ancient times Agragan was one of the numerous states or *janapadas,* which were like the city states of Greece. The *Mahabharata* and the Buddhist and the Jain literature are the chief sources of information about them. The state comprised Fatehpur, Sikar, Jhunjhunu, Nawalgarh, portions of Rajasthan in the west, Mahendragarh and the Hissar districts of Haryana in the south, some areas of Punjab in the north and the territory as far as Agra in the east. Agroha, which is now in ruins and forms part of the Hissar district of Haryana, was its capital.

Maharaja Agrasen is said to have lived up to the age of 193 and ruled for more than a hundred years. With the foreign invasions in India (beginning in 326 BC) began the downfall and disintegration of the state. Agroha was devastated during Shahabuddin Ghori's invasion in 1194, leading to the flight of the Agrawals and their dispersal in the neighbouring areas of Haryana, Rajasthan and Uttar Pradesh.

Agrasen attached great importance to family life and instituted eighteen *gotras* and restricted people of the same *gotra* from intermarrying, a custom which prevails even today. These *gotras* were not derived from Agrasen's eighteen sons, as is commonly believed by the Agrawals, but from eighteen leading families of Agrohas which were selected for this purpose by him.

The majority of Agrawals are Hindus but quite a number of them have embraced Jainism. This difference in religious affiliation does not constitute a barrier to marriage among these two religionists. An appellation popularly used as a surname by members of the Vaish community, particularly the Agrawals, is Gupta, Gupt, meaning profound or deep. A synonym very often used for the community is Bania, derived from the word *vanik,* meaning a trader or a shopkeeper.

Until two or three decades before the partition of India, the majority of Agrawals lived in the villages of Haryana, Delhi and a number of the adjoining districts of Uttar Pradesh and Rajasthan, in what is now generally referred to as Vishal Haryana. They carried on flourishing business there and exercised complete economic domination over the life of the other communities, particularly the agricultural. They were the bankers and the money-lenders and were perhaps the most respected and even feared people. But there has been a widespread feeling that the Banias exploited the ignorance and illiteracy of the villagers. Their critics charge them with irregularities and excesses in the maintenance of accounts and realisation of debts and loans.

Although most of the *mandis* and business centres in cities and towns of the northern states like Haryana, Rajasthan, Uttar Pradesh and Delhi are the real strongholds of the community today, Agrawals can be found in almost every state, particularly in Madhya Pradesh, Maharashtra, Orissa, Assam and Bengal.

By and large businessmen and traders, the Agrawals enjoy a fair share of representation in several other professions as well. If the community has produced numerous renowned businessmen and industrialists like the Dalmias, Modis, Singhanias, Srirams and Bajajs, it has also produced a number of eminent jurists, educationists, scientists, engineers, politicians, doctors, philosophers, poets and scholars.

Being engaged in one of the most lucrative professions, the Agrawals are generally looked upon as moneyed people. But except for a small percentage of rich businessmen and industrialists and some others, the hard core of the community consists of ordinary shopkeepers and tradesmen.

The Marwari Agrawals of Rajasthan excel the rest in business acumen. They have done particularly well in Assam and West Bengal where some have built huge industrial empires.

Theirs is a virile, dynamic community, full of life, drive and initiative which celebrates the various social, religious and national functions and festivals with great zest.

The Agrawals are orthodox and tradition bound. They visit Hardwar with their families for the ritual bath in the Ganga and do not normally miss such religious fairs as the Kumbh, the solar eclipse fair at Kurukshetra and the annual gathering at Garhmukteshwar. Those who succeed in completing the pilgrimage to the four religious centres (*dhams*) of Hinduism—Kedarnath, Sringeri, Puri and Dwarka—regard themselves as very fortunate.

The younger generation seems not to share the enthusiasm of their elders for religious and spiritual activities.

The Agrawal appears to combine in himself the materialism of the West with the religiousness of the East.

Social customs and practices among them are basically the same as those of other Hindus but the details vary from state to state. For instance, the rites and rituals of the Marwari Agrawals of Rajasthan are slightly different from those prevailing elsewhere.

For the Agrawal marriage is an occasion for great extravagance. Many families ruin themselves in the matter of dowry, an evil the community is particularly plagued with.

Though economical and rather miserly in personal affairs, they give away thousands in charity and often make generous donations

Top: A view the ghats at Varanasi.
Above left: Another view of the Varanasi ghats.
Right: Crowds at Prayag, the holy confluence of three rivers.

The four great Hindu pilgrim centres: (*Clockwise from top left*) Temple at Kedarnath.
Devotees at the Jagannath Temple at Puri. The temple of Sringeri in Mysore.
The temple at Dwarka in Gujarat.

Top left: A South Indian wedding. *Top right:* A Bengali wedding.
Above: A wedding in a North Indian village.

Hindu Festivals: (*Clockwise from top left*) Oil lamps being lighted at Dipavali. Traditional Janamashtami celebrations at Mathura: the 'Govindas' make a human ladder to reach the pot of butter in an enaction of the story of Krishna's life. The boat race — a part of the Onam festivities in Kerala. Durga Puja celebrations.

Top: Painting (from left) of Tansen, famous musician in Akbar's court; Surdas, blind 'bhakti' poet and Sant Haridas.
Left: Chaitanaya.
Above right: Masoleum of Kabir in Uttar Pradesh.

Above left: An image of Ramanujan.
Above right: A depiction of Goddess Saraswati in the Chenna-Kesava temple of Belur.
Left: Shiva's mount, Nandi.

Right: A Shaivite
sadhu.
Below left: A
Vaishanavite sadhu.
Below right: A bhikhu
at the Kumbh Mela.

Four great religious and social reformers of the nineteenth century: (*Clockwise from top left*) Annie Besant, founder of the Theosophical Society of India. Rammohun Roy, founder of the Brahmo Samaj. Dayanand Saraswati, founder of the Arya Samaj. Rama Krishna Paramhansa, founder of the Rama Krishna Mission.

and contributions for religious organisations and educational and charitable institutions,.

The Bania Community of Gujarat

Known as Vania in Gujarati, Vani in Marathi, Chettiar in Tamil, Sud in Punjabi and Komati in Telugu, this community is a conglomeration of people from different castes who were bunched in a single group because of their profession — dealing in grain.

The Vanias of Gujarat have forty subcastes almost all being further divided into the Visa (twenty), Dasa (ten) and Pancha (five), the first being said to be the highest in the Vania social order. Though the members of the Visa and Dasa eat together, they do not intermarry and neither has the type of association with the Pancha.

The Vanias make a strong claim to be Vaishs because they still have *mahajans,* and trade guilds, which are referred to in Sanskrit literature. There are 38 endogamous divisions of the caste and five have Jain sections, known as Shravaks, the others being the Meshris. Both Meshris and Shravaks used to eat together and intermarry till the revival of sectarianism in the nineteen twenties.

The Gujarat social restrictions are not confined to castes and subcastes alone but affect groups of towns or villages, known as Ekadas or Gols and marriage only within the group was permissible but as the rule was not rigidly applied and exogamous marriages were permitted with the permission of the Gol Panchayat, only a fine or a fee had to be paid for any violation.

The purpose of forming these Gols or Ekadas was motivated by practical considerations rather than narrow-minded bigotry. It was a form of protest against the hypergamy of urbanised families.

Despite the compartmentalisation of the Bania caste, the customs and ceremonies are much the same with the group as a whole. The widest difference is between the Meshris, who are Hindus, and the Shravaks, who follow Jainism. In the course of time, many customs and ceremonies, observed and practised a few decades ago, have fallen by the way. Polygamy was permissible, provided the man obtained the consent of the first wife but there are hardly any cases of polygamy now. Some Vania widowers marry and marriage with the deceased wife's sister is permissible but marriage with near blood relatives, common in some other communities, is prohibited as is divorce, though, in recent years, this has become acceptable.

In the past child marriages were in vogue, the girl being between 7 and 11 years of age. Now among Kapol Vanias, the age has been advanced to 16, the Ummads and Dawals extended it to 22. Only the Kutch Dawals, known as Letas, and some of the Panchas permitted widow marriage, which is generally frowned upon by all other Vanias even now. To some extent, the Vania wedding ceremony is the same as any other Hindu marriage.

The decision of the wedding date, which has to be some time between the 11th of *Kartika* Sud (October-November) and the 11th of *Asarha* Sud (June-July) is left to the parents.

Three or five days before the wedding day, the *mandav* ceremony is performed in both houses. It begins with worshipping Ganapati, followed by the installation of the family deity and the ceremonial erection of the *mandav* or marriage booth, into which the members of the family and friends throw red powder, milk, curds, betel nuts and a copper coin, accompanied with the chanting of mantras.

The women of both houses go in procession (singing wedding songs accompanied with musicians) and sprinkle sandalwood dust and flowers on a potter's wheel and bring home earthen pots to be used in the wedding ceremonies.

The most important persons are the mothers' brothers (on both sides) who carry gifts for the bride and bridegroom on the day before the marriage and superintend many of the marriage ceremonies.

At the bride's place the groom is met at the entrance by the bride's mother and some rituals take place.

Balls of cowdung ash are then thrown in the four directions and simultaneously the family Brahmana or the mother-in-law holds two earthen pots of curds, circling them seven times around the bridegroom and then places them in front of him. He then crushes the pots with his right foot and enters the marriage hall. The bride's parents wash the bridegroom's feet with milk, curds, honey, sugar and ghee. After this the ceremony follows the usual Hindu rituals. After the marriage has been solemnised, the couple is taken before the family deity and has to play the game of 'odds and evens' in which they try and guess whether the number of coins that each holds in turn in a closed fist is odd or even. This game has several other variations.

In another ceremony, the bride's mother worships the carriage of the couple by sprinkling sandalwood dust and flowers on it and places a coconut under one wheel which is meant to be crushed when the carriage moves over it. The pieces are gathered by the mother and handed over to the daughters.

There are other rituals among the various sects of the Vanias. Among the Oswals, the maternal uncle of the bride has to carry her four times round the bridegroom before placing her on his left.

Some variations in the marriage ceremonies of various sections of the community can, however, be observed.

When a woman is pregnant for the first time, various ceremonies are performed at the husband's home in the fifth and seventh months. On the fourth day of the latter, she goes to her parents' home and has a bath. On her return, her sister-in-law comes out with some red powder and a large piece of white cloth on which she has to tread and at each step taken, his parents drop a piece of copper and some betel nuts on it. The mother-in-law then performs a brief *puja* and the mother-to-be is then allowed to cross the threshold, taking care not to touch it. Her husband now holds her hand and together they go to bow before the family deity. About twenty days after this ceremony, she goes to her parents' home, where she remains till the child is three or four months old.

For ten days after the child's birth, the husband's family and friends send ghee, *gur* and spices to the girl's house daily. The *Chhathi Pujan* ceremony is performed on the sixtieth day.

On the twelfth day, when the mother worships the *baran balians,* twelve small heaps of rice are laid on a stool and next to each head is placed a betel-nut, a betel leaf and a copper coin and after *kanku* and flowers are scattered on them, they are given to the family priest.

In death, as in life, the Vania is bound by religious rites. On his deathbed he is required to give a Brahman *gaudan* or the equivalent value of a cow and has to announce a sum to be given in charity.

When the end draws near, he is bathed, dressed and placed on a freshly-washed portion of the floor of a front room, with his head to the north, till life ebbs away.

On his death, the body is removed from the house, head first, to a point halfway to the cremation ground. Here it is placed on the ground where some rice, some betel-nuts and a copper coin are placed on it. From here it is carried, feet first, to the cremation ground.

After the collection of the ashes and their immersion in a river, the place of cremation is washed clean and an earthen pot full of water is placed there which the chief mourner breaks by throwing stones at it through his legs from a distance. A cow is brought and milked there so that the milk falls on the cremation spot.

The father-in-law of the chief mourner sends rice, pulse and ghee to the bereaved household which, if the deceased was old, is cooked and eaten; if not, it is given to dogs. A widow's hair is cut off and the heads of all members of the family are shaved as are the moustaches (and beard) also if the deceased was young.

On the eleventh day is performed the most important death ceremony — mating a steer to a heifer; on the twelfth, cooked food is given to crows; and on the thirteenth a Brahmana is given a bedstead, bedding and some money.

Vanias are, generally speaking, staunch adherents of the Vallabhacharya sect. It is believed they were converted to this faith some 450 years ago. Except for the Agarwal and Ram Nagar Vanias, none of the others wear the sacred thread.

At one time they used to visit the Vallabhacharya temples daily but gradually with the spread of education among them and the weakening of religious control, worship at home was accepted as being proper.

In almost every Vania home, there is a *puja* room or a corner where the images and idols of worship are placed.

Vanias from North Gujarat and Kathiawar are sturdy and active, while those from South Gujarat are often slight and poor in physique. Some North Gujarat and Kathiawar Vanias have a moustache and those from South Gujarat have shaven their heads at the crown and in a line down to the back of the head.

They dress in colourful clothes which vary in different regions, the main variations being in north Gujarat, Kathiawar and Surat.

When going out men usually wear a *dhoti*, a jacket called *badan*, a cotton coat *(angarkha)* coming down to the knees and a shoulder cloth called *pichodi*.

In Kutch and Kathiawar, those who were in state service wore the loose *phenta*, probably due to Muslim influence. Others wear a large Rajputana type turban, while those in north and central Gujarat wear the tightly folded cylindrical turban, with numerous folds in front and several coils at the back.

The men and women are very fond of jewellery and well-to-do men as a rule wear a silver girdle and a gold armlet above the elbow and the richer they get, the more they add to their personal adornment. The women wear gold jewellery often set with pearls: *chak* in the hair, earrings, nose-rings, necklaces, an armlet above the left elbow, bangles of glass and ivory, silver anklets and silver toe-rings.

The Maheshwari Community

There are several legends about the origin of the Maheshwari community but the one generally accepted places the date of their origin as about four thousand years prior to the *Vikram Samvat*. It is said that in a village known as Khandala (near Jaipur) ruled Raja Sujat Sen. Once his only son went on a hunt with seventy-two Kshatriya fellowmen. Some *rishis* who were performing *yajna* were disturbed and cursed the royal party which turned to stone. On hearing the prayers of their wives, Siva (Mahesh) turned them into human beings again on condition that they would give up fighting and take to business. It is these seventy-two Kshatriyas who are supposed to be the original ancestors of the seventy-two *gotras* of the Maheshwaris. Later, three more *gotras* were added and now there are 989 sub-*gotras* and *nakhas*. Marriage in the same *gotra* is strictly forbidden.

The Maheshwaris number about three million and have played a notable role in the economic and industrial progress of the country. They are predominantly a business and mercantile community.

The chief language spoken by them is Marwari or Rajasthani but in other parts of India they have adopted the regional language and speak Punjabi, Gujarati, Marathi, Hindi and Telugu depending on the state of residence. They are originally from Rajasthan but have settled down in different parts of India in search of employment and business. Because of their industry, intelligence and adaptability they have built large industrial businesses.

The Maheshwaris remained a business community till the end of the nineteenth century. They had acquired many anti-social customs : dowry, child marriage and *purdah*. The first Maheshwari reformer, Raj Bahadur Shyam Sunderlal Loiwal (who was deeply influenced by Swami Dayanand Saraswati, the founder of the Arya Samaj), founded a Maheshwari Mahasabha which had its first session at Ajmer in 1892, which provided the impetus for the foundation of the All-India Maheshwari Mahasabha in 1908. Since then the Mahasabha has been crusading for social reforms. Many eminent Maheshwaris went to jail and helped in the *khadi* and *charkha* movements and one Krishna Sarda was hanged for his role in the struggle for freedom.

The Maheshwaris are a very enterprising community. The Birlas and Shivkissen Bhatter were the first Maheshwaris who, in 1918, ventured to start a jute mill. They faced great difficulties created by the British but through sheer perseverance they succeeded. Up to 1939 their mills were not allowed to be represented on the Indian Jute Mills Association's Committee. Similarly after independence, the Maheshwaris have started industries in different sectors of the economy.

The Maheshwaris are charitable in disposition. The Maheshwari Mahasabha has established the S.K. Jaju Memorial Trust for the purpose of distribution of scholarships, etc. There are several other philanthropic trusts started by various individual Maheshwaris. The institutions at Pilani are a symbolic example of individual Maheshwaris' contribution to the cause of education.

Certain special rituals and festivals are observed by the Maheshwaris. A rite which has great significance for the women is called Baditeej. It is celebrated on the third (*Krishnapaksha*) of *Bhadrapada* of the *Vikram Samvat* year when women fast and pray for the longevity of their husbands and unmarried girls pray for good husbands. Only the men cut *peenda* after which the women perform *puja* and break their fast.

Gorja or Gavraja is celebrated on the third day of *Chaitra* (Sudi) when Siva and Parvati are worshipped. Unmarried girls worship the goddess Gorja with *gulla* (the inside of green grass) for sixteen days and married women for eight with *doob*.

Raksha Bandhan in this community is celebrated twenty days after the usual date of its celebration on the fifth of the second half of *Bhadrapad* and is known as Bhai Panchami or Rishi Panchami.

Jaystha Sukla 9 of the *Samvat* year is celebrated as Mahesh Navmi to commemorate the birth of the Maheshwari community when Mahesh is worshipped.

Two special customs are different from other marriage rites of the Hindus: *Mamapheras,* when the maternal uncle takes the bride round the bridegroom four times. The remaining three circles are completed around the sacred fire. The Maheshwari bride must wear ivory bangles for a couple of years or at least for forty days after her marriage.

When a member of the family dies, the sons, the grandsons and great grandsons on both the paternal and maternal sides, have their heads shaved. In other Marwari communities only the sons are required to do this.

The Marwari Community

The Marwaris come from the 'region of death', Marooa-war or Marwar, the desert area of Rajashtan, where in summer the sun beats the earth into a 'sheet of iron' and turns the sky into a 'canopy of brass'. Today, they control almost 60 per cent of the assets of Indian industry in a broad spectrum   of productive activity. They have been providing entrepreneurial leadership to the country from before and after Independence. They belong to the merchant community of Rajasthan and their competence in trade and business is proverbial.

Many of them spread out *via* the Ganga, a congenial route, as Hindi, the language spoken along the river, was their main language, the culture was also a common one and there were several places of pilgrimage along the route which attracted them. In Calcutta they prospered, having established the jute and tea industries. In most cases they had no formal education, so the professions were closed to them but their strong point was arithmetic and many of them became brokers.

James Tod, the best-known chronicler of Rajasthan, has mentioned 128 merchant or commercial communities and groups belonging to that region but the number could have been as high as eighteen hundred. According to the census of 1901, five million people in India returned Marwari as their mother tongue. Today, three communities that are believed to be dominant in the commercial sphere are the Maheshwari, the Agrawal and the Oswal, all the three claiming to be of Rajput descent. The Maheshwari tradition is that, during one of their battles, though Vaishnavas, they prayed to Siva, to help them which he did on the condition that they would forsake the sword and take up the pen, the badge of the peace-loving merchant class.

The Agrawal trace their descent from King Agrasen whose capital was at Agroha in the Punjab. He is said to have had seventeen sons whom he wanted to marry to the eighteen snake daughters of a king named Basak but as there was one son less, he took a portion of the eldest and made up the deficit thus establishing eighteen clans.

The Oswals, who are mainly Jains come from the town of Osian, forty-eight kilometres. from Jodhpur. They also trace their descent from a number of Rajput clans. Formerly there was no intermarriage between these communities, not even between similar groups like the Oswals and Poswals (both of whom are Jains claiming Rajput descent) but such restrictions are breaking down today.

The Marwaris were influenced by the tradition-bound standards of the court at Udaipur. The women observed strict purdah and the houses (*havelis*) they lived in, cut them off completely from the world of men, even their own men, as they were not allowed to enter the men's section in their own homes. Some strict customs were observed in the women's section. A daughter-in-law could never approach the mother-in-law without covering her face or speak to her without the presence of intermediaries. Yet in their own way the women shared with the men the responsibility of meeting family, caste and other obligations. They were made aware from a young age that the family prestige depended on their character and behaviour.

A wife was expected to behave with great restraint even when receiving her husband returning home after a long time.

Festivals were celebrated with great regularity and were full of the gaiety, colour and song that are to be seen in Marwar weddings even today.

The Marwari bridegroom holding a sword, wearing a turban, jewellery and a coconut tied to his side, mounted on a mare, is customarily led in a procession to the bride's house. He touches a decoration fixed on the door with a *neem* twig or, in some groups, with his sword.

The ceremonies that follow are elaborate, many of them common to other Hindu communities, as are also the 'games' that are played by the couple such as fishing for a ring in a pot of milk or untying the knots on a *rakhi*. The first time the hands of the couple meet, the mother-in-law places freshly ground *mehndi* (henna) in them. It is also customary to decorate the hands and feet of the women on all festive occasions with beautiful floral patterns with *mehndi*. When the bridegroom returns to his house with his bride, seven *thalis* are placed in a line which he pushes aside. The bride follows in his footsteps picking them up one by one, making as little noise as possible, thus symbolising her desire to merge quietly in her new household. At the birth of a son, a *thali* is sounded to proclaim the news but silence announces a daughter's arrival.

The chief festivals are Vasant Panchami, Holi, Gangor, Teej, Rakhi, Dussehra and Diwali.

Jainism, which was adopted by many of them influenced their attitude towards the acquisition of wealth as the Jain doctrine of *anekanisvada* (many-sidedness of reality) gave them a broader outlook on life than the average Hindus. Though they had been established as bankers in Northern India since a long time and their connection with Bengal began in the eighteenth century with their association with the nawabs of Bengal as their bankers.

With the coming of the British, a gradual but definite change took place. The centre of trade shifted to Calcutta and from being initiators of trade they slipped into the position of middlemen. They retained control but only a small percentage of the profits. The main commodities they dealt in were indigo and opium grown in the Malwa Plateau and exported in great quantities to China at the beginning of the nineteenth century. The Marwari, with his already sound financial base became adept at developing the mechanisms of the trade. They had a unique system of transmitting the market rates of opium from Calcutta to the heart of Rajasthan within an hour's time. The transmission was carried out through flashing mirrors stationed at various points for a monthly fee of fifty rupees.

A hundred years later, they controlled the cotton mills in Bombay and the jute mills in Calcutta. They lived frugally in communal *basas* with case boxes and red ledgers as their main business equipment. They worked as *banians* or guaranteed brokers to the big English firms, wielding great power as the intermediaries between the producers and the consumer.

Their talent for taking commercial risks and for working together (which gave them access to reserves of capital as well as information) combined to make their fortune, acquired mostly through speculation. The Birlas alone are said to have acquired from Rs. 20 lakh to Rs. 80 lakh during the Second World War. When the British started leaving India, it was left to the Marwaris to walk into the industrial field. Since then the rise in their fortunes has all but skyrocketed and their history suggests that their genius lies in making every situation work for them.

The Patel Community of Gujarat

According to a local saying the Patidar or Patel of Gujarat 'grows gold'. He makes it through trade, commerce and industry. Sharp business acumen, resourcefulness and energy are the hallmarks of the Patidars and are undeniably the chief cause of the extraordinary affluence and success of this community of Gujarat.

Patels are ambitious, intelligent, independent, hardworking and hospitable, thrifty as a rule but excessive spenders on occasions like marriage and death.

Sharing a common ancestry with the Punjabi Jats, the Patidars are mostly sturdy men of medium height and sallow complexion.

Blessed with a very fertile region for their home, this community in Kaira District has combined hard work and enterprise to give meaning to the "green revolution". Today the Kaira District is thickly populated, has a high degree of literacy, is the most intensively cultivated, progressive and prosperous district in Gujarat. The yield per acre is one of the highest in India. The intelligent adoption of a large number of new agricultural methods and technology speak for their enterprise. Nowhere else has co-operation been so successful as in this region. The Kaira District's Co-operative Milk Producers Union better known as the Amul Dairy, is one of the most successfully functioning in India today.

The Patels have also been outstanding in the fields of trade and industry. They have been pioneers in textiles (the Mafatlal Group), chemicals (Alembic) and engineering industries (Jyothi, Hindustan Tractor, etc.). In fact, the name 'Patel' is synonymous with big business. The tobacco business is virtually a monopoly of the Patels. Many of them are established in several African countries and trade with and in South and East Africa is the basis of their fortunes. With the profits ploughed back into the village signs of prosperity are visible. Ownership of some land and a house is a matter of status with a Patidar no matter how wealthy he may become. Many a Patidar in the Charoter villages might own a concrete three-storied house, a Mercedes Benz and a refrigerator.

Though the Patidars are a closely knit, self-reliant community, they are non-communal and contribute to deserving objectives of other communities as well. Most Patel villages have schools, hospitals and other charitable institutions.

The Patidars were and continue to be in the vanguard of the political movements in the country and have produced such outstanding leaders as Vallabhai Patel and his brother, Vithalbhai Patel, Darbar Gopaladas Desai and Motibhai Amin. Their influence also led to the spread of education and to the removal of many social abuses like untouchability, low status of women and female infanticide. The Patidars are also noteworthy administrators and civil servants.

Bhulabhai Desai (d. 1970) laid the foundation of the rule-based Vallabh Vidyanagar University and was the founder chairman of the Swatantra Party in Gujarat.

Eshwar Patlikar, Pitamber Patel and Pannalal Patel have enriched Gujarati literature. Yogendra Desai and Chandralekha are dancers of a high order and Kanti Patel, the sculptor, and Balakrishna Patel, the painter, are well-known in the sphere of art.

The Patidars trace their ancestry to Lava and Kusha, the sons of Rama. According to the Barots, the minstrels of Gujarat, the Lava Patidars are the descendants of Lava and the Kadwa Patidars of Kusha. Historically, it is said that they are the descendants of the Hunas and Gujars who came to Gujarat from the West in AD sixth century. Another theory, however, is that they are originally Jats from the Punjab who migrated to Rajasthan and thence to Gujarat, after the successive Muslim invasions.

The two main subcastes among the Patidars are the Lava and the Kadwa and there is no intermarriage between them. Though originally they were all primarily agricultural, the Lava Patidars did not themselves work in the fields while the Kadwas did.

The Lavas are further subdivided into Kanbis, Anjanas and Chowdharies, the first being cultivators and the other two traders.

Patidar weddings are arranged on a grand scale. At the *sagai* or engagement ceremony, the custom of *matli* involves the sending of over eighty kilograms of sweets to the bridegroom's place. In the dowry, the girl is supposed to be given a minimum of 250 grammes of gold and 25 to 30 sets of clothes, though the figure usually goes up to 51 or 101.

After the *matli* comes the *chandlo* ceremony, when again the girl's parents make cash presents to the boy's family. On the day of the marriage the *barat* arrives in the evening and after an exchange of garlands there is the *hasta milap* (the main ceremony). After each round of the sacrificial fire the bridegroom's palm is crossed with gold.

The death ceremony is another occasion for heavy spending. The women mourners follow the funeral procession in single file. Mourning continues for nine days. Men come to mourn (*koko*) and sit together outside and women mourn inside the house. The mourning is called *kan-mokan*.

6

OTHER HINDU COMMUNITIES

Chandraseniya Kayastha Prabhu

The members of the Chandraseniya Kayastha Prabhu community number over one hundred thousand and are scattered all over India, their largest concentration being in Maharashtra (the Deccan coast, Konkan and the coastal Kolaba District and Baroda).

Their origin is controversial. The name Chandraseniya is a corrupt form of Chandrashreniya (people from the valley of the Chenab in Kashmir). The term Kayastha originates from the region around Ayodhya, which was called Kaya Desh, where the Chandraseniya Prabhus settled. 'Prabhu' denotes a high government official. Traditionally, they have been record keepers and scribes. They were appointed by Shivaji as custodians of his forts and held high offices in Peshwa and Mughal times but later shifted their allegiance to the Nizam, the Gaekwads and Holkars. With the advent of British rule they became clerks and *vakils* and took up service in the army.

Navaratri is the most important festival of the community when a little girl often above the age of three, is dressed as a *devi* and worshipped as a Kumarika.

A religious community, the Kayasthas worship Ekvira of Karla who is the Kuladaivata.

They have the Upanayana ceremony and are Vedadhikaris (having the right to read the Vedas).

The Coorgi Community

Coorg, the home of the Coorgis, is a small beautiful district on the Western Ghats of Karnataka. Some say that the Coorgis or Kodavas came from the Indus Valley and are Aryans. Others hold that after Alexander the Great had abandoned his eastern campaign, the Scythians in his army came to the south, married local beauties and settled in the remote hills of Coorg. Still another version is that they are the descendants of Arabs. But the Coorgis are Hindus and, as a martial race, belong to the Kshatriya community. Due to long personal contacts with the westerners, the Kodavas or Coorgis have also become westernised.

Their ancestral houses resemble old fortresses and are surrounded by rich fields and gardens where oranges, pepper and coffee are grown. The entrance to each house is by carved stone gates.

Every Coorgi village has a headman who looks after travellers coming to the village, sees that the lands are properly cultivated and helps the villagers in times of misfortune.

Coorgis are a conservative people and marriages are arranged by the parents. Kodavas do not observe the dowry system but parents give their daughters jewellery, etc., and what cash they choose to give.

The women wear the sari in a peculiar way pleated at the back. The story goes that the goddess, Paravati, appeared before the Coorgis in the form of a river and came with such force that the pleats in this dress, which are normally in front, were pushed to the back.

The Coorg District has produced two of India's greatest generals, Cariappa and Thimayya. Its tradition and culture are in many respects, unique.

The Dogras

The Dogras, numbering nearly one million are concentrated north of the River Sutlej (in Jammu, Himachal Pradesh, Kashmir and

Punjab) and have carved out India's northern frontier along the Karakoram.

According to one tradition, the word Dogra is derived from *duggar*, which is ascribed to *dvigarta,* implying a land of two lakes, the Mansar and Saruinsar. The historical tradition rests on two Chamba copper plates of the eleventh century that have been found which mention Durgareshwar, the lord of Durgar. It is said that Durgareshwar, once attempted to conquer the Chamba Kingdom so the name may well be derived from *durgaradesha* (the difficult terrain). In any case, the word 'Dogra' does not denote a caste but is a term embracing Hindus of all castes as well as Muslims and Sikhs living in the Dogra region and speaking Dogri.

The Dogra region is famed for its miniature paintings. The Pahari school, which included the Poonch, Jammu, Basohli, Guler and Kangra styles, created beautiful and highly stylised combinations of colour and line, expressing delicate and sensuous feeling and intense passion. Many of these paintings depict the moods of lovers in a romantic setting.

The Dogras excel in martial arts. However, in addition to their joining the defence forces in large numbers, they have also entered other spheres of economic and political activity. Dr. Karan Singh, the youngest person ever to become a member of the union cabinet, and at one time the ambassador to the United States, is a Dogra.

The Garhwalis

The domain of the Garhwalis comprises the four districts of Garhwal Chamoli, Tehri and Uttarkashi in the state of Uttar Pradesh, with its massive snowbound ranges bordering on Tibet. Life in the Garhwal hills is not idyllic and for the simple and poor people that they are, it is one long struggle.

The Garhwalis number more than one million in population and the region can not sustain many more people. Most Garhwali cultivators are poor but they are sturdy, have wonderful powers of endurance and manage to wrest a precarious living from the unhelpful Himalayan soil.

A typical Garhwali village has rough stone houses straddling the spur of a hill above the fields or a stream, with half a dozen families each possessing a few acres of land on which everyone works. The women do most of the work in the fields — the ploughing, the sowing, the weeding and the reaping. As the land does not provide enough, the men have to take up work in the plains or join the army. From an early age, children help in the fields, graze cattle or carry milk to the market. But the hunger for learning is always present and many children walk five or six miles to school every day.

Their food is simple — milk, lentils, a few vegetables, a little fruit and, rarely, sheep or goat. Medical facilities hardly exist, except in the bigger villages, where sometimes there is an ill-equipped dispensary with a compounder in charge. People have to walk great distances to reach a hospital; sometimes sick people simply stay at home until they got better — or fail to do so.

Many of the roads are either mule tracks of footpaths and although several remote areas have been opened up, large tracts of Garhwal cannot be reached except on foot.

Some villages have primary or middle school but to send a boy to college (which means sending him to live in a town in the foothills) involves great expense for the parents. Very few can afford to do this. Those who manage to receive good education, generally do rather well. There are many Garhwali scholars and educationists of note and many also achieve prominence in public life.

Garhwalis have their pleasures too. Almost everyone can sing. Among musical instruments, they favour the *bansri* (shepherd's pipe) and the drum. Many songs deal with the homesickness of those who are separated from their parents and their home in the hills. They have a tradition of *hurkias* (bards) and story telling is still popular in villages where there are few other forms of entertainment. Scholars like Tare Datt Gairola, Shyam Chand Negi, Govind Chatak, Mohan Lal Babulkar and Radhakrishnan Vaishnav have documented many Garhwali folk tales, songs and proverbs. There are also a number of Garhwali poets and short-story writers working in Hindi: Ram Prasad 'Pahari', Santosh Narayan Nautiyal,

H.D. Bhatt, Ganga Prasad 'Vimal', Bhajan Singh, Bhagwati Prasad Panthani and Purashottam Dobhal, the playwright.

For the story of Garhwali art, we must turn to Mukandi Lal's *Garhwal Painting*, which traces the development of the Garhwali (Pahari) school of painting which has an acclaimed place in the country's art tradition with its themes from the great religious classics, its tender depiction of women and its impressionistic treatment of Himalayan flora. Modern Garhwali artists have made notable contributions to painting and sculpture.

A religious festival or a village fair will attract people from places within a radius of sixteen to twenty-four kilometres. and it is on these occasions that the Garhwali women dazzle the eyes with their gay clothes, heavy silver nose-rings and earrings and colourful head scarves.

Marrying a daughter off is really no problem in Garhwal. A dowry is unnecessary since there are fewer women than men.

The early history of Garhwal is obscure but three castes were known: the Brahmanas, the Rajputs (including the Khasias) and the Doms. The number of Brahmanas has always been rather small. There is no hereditary caste of sweeper in the hills and most of the people listed as Sudras are really weavers, carpenters and other artisans and craftsmen.

It appears that the principal Rajput families in the Himalayan districts were the Palas of Garhwal, the Chands of Champawatgarh and the Katyura princes, who originally lived at Joshimath in Garhwal and later migrated to the Katyur valley in the Almora district. In spite of the rajas, the real masters were the turbulent races on either side: the Rajputs, the Gujars, the Sikhs and the Gorkhas—who levied heavy ransom and tithes on the unfortunate cultivators. It was the conquest of Garhwal by the Gorkhas that led, indirectly, to British intervention in this area.

The ambitious Gorkhas of Nepal captured Almora in 1790 and then carried their invasion into Garhwal. Srinagar (Garhwal) was taken in 1803 and the king, Parduman Sah, fled to the plains. By pawning his property and his throne, he got together a new army, returned to the foothills and attacked the invaders. He was defeated and killed.

The rule of the Gorkhas in Garhwal was very severe, cultivators being sold as slaves at the Hardwar fairs, for anything from Rs. 10 to Rs. 150 a head, according to age, condition and sex. As the average price of a horse was less than about Rs. 300, it is no wonder that the Garhwalis welcomed British intervention.

The British found the Gorkhas very stubborn opponents but the small fierce men from Nepal had stretched their lines of communication too far and they were eventually driven out of Garhwal. In 1815, the British reinstated Raja Sudershan Sah of Tehri, the portion of his territory which lay to the west of Alaknanda was restored to him and the British retained the lands to the east (the district of Pauri-Garhwal).

Garhwalis are gallant fighters. Of the 2/39th Garhwal Rifles, Gobar Singh Negi was only nineteen when he was killed by the enemy in 1915 in World War I. He died fighting with exceptional gallantry and was the youngest Garhwali recipient of the Victoria Cross. There is a memorial to him at Chamba, in Tehri-Garhwal. Another Garhwali (Naik) Darwan Singh Negi won the Victoria Cross for conspicuous bravery during the battle at Festubert on 23 November, 1914. Their valour and sacrifice have always been a source of inspiration to the Garhwalis.

The Gorkhas

The original Gorkhas came from the small town of Gorkha in Nepal. History narrates that when Allauddin Khilji laid siege to Chittor, the Rajputs put up a fierce resistance. But the fortress fell in 1303. The surviving Rajputs trekked northwards to the hills. While travelling from place to place in the mountain ranges, they found the Magar and Gurung tribes cultivating rice and maize on the lower slopes or tending cattle and goats higher up on the mountain sides. They settled down in this place and lived in thatched circular huts, wore homespun cloth, spoke Magarkura and Gurungkura, the tribal dialects and practised the Buddhist faith.

These Rajputs had brought their Brahmana priests with them and together they began converting the local people to Hinduism. This gradual process continued for four centuries and before long

Hindi became a local dialect. They also took over large tracts of land in Nepal.

Drabya Shah, a descendant of the early Rajputs, conquered Gorkha in the sixteenth century. After a span of nearly two hundred years, Narbhupal Shah ascended the throne. The most powerful in the line was Prithvi Narayan Shah, who vanquished the neighbouring kings and held sway over Nepal. It was the hour of Gorkha supremacy.

When Prithvi Narayan died in 1770 the lesser Gorkha generals took over and extended their military operations into the state of Sikkim and further on as far as Darjeeling. In 1792 the Gorkhas had a brief encounter with the Chinese but were thrown back by General Fu Kang. An attempt to take over the Kangra valley too proved futile as the Gorkhas were outnumbered and driven back by the raja who sought the assistance of Maharaja Ranjit Singh.

The Gorkhas infiltrated southwards and occupied British territory, including Gorakhpur. The Governor General of India sent out warnings to which the Gorkhas paid no heed and the British declared war on them in 1814. After a stiff battle, the Gorkhas were finally defeated and Dehra Dun, Almora and Gorakhpur became British Gorkha regimental centres.

When the 1857 upsurge broke out, the 2nd Gorkhas, called the Sirmoor Battalion, were called upon to fight for the British. They joined the British forces at Alipur, thirty-two kilometres north of Delhi. Nearly four thousand freedom fighters, with one hundred heavy guns and sixty field guns, defended the city. The fighting continued for two weeks in which over a hundred Gorkhas were killed.

The Kumaon Battalion was put into action along with the Sirmoor Battalion and the British were able to suppress the attack. The 4th and 5th Gorkha Rifles were raised during this action. Queen Victoria presented a gold-gilded truncheon to the Gorkhas in recognition of their valour.

The Gorkha soldier is extremely hardy and has a great sense of loyalty and dedication. Generations after generations of young Gorkhas have enlisted in the defence forces. Their motto has been, *Kafar huru bhanda maru nikos* (It is better to die than be a coward).

At the end of the nineteenth century the Gorkhas had served overseas in Malaya, Burma and Cyprus where they were acknowledged as the fiercest fighting men. At the beginning of the twentieth century they were called to fight in China during the Boxer uprising.

When World War I broke out, there were ten Gorkha regiments each with two battalions, with regimental centres at Dehra Dun, Almora, Bakloh, Shillong, Quetta and Dharamshala. Young Magar and Gurung boys came down from Kaski and Lumjung, Ghandrung and Baglung, to Gorakhpur for their initial training.

At the outset of World War I, Maharaja Jang Bahadur Rana of Nepal sent twenty-five thousand Gorkhas to support the British army. The strength of the Indian Army's brigade of Gorkhas was multiplied eight-fold. During the four years of the war, the Gorkhas fought in France, Mesopotamia, Gallipoli and in many places in western Europe. As part of the Indian Corps in France they fought at La Bassee, Festubert and Givenchy.

Rifleman Kulbir Thapa of the 2nd Battalion, 3rd Gorkha Rifles (2/3 Gorkhas) won the first Victoria Cross for action at La Basse; the second being won by (Naik) Karni Bahadur Rana of the same regiment.

During World War II the Gorkhas fought the Germans and were sent to the Middle East, Malaya, Basra and Tehran. They took part in the famous battle of El Alamein in Libya and fought in Tunisia as well. Several Gorkhas received the Victoria Cross for their gallantry in this war.

The partition of India in 1947 brought about many changes in the set up of the defence services. The Gorkhas, being Hindus, remained with India, the 2nd and 6th Gorkhas, consisting of the Gurungs and the Magars, and the 7th and 10th Gorkhas, comprising the Rais and the Limbus, were sent to Malaya as part of the British Gorkhas.

During the winter of 1947-48, the 5th Gorkhas fought the tribal invaders in Kashmir. The brigadier who directed the operations died the following year and was posthumously awarded the Maha Vir Chakra.

The 5th Gorkhas received five more gallantry awards and eight mentions-in-despatches.

In 1961, when the Chinese tried hit-and-run tactics, the 1/8 Gorkhas were on the far side of Leh. In July and August of 1962 they fought the Chinese for the out-posts near Lake Pangong and it was during this action that (Major) Dhan Singh Thapa was awarded the Maha Vir Chakra. Other Gorkha battalions also fought in this war.

There are seven Gorkha regiments — the 1st, 3rd, 4th, 5th, 9th and 11th — with the Indian Army, the 2nd, 6th, 7th and 10th being with the British Army. The 1st and 4th have their regimental headquarters at Sabathu, while the 3rd, 8th, 9th and 11th have their headquarters at Dehra Dun.

The Gorkhas are short, stocky and have slanting eyes. Both men and women are fond of horses, rum and cigarettes. They are the fiercest, the most dreaded fighting men in the world on the battlefield but otherwise they are gentle, family-loving men with a passion for football and boxing.

The Gorkhas are divided into various groups who differ from each other in many respects, including in features and customs but possess a common character which binds them into a distinct 'race'. They are settled in many countries but their largest concentration is in India, with Dehra Dun as the major centre of their activities.

The festivals of the Gorkhas are described briefly below.

Dussehra is a time for family reunions and the gathering of the clan. The first day is called *jamare aunsi,* when barley seeds are planted by the *bahuns* (priests) near the spot where the festivities are to take place. The *agni kund* is lit and a *havan* is performed throughout the festive period.

The Goddess Durga is worshipped from the second to the sixth day and on the seventh they invoke the blessings from the flowers (*phulpati*). The weapons are garlanded.

The eighth day is *kalaratri,* the dark night, the night of merriment when the Gorkhas dance in their traditional dress.

The day of sacrifice, *balidan,* is the ninth and the most significant day. It commemorates Rama's slaying of Ravana, also the destruction of the buffalo demon by Durga, which is symbolised by the sacrifice of a buffalo.

The tenth day is Vijayadashmi recalling Rama's return to Ayodhya with Sita and Lakshmana. Green shoots of barley, planted nine days earlier, are plucked and placed in buttonholes or behind the ear. This is a day of great rejoicing in Gorkha homes.

When a Gorkha gets married a girl is chosen for him by his family — one who belongs to the same section of the people and if possible to the same village. Contrary to the popular belief, Gorkhas do not practise polyandry. In fact, a Gorkha can, and at times does, have more than one wife.

Divorce among the Gorkhas is easily arranged. A request is considered by a committee of elders who fix a compensation to be paid by the husband to the wife.

When a child is born the name-giving ceremony is a big event. A clan name is chosen — Pun, Gurung, Rai, Limbu, Thakur, Thapa, Chettri or Pradhan. During the weaning ceremony, the *bahun* (priest) gives cooked rice to the infant. The child's going to school is another occasion for celebration.

While the majority of Gorkhas join the army, the more educated take up different vocations. Even the women are now taking up employment and there are Gorkha nurses, teachers and host-esses.

The Jat Community

The Jats who number over fifty million make excellent soldiers and farmers. They are found in an area stretching from Punjab to the Chambal (Dholpur), and from the Yamuna to the Luni in the desert of Rajasthan. In Punjab, the Jat speaks Punjabi; in western Rajasthan, Rajasthani; in eastern Rajasthan, Bharatpur, Dholpur and western Uttar Pradesh, Braj Bhasha; and in Haryana, Haryanavi. In all these areas they constitute the most prominent agricultural community.

Jats are God-fearing rather than religious, conservative rather than orthodox. Almost all the women are vegetarians and observe *purdah* in the presence of elders but not otherwise. The dowry system prevails but is on the decline due to the influence of the Arya Samaj. Dussehra is the most important festival of the Jat community and is observed with dignity and traditional ceremony, including *shastra pujan* (worship of arms). Holi is a festival of abandon and merrymaking. In eastern Rajasthan and western Uttar Pradesh the Jats worship Krishna and Hanuman; in Haryana and western Rajasthan many are Saivites; and in Jodhpur, Vir Teja, the legendary Jat hero and miracle worker is also worshipped in Teja *mandirs*.

The Jats were of Aryan stock and made the northern plain of India their home. They brought with them certain institutions, the most important being the *panchayat* and the custom of marrying the widow of the elder brother. They marry within their own community but not within their own *gotra* or sub-caste.

The brunt of most foreign invasions into India was borne by the martial races of the Punjab, Haryana, Rajasthan, and western Uttar Pradesh, including the Jats of these regions, who not only tilled their fields but also defended the country. The first Hindus known to the Arabs were the Jats. Mahmud of Ghazni was harassed considerably by the Jats of Sind and western Rajasthan and his seventeenth expedition was forced to chastise them. After the defeat of Prithvi Raj Chauhan (1192) the Jats of Haryana, under their chief, Jatwan, revolted against the Muslim commander of Hansi, the revolt being serious enough for Qutbuddin to intervene personally. Taimur dealt severely with the Jats during his invasion in 1398 and called them "a robust race, demon-like in appearance and as numerous as ants and locusts, a veritable plague to the merchants and wayfarers."

On his march to Delhi, Babar found the Jats of northern Punjab an irritant. The Mughals had firm control over North India and came down with a heavy hand on dissenting elements. It was during the latter half of Akbar's reign that the Jats of the Braj region (Mathura, Brindavan, Govardhan, Bharatpur and Agra) caused him some trouble so he attacked them several times and his officers went to their villages to kill and behead them. In order to defend themselves, the villagers hid in the thorny scrubs or retired behind the slight walls surrounding their villages. The women reloaded their husbands' matchlocks and handed them the lances.

Organised Jat resistance took shape during the latter half of the reign of Aurangzeb when his severity aroused their wrath and that of the Marathas and the Sikhs. The Jats of the Braj region lived and suffered under the direct shadow of the Delhi empire. They could not bear to see some of their most holy places like Mathura, Brindavan and Govardhan being desecrated. In 1666, they rose in revolt under Gokal, the Jat zamindar of Tilpat. Gokal was finally killed.

It was during the last two decades of the reign of Aurangzeb that the Sinsinwar Jats of Bharatpur under individual village headmen like Bhjja Singh and Churaman continued their depredations near Delhi and Agra and became powerful enough to carve out the little kingdom of Bharatpur for themselves by 1720. Bharatpur was hemmed in on the west by the Rajput kingdom, on the north by Delhi and the surrounding districts and on the south-east by the Marathas.

In 1721, Sawai Jai Singh II captured Churaman's strong-hold in the village of Thun (in Bharatpur) and the latter committed suicide. Till the middle of the eighteenth century there was no Jat state or ruler, only powerful robber leaders.

It was left to Badan Singh, Churaman's brother's son, to bring the scattered units of the Jats together into a real cohesion and to establish his authority over almost the whole of Agra and Mathura districts. He allied himself with the Jaipur rulers and by his shrewdness and foresight soon became the sole lord of territories and wealth which had so long been dispersed among the Jat chieftains. The disarray in Delhi assisted his activities. He fortified his villages and built the famous forts of Deeg, Kumher, Bharatpur and Weir. After the invasion of Nadir Shah, the Jat dominions expanded further. As the Delhi government could not effectively resist this expansion, the four forts in Bharatpur soon came to be known as the most impregnable forts of India.

Although illiterate, Badan Singh was endowed with some aesthetic sense and it was he who began work on the beautiful garden palaces of Deeg. He died in 1756 and was succeeded by his adopted son, Suraj Mal, who extended the authority of his kingdom of Bharatpur to the districts of Agra, Dholpur, Mainpuri, Hathras, Aligarh, Etawah, Meerut, Rohtak, Farrukhabad, Mewat, Rewari, Gurgaon and Mathura. Suraj Mal was the greatest warrior and statesman that the Jats had produced. He had great diplomatic skill, military judgement, political sagacity, guile, courage and resourcefulness. His untutored genius turned Bharatpur into an impregnable stronghold and around it grew a prosperous city.

He was killed in a surprise attack on his men near Delhi on 25 December, 1763.

At the time of his death, his kingdom included Bharatpur, Agra, Mathura, Alwar, Dholpur, Aligarh, Hathras, Mainpuri, Rewari, Meerut, Gurgaon, and the outskirts of Delhi. With his death and the rise of Maharaja Ranjit Singh, who became the undisputed overlord of the Punjab (about the first decade of the nineteenth century) power and glory departed from Bharatpur.

Suraj Mal was succeeded by his son, Jawahar Singh, who, as a young prince in 1757, had stood against Ahmed Shah Abdali's armies at Chaumuha when about ten thousand Jats laid down their lives to save Mathura. After nine hours of bitter fighting, though broken, they did not bend.

There was one final grand moment in the history of Bharatpur that made it a household word in India. Between January and May, 1805, the British army suffered four defeats at Bharatpur and the fort could not be taken. It was taken in 1826, following a war of succession. A few years earlier the Ranas of Gohad of the Chamba region had made their peace with the British and made Dholpur their capital.

Although the 1857 revolt began in Meerut, the Jats did not play a leading role in it. They tilled their fields and some fortunes were made. Recruits to the (British) army were not wanting.

After the First World War, their leader Chaudhari (Sir) Chhotu Ram (1885-1946), a man of vision, foresight, openness of character and subtlety of mind, was largely responsible for their awakening. He channelled their energies into fields other than farming and military service. He opened schools and colleges and it was under his inspiration that the Jats took to law, teaching, business and politics. The zamindars of Kiratpur, Sahanpur, Pisawa, Kuchesar, Lakhimpur, Mursan and Unchagaon in Uttar Pradesh began to take an active interest in the last two spheres.

The Kumaonis

The people of Kumaon are poor, honest, hardworking and self-respecting. Their home is in the beautiful foot-hills of the central Himalayas in Uttar Pradesh. Agriculture and trade in timber are their main occupations. They have a rich tradition of folk art and music and a high percentage of literacy.

Kumaon covers the districts of Naini Tal, Almora and Pithoragarh in Uttar Pradesh which came into being in 1814 when the British overcame the Chand Rajas. Legend had it that during the prehistoric era, the Kinners, Kiratas, the Khas and the Vedic Aryans were the rulers of this area. During the sixth century BC they were invaded and conquered by a people about whom very little is known. During the Mauryan period the rulers of this area probably accepted Mauryan sovereignty. During the Vardhan empire this area was under its influence. For two centuries after Harshavardhana, the region was ruled by the Tibetans. In the middle ages the Katyur dynasty ruled the area for over a century. Anek Mali, a Nepalese, invaded Kumaon in 1191. Two centuries later the Chand Rajas ruled over the area till they were defeated by the Gurkhas around 1790 and in 1815 the British annexed Kumaon and established themselves in the region.

Kumaon covers an area of 13,024 square kilometres. Situated in the Himalayan foot-hills, it is flanked by Himachal Pradesh on the North-West and by Nepal on the East. On its north is Tibet and on its South the plains of Uttar Pradesh. Its rivers are snow-fed and flow throughout the year. Among the well-known rivers are the Kosi, Kali Pindari, Ramganga, Saryu and Gomti.

The original Kumaoni was Vedic Aryans or Nordic. The speech was Sanskrit. Kumaonis have their own dialect (based on Hindi) with marginal phonetic variations in different regions, but they are equally at home in Hindi.

The people are divided into the usual four Hindu castes and a number of subcastes. The Joshis and Pants of Kumaon are said to have come from Maharashtra and the Kshatriyas from Rajasthan during the last days of the Mughal empire and during the Maratha period.

The Kumaonis are handsome people, generally light complexioned, slightly built, with black, brown or light-coloured eyes, brown hair and long straight or aquiline noses. They are simple, unsophisticated, hospitable, and attached to the hills. Their land is beautiful with the hillsides contoured in terraced fields. The Kumaonis are orthodox and cling to their old customs.

Kumaonis celebrate all the main Hindu festivals — Holi, Diwali, *Janmashtami*, Rakshabandhan and Dussehra. There are a number of fairs connected with religious festivals which are celebrated in different parts of the region — Makar Sankranti at Jageshwar, Bageshwar, and Thai; *Janmashtami* at Devidhura; Nandashtami (Nanda Devi Fair) at Almora, Naini Tal and Pithoragarh; and Vrishchik Sankranti at Jauljibi.

The Nanda Devi fair is celebrated only in Kumaon. In Naini Tal and Almora there are temples dedicated to Nanda (Parvati), the family goddess of the Chand rajas.

On the day of the festival, in Naini Tal and Almora, her image is paraded in the streets and then taken to her temple where a *havan* is performed and buffaloes and goats are sacrificed. Haryala is another festival which is celebrated only by the Kumaonis. Ten days before the festival, five kinds of seeds are sown in a basket full of earth, to the accompaniment of *puja*. Water is sprinkled on them twice a day. On the ninth day, the women of the house and the priest perform a special *puja*. On the Sankranti day, *puja* is again performed and the yellow stems are cut and offered to God. The shots are worn by everyone in the household, on the head or the wrist.

Marriages are arranged if horoscopes tally. On the appointed day, the bridegroom's party goes to the bride's house in a procession with the bridegroom riding a horse to music from various local instruments: the *ransingha* (horn), *damua* (drum), *nagara* (middle drum) and *mashakbeen* (bagpipe). Dancers with swords in their hands and flag bearers with red white *nisan* and a few others carrying boxes with gifts for the bride form the *barat*. The groom's party is welcomed by the bride's father at the gate of his house. The women of the house make beautiful coloured patterns (*alpana*) on the ground to welcome groom. While he stands on the *alpana* he is given gifts by the bride's father. The main ceremony is performed at night when the father gives his daughter away (*kanyadan*) which is followed by *saptapadi* (going round the sacred fire seven times). Next morning the marriage party returns to the bridegroom's house with the bride.

The birth day of a boy is considered to be a big event. When the child is six days old a ceremony (*chhatti*) is performed. There is a big feast at night and singing and dancing by the women of the family. When the child is twelve days old, he is given a name according to his horoscope. The name is whispered into the child's ear through a conch shell by the family pandit and other close relatives. The sacred thread ceremony is generally held when the boy is in his teens. At the beginning and end of every ceremony conch shells are blown, bells rung and the guests put vermilion paste on each other's forehead. The death of a relative is mourned from three to ten days according to the closeness of the relationship.

The primary occupation of the people is agriculture but the holdings are small and in spite of back-breaking toil in the small terraced plots carved out of the hillside, the return from the land is meagre. There is no industry worth the name and hardly any other means of employment. The people are very poor. Only the forests which are widespread, provide work to a number of people, specially the landless peasants. A large number of families, living nearer the plains, make ends meet by coming down during the winter months and working in farms and forests. Young men are always eager to be employed in the defence forces or in the government service. In order to earn something they even take up menial jobs outside Kumaon in tea shops, hotels, homes, etc. As a result, only elderly people and young women and children are left in the villages and it is the women on whom all the work of tending the fields fall. They have to work very hard from morning to night.

Kumaon has a high percentage of literacy and a long tradition of learning and education. It has produced gifted and eminent people who were distinguished in many walks of life. The community also played a prominent role in the freedom struggle and produced some notable national leaders.

Many great Indians have been drawn to Kumaon, among them Rabindranath Tagore, M.K. Gandhi, Lajpat Rai, Jawaharlal Nehru and Vivekananda. The American painter, Earl Brewster, made Almora his home; Nixon (Krishna Prem) an Englishman and a convert to Hinduism, lived in an *ashram* in these hills. Over the years, the number of tourist centres in the Kumaon hills has grown although many beautiful spots are still unexplored.

Naini Tal is a lake resort in this district that is at a height of 1,925 metres above sea-level. The place was "discovered" in 1841 by an English merchant (Barron) who gave a detailed account of the lake and the surrounding hills in the *Agra Akhbar*. The British Government developed it and made it the government's summer capital of the then United Provinces. Ranikhet was developed by the British in 1869 as a cantonment. Almora and Ranikhet command a view of the Himalayas that is superb. Nanda Devi which has an altitude of 7,818 metres; Trisul of 7,122 metres; Nanda Ghunti of 6,429 metres; Hathi Parbat of 6,729 metres; Gauri Parbat of 6,716 metres; Mana Peak of 7,259 metres; Kamet of 7,758 metres and Panchkoti and Nilkantha can be seen from here. A few kilometres away from Ranikhet are the Chaubatra Gardens, famous for their apples and other hill fruits.

Almora is the oldest city of Kumaon. It was founded in 1563 by a Chand raja. After the Chands, the Gorkhas occupied it till the British annexed it in 1815. It is 1,646 metres above sea-level and is surrounded by four hill ranges; Banari Devi, Kasar Devi, Shyahi Devi and Katarmal hill. Almora has still retained some of its old-world atmosphere.

In Dwarahat, which is about 75 kilometres from Almora and which used to be the seat of the Katyuri rajas of Kumaon, there are a number of temples which were built in the middle ages, as there are in Bageshwar, about 19 kilometres from Baijnath. Baijnath is famous for its temples which were built about the twelfth and thirteenth centuries and have life-size statues of many gods.

Punyagiri-Tanakpur has a very old temple situated on the top of a hill overlooking the River Kali and is one of the oldest temples of Kumaon. Pithoragarh town has grown rapidly after becoming the headquarters of a district called Pithoragarh.

The Pindari glacier is about 118 kilometres from Almora. It is 3,963 to 4,268 metres above sea-level. It is 4.8 kilometres long and about 366 metres wide. The Milam Glacier is on Pindari's opposite side. It is the biggest glacier in this region. Ramgarh, which is 26 kilometres from Naini Tal, is about 1,790 metres above sea-level and is famous for its apple orchards.

Mukteshwar is about 51 kilometres from Naini Tal and is 2,787 metres above sea-level. It is famous for its beautiful forests and the view of the snows and the government veterinary institute. Bhowali is 11 kilometres from Naini Tal and has lovely pine and oak forests.

The Kumaon Regiment is one of the oldest regiments in the country and was founded in 1780. Its men fought bravely during both the world wars, a number of whom were recipients of the Victoria Cross, were mentioned in despatches and were decorated.

The Khatri Community of North India

The Khatris are a community of the Kshatriyas who were based in the Punjab. Most of them became traders and some established small kingdoms.

The Khatri tradition of doing business has continued since then. Punjabi businessmen are mostly Khatris (such as the Mahindras of Mahindra and Mahindra; the Thapars of the Karam Chand Thapar group; the Nandas of Escorts; the Kapoors of Atlas Cycle Industries; and others).

They are divided into a certain number of *gotras,* each bearing the name of the *rishi* patriarch concerned and each *gotra* following a particular *sutra* of a particular *shakha* of one of the four Vedas. Thus the Kapoors (one of the three *Dhaighars*) belong to the Kaushik *gotra* and follow the *Yajur Veda,* their *shakha* being Madhi-vandni and their *sutra* Katyayana. Some other *gotras* are Kashyapa, Bharadwaj, Kaushaliya, Angira, etc.

The Kshatriyas of the various *gotras* were subdivided into the Suryabansi, Sombansi (or Chandrabansi) and Agnibansi subsects, each having further *gotras.*

A large number of Khatris from Punjab revere Guru
Uttar Pradesh they have become Vaishnavas though are
Varanasi. The Arya Samaj has attracted many to its fold. In Agra,
they have declared themselves. to be Radhasoamis and a few
venerate the Muslim saints buried at Jaleswar, Amroha, Bahraich,
Ajmer and Fatehpur Sikri.

Despite the variety of their religious leanings, they have two
basic religious convictions in common: a faith in the *Vedas* and
Vedic rites and an intense devotion for *Shakti* (power) who is
worshipped in every Khatri family under one of her many names—
Barah, Chandika, Durga, Gauri, Rohani, Parbati, Jwala, Naina
Devi, Jogmaya, Bindabasini and Kali.

The Sikh gurus were all Khatris. Guru Nanak was a Khatri of
the Vedi clan. The last six gurus, including Guru Govind Singh,
were Khatris of the Sodhi clan.

The Maratha Community

Maharashtra occupies one-tenth of the land area of India. It marks
the southernmost boundary of the spread of Sanskrit based
languages, Marathi being the last of these to be encountered. It is a
culturally significant region because it is the link between north
and south, between the Indo-European culture that invaded India
about three thousand years ago and the Dravidian culture that was
indigenous and which these invaders pushed south. In its language
and culture it accommodates both.

The Marathas (a community since the 1911 census) comprise
Kuli Marathas as well as Kunbis and represent the largest (twenty
million) single community of Maharashtra. A Kuli is a group, all
the members of which generally bear the same name. They vary
from light brown to very dark in complexion, are of medium
height and generally have high cheekbones and dark eyes. They
seem to belong to Marathwada i.e. Daulatabad, Aurangabad, Beed
and Parbhani and have been landowners and soldiers in Maharashtra for many centuries.

They worship various forms of Siva and his consort, Parvati.
The worship of the "Devak" is found only among them. It has

totemistic origins and consists of a certain tree or leaves of five trees or an animal or an inanimate object which is worshipped by the members of one Kuli.

The *Kuladevata* or family deity, is worshipped on all special occasions (like weddings or naming ceremonies), and is visited during the special *tirtha* (pilgrimage) during their festivals.

The Kunbis were originally land workers, the proportion of Kuli Marathas to Kunbi being roughly 45 : 55.

Shivaji Bhosle, the most eminent Maratha, was born in 1630 and it was he who first made the bid for establishing a Maratha kingdom.

The community is, perhaps, the most powerful community in Maharashtra, not only because it is the largest but because it has entered modern post-independence politics with an aplomb that can come only of many generations' experience in the art of ruling and manoeuvring.

The Sindhis

After the partition of India in 1947, over a million Sindhi Hindus left their homes in Sind and became dispersed all over India, many settling down in major trading centres such as Bombay, Calcutta and Kandla.

They became divided into two major groups: the Bhaibands and the Amils. Though they were originally workers on the land, the former have become a trading and shop-keeping community. The latter had always been, and still continue to be civil servants, teachers and scholars. They considered themselves the ruling class, though often their impecunious members would seek employment with the Bhaibands. Most of the Muslim rulers of Sind had Hindu *dewans* who were Amils. These two groups cannot be classed as castes as they are fluid and interchangeable in the sense that families from one can enter the other and *vice versa* if one of the professions of the group being entered is practised for a generation or so.

The present family names of Sindhis are derived from an ances-tor, usually a great-grandfather. Some take the names of the professions followed. There is no taboo regarding marriage between the two groups. Economic factors may isolate certain Bhaiband families into an endogamous group but this constitutes no 'caste' bar. While in Sind, very few members of the land-owning or trading Bhaiband community had attained higher education.

The Sindhi is adaptable. Not having a highly ritualistic or literary tradition of his own, he wears what those around him wear and worships as they worship. In Maharastra, he will attend a Ganapati *mela,* in Uttar Pradesh a *Janmashtami* gathering, in Bengal, Durgapuja and in the South, Pongal. He has sturdy self-reliance and as a result of his lack of roots, he overvalues economic security and ostentation. Having been deprived of their original work connected with the land, the Sindhis have taken up trading, banking and small independent enterprises, all occupations that depend on resourcefulness and the use of one's wits.

Religious rites for the Sindhi Hindu community are the same as for most other Hindu communities in the country. All the boys wear the sacred thread and have the *mundan* ceremony.

After marriage, when the bride is brought to her new home, she is made to sit by a mound of salt. Then her husband's relatives plunge their hands into the salt with her and 'measure the salt'. This is called *dattar mavan* and is done to ensure future harmony between the bride and her new relatives. When married, she is given a nose-ring set with two pearls and a ruby by her husband as a symbol of her new status and her mother gives her ivory bangles.

This jewellery is taken away and the bangles broken if she becomes a widow. In the olden days a widow had to sleep on the floor for twelve months, wear a red *gharara* (skirt) given by her mother and could not leave the four walls of the house but now these restrictions are seldom imposed.

Chetichand, a typical Sindhi festival, falls at the end of *Phalguna* and heralds the new year which commences with the month of *Chaitra* and is the usual spring festival that is celebrated in India. On this occasion the Sindhis worship water, for them symbolising the Darya Shah, the river Sindhu. They put water in a large *thali* or vessel and make a *diva* (lamp) of *atta* (flour) and light four wicks in it. After performing *puja,* sweets are distributed as *prasad* and amidst dancing, singing and merry making, the lamp and the *prasad* are immersed in the water.

Another Sindhi ritual is *handa*. While rice cooks in an earthenware pot on an open fire, Brahmanas chant special mantras and perform *puja* at the end of which the mouth of the pot, which is tied with a piece of cloth, is opened. It has been observed that when uncovered, the *handa* splits into four equal parts.

Their everyday food, which is simple and requires little preparation, is generally *khichri* (made of rice and dal) vegetables, curds, etc. On special occasions they eat special food (such as *pulav, malpura* and meat). They eat fish and all kinds of meat except beef.

In spite of all their ostentation, their fondness for wealth and its trappings and their simple taste in matters of clothing, jewellery and food, they are exuberant, lavish and resilient and are the backbone of the country's middle-class economy.

The Nayar Community

Traditionally a martial people, the Nayars have made history in Kerala. Today they are more distinguished as bureaucrats, writers, artists, administrators and diplomats. They are the only matrilineal community in the country. Under the *marumakkathayam* system, the property rights of the joint family are vested in the female members and are passed on from mother to daughter, though the property is managed by the oldest male relative of the family, who is called the *karanavan.*

After marriage a daughter does not go to her husband's home but remains in her own ancestral place (*tarawad*) and the husband comes to visit her, remaining a member of his own *tarawad.* The first duty of a husband is not to his sons but to his nephews. This custom and the *marumakkathayam* system are both dying out but a child still takes its mother's family name and is entitled to a share of the matrilineal property, should it be divided.

Nayars are essentially non-Aryan in their customs, manners, social structure and family set up and their ways of living, traditions and beliefs are also quite distinct from those of other Malayalis.

They have their own marital arrangements, succession laws and discipline and involvement in the arts and culture such as the dance drama, Kathakali. They were a class of professional warriors with a high skill in swordsmanship, who formed, themselves in times of battle into suicide squads called *chavers,* despised manual work and left the ploughing and tilling to tenants or hired hands.

By the time the Brahmanas arrived in Kerala, about the first millennium, the first known rulers of Kerala, the Cheras, who were Nayars, already had an established kingdom there.

The Nayar community has many subcastes, the majority being land-owning. As warriors the Nayars were unequalled and their sense of loyalty was legendary. Attached to the house of each village headman was a *kalari* in which young men trained in the art of combat and defence.

Marriage among the Nayars has a somewhat different meaning from marriage in other communities and is not so much a religious as a social ceremony. The term *sambandham* used originally for marriage meant a connection or alliance (for consummation) or union. Temple marriages, especially at the Guruvayur temple, are popular and inexpensive. There is an exchange of garlands and sometimes of rings and the bridegroom ties a *mangalasutra* around the bride's neck and the traditional presentation of saris takes place. There is no chanting of mantras and the ceremony is over in five minutes. It is both touching and impressive in its simplicity.

Nayars are Dravidians. Many have a lighter complexion than the Tamil Dravidians and resemble North Indians in their facial structure which may be the result of interbreeding with the Namboodiri Brahmanas.

They also have some shared characteristics with the ancient Naga people (whom the Aryans first encountered when they invaded north India) who worshipped the Naga, the serpent deity of the underworld and took their name from this cult. The Nayars have also preserved the serpent cult till today.

Every Nayar *tarawad* has a clump of bushes before which a lamp is lit every evening and some milk placed as an offering to the snake deity. Next morning, if it is seen that the offering has been accepted, there is satisfaction. If for some reason the forked-tongued creature has ignored the milk, there is general gloom and introspection. The belief is that the snakes belonging to the shrine of a *tarawad* are protectors of the family and will not bite anyone.

Personal hygiene is not merely a way of keeping clean but a way of life for the Nayars. The daily oil bath is a compulsory and complex ritual that can take up to two hours.

Among Nayars there are more than a hundred endogamous subdivisions, separated according to region and occupation, among whom marriage till recently was taboo.

While the rest of Hindu India celebrates Diwali with new clothes, fire-crackers, sweets and gambling, Nayars have only a special ceremonial oil bath on this day. Onam, in September, is their big festival. This is a harvest festival and the emphasis in its celebration is on festivity and fun, songs and laughter rather than on the religious aspect.

Nayars are not vegetarians by religion or compulsion. However, on auspicious or festive occasions only vegetarian food is served, preferably cooked by Brahmanas.

Other celebrations in a Nayar family are those marking the important stage in the life of the daughter of the house such as when she attains puberty and when she or a number of girls of the clan have a 'mock' marriage. Their real marriage being a simple affair with no feast, ritual or pomp, here she has all she could wish for from a real wedding.

The "bridegroom" is a respected old man from the neighbour-hood, whether married or not. He ties gold *talis (mangalasutras)* around the necks of the girls and his part is over. The honorific suffix *amma* is added to the girl's name after this. Nowadays this old ceremonial has been given up and it is observed on the occasion of the real wedding itself.

Motherhood and the birth of a girl naturally have a special sanctity among the matrilineal Nayars. The line of a woman with no daughter ends with her but though sons are also recognised now as having a place in the family, there is still nothing like having a daughter to whom the family wealth and property can be passed on.

The contribution of the Nayars to the arts—dance, drama, music, Malayalam and Sanskrit literature, has been tremendous. Dancing was part of the training received by young Nayar warriors in the feudal age. Elements of this *shastrakali* can be seen in Velakali which re-enacts the battle scenes of the *Mahabharata* and is performed in Trivandrum by Nayar youths. Kathakali, a unique style of the dance drama, performed in temples in night-long sessions by the light of flickering brass lamps, is part of every Nayar's life even today and is his introduction to and his association with all the glorious epics and legends of the past.

Krishnattam, performed regularly by trained dancers at the Guruvayur temple and Ramanattam, Kudiyattam and Ottam Thullal, are some of the surviving dance forms which can be seen in Kerala today.

Malayalam literature has been greatly enriched by the contributions of Nayar writers, who include nationally known poets like the revolutionary Vallathol and novelists like Thakazhi S. Pillai. Kathakali is another art in which the names of the Nayars is foremost.

The Nayar still puts a priority on learning — the women are educated and can discuss anything from the division of ancestral property to serious matters in politics.

Nayars of old were divided into castes according to occupation. They lived together as a self-sufficient community. A majority of them were landowners, though they played a vital role as fighters.

Attached to the house of each village headman there was a *kalari* (roughly, gymnasium) in which youths were trained in the arts of combat and defence. Training consisted of rubbing the body with a mixture of different oils, physical exercises and practice with stick and sword. Even today there are some *kalaris,* especially in North Kerala.

As warriors Nayars were unequalled and their sense of loyalty was legendary. There was an old custom testifying to this by which Nayar volunteers signified their vow to burn themselves on the day their king died and this vow they faithfully fulfilled. Barbosa refers to a regiment of women soldiers in Kerala.

The Nayars are not really Sudras. Logan, in his *Malabar Manual,* says that the Nambudiris respected the Nayars as kings. They were owners and controllers of temples and enjoyed all the privileges of the high-caste Hindus.

The Nayars have two distinctive characteristics — a strong sense of pride in the clan and a healthy respect for women. To the Nayar, the *tarawad* (the undivided matrilineal family) is all important. It connotes for him upbringing, pedigree and pride in lineage and a sense of belonging. He learns to respect the women in the house and carries the same respect over to all women.

The Nayar woman has for centuries been used to long periods of managing the home by herself, the man being away and has consequently acquired the strength, dignity and poise that comes naturally to women used to asserting their authority. The man too accepts the idea that the very structure of the social fabric rests on the women.

The Sudras

The Sudras (Scheduled Castes and Other Backward Classes) were the group most discriminated against in India being the *avarnas* or out-castes of Hinduism. They number more than 150 million. Classified as Scheduled Castes and Other Backward Classes, they did the dirty work for everyone, cleaning the lavatories, disposing of the dead animals, washing other people's clothes, making and repairing their shoes, tilling their land, etc. They lived in squalor on the outskirts of villages not even allowed to take water from the common well. A high-caste Hindu would neither touch them nor go too close to them for fear of becoming polluted.

Saints and social reformers have preached against untouchability notable among whom were Tukaram, Ravidas (himself an un-touchable), Kabir and Nanak, who condemned the practice as ungodly. In the nineteenth century, Phule allowed 'untouchables' access to his well and opened schools for them. Sri Narayana Guru (himself of the Scheduled Caste) fought for them and preached the doctrine of "one caste, one religion, one God".

Mahatma Gandhi called them Harijans (people of God) and made Harijan uplift an essential part of his campaign for freedom and national reconstruction. Temples were thrown open to them in the princely state of Travancore in the nineteen thirties and in many parts of British India when provincial autonomy was introduced. Dr. B.R. Ambedkar, himself a Mahar (one of the Scheduled Castes) demanded separate electorates for his people but this was opposed by Gandhi who went on a fast to uphold the principle of joint electorates. In 1956 Ambedkar and thousands of his followers embraced Buddhism.

With independence, untouchability was abolished by law but there has been hardly any radical change in social attitudes. On the governmental level much has been done to improve their lot. Their children are encouraged to go to educational institutions and are given special concessions but the literacy rate among them is half the national average. They are specially protected by the Constitution of India and a certain percentage of jobs is reserved for them at all levels of government service but often because they are not properly qualified, the vacancies remain unfilled. Nevertheless the lot of these groups has improved during the last thirty or forty years.

Caste prejudice in India is still very strong and ingrained and changes for the better can only be effected slowly. These castes form the majority of India's landless labour and they will have to be provided with land if their economic status is to be improved. The extent of their holdings (of the nine million who own land) is less than five acres so their condition leaves a great deal to be desired.

The Bunt Community of South Kanara

The people of south Kanara (Karnataka), the Bunts, live on a small strip of land locally called *Parasurama Srishti* (the creation of Parasurama). Their population is about 3 million.

The Bunt community is regarded as the single most important and advanced section in the district for its traditional leadership, agricultural knowledge and prowess. The men are good-looking, aggressive and warrior-like, the women, beautiful and independent of character.

The origin of this agricultural community, the single-largest caste after the Bilawa (originally the toddy-tapper caste) is still obscure but it is known that the Bunts belong to a fighting race.

The Bunts of Tulu Nad (north of the Chandragiri river in the Kasargod *taluk,* in Kerala, and south of the Kallianpur river in the Udipi *taluk*) and the Nadavas (a Kannada-speaking people of the same caste, spread over the Udipi and Coondapur *taluks*) are, considered Sudras. The Nadavas were agriculturists and traders and are now called Bunts. The Bunts are Sudras, although they played the role of Kshatriyas early in the Christian era when they and the Nadavas were the military chieftains of the area. Their lands were given to them as gifts by the rulers for the services rendered in wars and they gradually became agriculturists.

When the Vijayanagar dynasty came to power in South Kanara in 1336, a number of minor Bunt and Jain feudatory chieftains were already well established.

Another theory, based on the different surnames of Bunts like Shetty (Sethi), Rai and Bhandari, is that the origin of the Bunts may have been in north India. The language spoken by the Bunts is Tulu — one of the five Dravidian *bhasas* but it does not have a script.

Being a fighting people who had to be away from their properties for long periods, the Bunts (as most of the non-Brahmana communities of the region) evolved the *aliya* (nephew) *santhana* (family line) system by which all the property was vested in the female members who managed the farms while the title remained with the males. The entire family property remained undivided and intact as it devolved upon the sister's son of the deceased holder. A 'family' consists of a mother and her offspring and the father is an 'outsider', an ideal co-operative venture. Unlike many other communities, the birth of a girl is welcomed since she perpetuates the family line.

Till recently there were instances of over a hundred persons of such a family living under one roof with a common kitchen. Agriculture was practised on a co-operative basis under the *yajaman* (head) of a *guttu* or *beedu* (Bunt memorial house).

Intermarriage between people belonging to various *guttus* and *beedus* was prohibited but this restriction is dying out gradually.

The British made the Bunts *patels* (village headman). On account of a peculiar *ryotwari* tenancy system, by which even a small holder was dispossessed of his land, as from generations it was actually held and cultivated by the tenant, hundreds of Bunts found themselves in distress as they could neither get the rent nor evict the tenant.

Despite land reforms and economic stress, the Bunts even now own most of the cultivable land and command the traditional leadership and respect of the villages. Bunts still have a majority representation in most *panchayats, taluk* boards and even in the State Legislature. Successive ministers representing the district have been Bunts. Political power naturally belonged to them because they always shared the joys and sorrows of the people, particularly the tenants.

Bunts are non-vegetarian but some important families, the Ballals and Kurla Hegdes, the heads of families abstain from eating flesh and imbibing intoxicating drinks. These groups wear the sacred thread.

It is said that there were no temples in South Kanara before the Brahmanas were "imported" by an invading king. But when they were built, their lands remained with the Bunts.

Along with the other non-Brahmana communities of south Kanara, Bunts are noted for their *bhuta* (demon) worship. There is no Bunt house without a place meant exclusively for a demon. Unlike other Hindu communities, Bunts have no guru or swami of their own. Since the demon is their main deity, there is no compulsion about visiting temples, although this practice has come into being in recent times. Bunts are neither tied to any religious custom nor bound by any Vedic ritual.

The Bunts love manly and outdoor sports. Buffalo racing (*kambola*) and cock-fights (*koridatta*) are two of their recreations.

The folk dance drama of the district, the *yakshagana,* has been promoted and nourished mainly under the guidance of the Bunts, a form of dance that has received nation-wide acclaim. Some Bunt houses have their own troupes and many Bunts have made notable contributions to this form of the dance.

A marriage solemnised under the *aliya santhana* system is not a marriage in the strict sense of the term and based more on custom than on the Aliaya Santhana Act. Divorce is granted after six months of the application and, under the Act, there is no system of alimony or maintenance. Nevertheless, despite this liberal provision there has been hardly any instance of separation worth mentioning.

As the girl given in marriage was the chief inheritor of property and got valuable jewellery from her mother, the dowry system was unheard of till some fifty years ago. Nowadays, it has become a common practice in this community as well. Only a few families have set an example by not giving or taking dowry and a few have gone a step further by giving their girls in marriage to Vokkaligas, who are regarded as being closest to the Bunts. The marriage ceremony today is a simple and inexpensive one though in the past it was a long drawn out affair.

Mumbai has the largest number of Bunt residents outside the district. Some of the Bunts who have migrated to Mumbai and other places have shown initiative and enterprise. Several Bunts have become poets, doctors, journalists and politicians.

The Ezhava Community

The Ezhavas belong to the Backward Community and, numbering close to ten million, form 30 per cent of the population of Kerala and have gained a position of strength in the social and political life of Kerala. Originally their occupation was toddy-tapping but now poets, philosophers, ayurvedic physicians and astrologers are to be met with among them.

Suppressed by the Brahmanas and the Nayars and regarded as outside the fourfold structure of the caste system for centuries, by their own efforts they have removed themselves from the stigma of untouchability.

Though traditionally out-castes among the Hindus of Kerala, they enjoyed the respect and regard of royalty. Their religious practices have been influenced by Buddhism and widespread adherence to Saivite and Tantric ritualism. Though they are usually known as a community of farmers and toddy-tappers, they have also a tradition of scholarship in Sanskritic subjects.

There are various theories which suggest they might have had a foreign origin, which are somewhat fanciful. One such is that they introduced the coconut into Kerala. Another is that an ancient ruler of Kerala, Cheraman Perumal, invited a section of people, called Chekons, to his kingdom from Ezhathu Nadu (Sri Lanka) — hence the name Ezhava. Still another states that their name, Thiyyas, is derived from Theevy, a corruption of the Sanskrit *dvipa* (island) — again, Sri Lanka. The word 'Ezhava', probably mentioned for the first time in the ninth century, appears in the Tariaspally inscription of the Emperor Sthanu Ravi and later in the Tanjavur inscription of Rajaraja Chola where it was used as the name of a community. The Sangam classics, like the *Silappadhikaram* and *Manimekalai*, do not contain any such term but they mention 'Uzhavars' (cultivators) and the phonetic closeness between the two words (Ezhava and Uzhava) is obvious. A possible inference is that the castes of South India had already come into existence a couple of centuries before these inscriptions as a result of the influx during the pre-Christian era of Aryan Brahmanas. But their impact then was not as great, as Buddhism was the predominant religion. Kerala was first ruled by the Chera dynasty and the Cheras were Villavas or Ezhavas. When, eventually, the Brahmanas got the upper hand, the social structure changed but the Ezhavas refused to submit to them and paid for it dearly.

The name 'Ezhava' is said to apply to those who inhabit Quilon and the southern parts of Kerala, those who live between Quilon and Cochin are known as Chovans, the Thiyyas being spread over the north of Cochin, especially in Malabar.

The martial character of the Ezhavas might have been an inheritance from the Villors (archers) of ancient Tamilakam. The first mention of this is in the legends of the Chekavans or Chakors (from which the name Chovan is derived) celebrated in the heroic songs of Malabar.

The reputation of the Ezhavas in the fields of medicine and astrology rests on the fact that they were Buddhists. The *Ashtanga-Hridaya* is the most popular Ayurvedic treatise in Kerala and its author, Vaghbhata, was a Buddhist who spent some years in the Southwest of India. The Ezhava physician, Itty Achuthan (who belonged to Shertellai in the Alleppy District) helped the Dutch governor-general in India (Henri Van Reid) in the compilation of the encyclopaedic *Materia Medica* in Latin, published in Holland in 1678 in twelve volumes, with meanings in four languages.

Yogamrutam, an Ayurvedic work held as a classic by Malayali physicians was written by Uppottu Kannan in the last century. Thayyil Krishnan Vaidyan of Alleppey published a unique medical dictionary, the *Aushadha Nighantu,* in 1906, which the government of India has published in Sanskrit.

Since their origins go back to the dim past, the customs and beliefs of the Ezhavas and Thiyyas are primitive. The old Tamil background gave them the god Subrahmania and the goddess Kali and Buddhism introduced Chathan, Chithan and Arathan — all Sanskrit synonyms for the Buddha.

An art form, especially obtaining in the Cannanore District among the Thiyyas, is known as *poorakkali* which is associated with the celebration of the Pooram festival (held during March-April) when sophisticated dances are presented and recitations of Puranic stories and scholarly disputations on ancient *sastras* like Vyakarna, Tarka (logic) and Vedanta are held.

Among Ezhavas marriage takes place after the girl attains puberty and the proto-Austroloid custom of taking the uncle's daughter as bride is often followed. Polygamy was also practised. Marriage customs vary from region to region.

The Thiyyas of north Malabar were matrilineal, those of south Malabar and Cochin were patrilineal and the Travancore Ezhavas were of mixed lineage. The Ezhavas have a penchant for reform and revolution and some of the outstanding leaders of religious, cultural and social changes have sprung from them.

The Gujar Community

The Gujars belong to the north-western parts of India. They are mostly Muslims, a few being either Hindus or Sikhs. Traditionally they have been cattle breeders and milkmen. During the times of the Turkish, Afghan and Persian rulers, they earned notoriety for preying upon stragglers, the dead and the wounded left on battlefields.

They were usually associated with herdsmen and shepherds and were a pastoral people with no fixed abode. A large number of Gujars have now settled down and taken to farming and combine agricultural work with animal husbandry. They are simple, thrifty and industrious but have little ambition and desire nothing better than to be left alone in peace with their cattle and fields.

Although they rise with the dawn, they do not work for long stretches at a time and do not seem to be very particular about increasing the yield of their fields.

The Gujars are cultivators only in the plains and bad cultivators as they are more given to keeping cattle than following the plough. In the hills they are mainly pastoral, selling milk and *ghee*.

The Gujar is well built, with the physical characteristics of the Jat. Gujars and Jats, eat and drink in common. The close resemblance between them suggests that they — and perhaps the Ahirs — are from the same ethnic stock.

According to one view, the Gujars are identified with the Kushans, Yuchi or Tochari, a tribe of eastern Tartars. About a century before Christ, their chief conquered Kabul and the country round about Peshawar and his son, Wima Kadphises, extended his sway over whole of the upper Punjab and along the banks of the Yamuna as far as Mathura and the Vindhyas. His successor, Kanishka, the first Buddhist Kushan Indo-Scythian ruler, annexed Kashmir to the kingdom of the Tochari.

There is a record of three princes of the Gujjara race, of whom the last reigned in middle of the fifth century. An ancient kingdom, named Gujjara, existed to the east of the lower Indus for at least four centuries (AD 400 to 800). The Gujars are the only people whose tribal names seem to offer a clue to their descent from the Kushans. Another view is that they were always in India.

In the late nineteenth century they were found in great numbers in every part of the north-west of the country, from the Indus to the Ganga and from the Hazara mountains to the peninsula of Gujarat. They have also spread to the riparian lowlands of the Yamuna in considerable numbers.

Throughout the hill country of Jammu, Chibhal and Hazara and in the territory lying to the north of Peshawar, the Gujar herdsmen are found in great numbers. Here they are a purely pastoral and nomad group, who practise transmigration, taking their herds up to the higher ranges in summer and descending to the valleys in the cold weather.

Gujars are largely Muslims, some of whom have retained certain Hindu observances. Hindu Gujars are found in pockets but they are relatively a minority. There is a view that the cult of the child Krishna, who loved milk and butter, may have originated with the Gujars who were a pastoral people dealing in milk and milk products. This cult is evident among the traditions of the Ahirs, certain groups of whom (Nandbansi and Gualbansi) appear to be of Gujar origin.

In certain parts, Gujars date their conversion to Islam from Hinduism to the time of Aurangzeb. They still observe Hindu rites and on the birth of a son the women make an idol of cowdung (*govardhan*) which is worshipped.

The social customs of Hindu Gujars are much the same as those of the Hindus and those of the Muslim Gujars like those of the Muslims. They also have certain special customs of their own. The Gujars of Nakodar Tehsil (in Jullundur) have a marriage custom called *pind walna*. In a sort of game, the young men from the bridegroom's party gallop around the village and the men from the bride's side try and prevent them from doing so. The person who is able to ride round the village is given a present by the bride's parents. This custom is perhaps, a survival of the tradition of 'marriage by capture'. A day or two before the wedding, *madha* worship is held, the beam of a plough being pitched before the entrance to the house with a little straw tied to it. A large earthen jar, with a smaller one full of water placed on it, is placed beside the beam, a red thread being fastened round the uppermost pot. This is supposedly a fertility charm.

Child marriage is fairly common among the Gujars. Caste barriers and untouchability are declining gradually. A comparatively wealthy Gujar family may own a camel, a horse, two oxen, two buffaloes and a few goats. Being pastoral some Gujars observe a regular *siapa* (mourning) on the death of a buffalo. The women mourn almost as if they had lost a relative.

The dialect of Gujars — Gujari or Gojari — is akin to Hindi. It has strong affinities with the language spoken in Jaipur and is akin to Rajasthani. Gujari is spoken mostly by the Himalayan Gujars, including those of the Sivalik hills in Hoshiarpur but elsewhere they generally speak the dialects of the people among whom they live.

The Lingayat Community

The Lingayat sect was founded by Basava in the twelfth century. The Lingayats are Virasaivites or militant Saivites, one of the most well-organised Hindu communities. Sudras by caste, they are predominantly a community of peasants, many engaging in trade and industry. They play a dominant role in the economic, educational, social and political life of Karnataka.

Their contribution to the religion, philosophy and literature of India is of long standing. They have contributed to the Sanskrit, Kannada, Telugu and Marathi literature. Vachana, a unique form in Kannada literature, has its origin in the Shivasasharanas of the twelfth century. It gives utterance to liberal values such as the dignity of labour, liberty, fraternity and freedom from caste. The Vachanas of Basava, the *Akkamathadevi* and *Siddharameshwara* are held in special esteem and the *Surya Sampadana* is the quintessence of Virasaivism.

Harihara, Chamerasa, Sarvajnya, Raghavanka and Kereya Padmaras brought about a renaissance in Kannada literature. Among mystic poets Nijaguna Shivayogi and Mayideva are outstanding. The rich literary tradition of the Virasaivites is being kept alive today by many writers.

Over 80 per cent of the educational institutions in Karnataka are supported by the Lingayats as are many associations and societies that look after the educational needs of the people. Outstanding educationists from this community have played a special part in the spread of education.

As rulers, ministers and soldiers, the Lingayats were the moulders of the political scene in the past. The Kakatiya kings of Andhra Pradesh, the Sangama kings of the Vijayanagar empire, the rulers of Kaladi Kodagu, Belavadi, etc. were all Lingayats. Lingayat queens like Rudrammadevi, Channamma Kaladi, Mallamma of Belavadi and Channamma of Kittur have made a mark in history by their heroism. Channamma of Kittur fought the British earlier than did the Rani of Jhansi.

The cardinal principles of Lingayat philosophy are *Shad-sthala* (the six-fold spiritual hierarchy), *ashta-varans* (the eight-fold spiritual aids to Lingayat faith) and the *pancharas* (the five-fold disciplines of life). They believe that God is real and that the goal of life is to attune oneself to the Divine and bring harmony into life.

The metaphysical aspect of the Lingayat philosophy is known as *Saktivishishtadvaitta,* according to which the soul has the potential power to become God, the means to this being religion. The phenomenal world has its own importance and role to play in the spiritual evolution or growth of the *atman.* Matter, pain and pleasure are meaningful. The body is the temple of the soul. All occupation is a means of worshipping the divine. Whatever there is, is a gift of God to be used for one's salvation.

All Lingayats, even the women, wear the sacred thread. The community observes all major Hindu festivals such as Vijay-adashami, Sankranti, Ganesh Chaturthi and Diwali.

They acknowledge only Siva and not Brahma and Vishnu. They revere the Vedas but disregard the later commentaries on which the Brahmanas rely.

They claim to be free from caste distinctions but caste is observed among them. They adjure sacrifices, penance, pilgrimages and fasts.

Marriage is a sacrament. Most marriages are arranged through intermediaries though there are stray cases of Lingayat boys marrying Muslim or Christian girls after their initiation into the Lingayat fold. If the boy embraces the girl's religion, he is ostracised. The marriage of a boy to his sister's or his maternal uncle's daughter is socially acceptable. The marriage ceremony is performed by the *ayyanawar* (priest) who chants mantras. There is no *saptapadi* in a Lingayat marriage. Immediately after the marriage ceremony, the bride goes to her parents and the bridegroom to his relations. The consummation takes place on the following Wednesday or Saturday. In the first year of married life excessive indulgence is restricted by certain long-standing customs.

The dead are buried, not cremated, and there is no mourning period nor are the yearly *sraddha* ceremonies performed as among the Hindus. The Lingayats believe in rebirth.

The Mahar Community

The Mahars form nine per cent of Maharashtra's population.

In 1956, over 80 per cent Mahars became Buddhist, under the leadership of Dr. B.R. Ambedkar, to free themselves from the shackles of caste and to remove the stigma of untouchability by building a new religious and cultural identity for themselves outside Hinduism.

It has been claimed that the Mahars were the earliest settlers in Maharashtra but were pushed out by the invading Aryans; also that they were Kshatriyas, degraded during the great Mahadurga famine for eating beef. Outside the *varna* system and lower than the Sudras, the Mahars were denied access to Vedic Hinduism and the Hindu temple was closed to them. Their gods were the 'lower' deities such as the village pestilence goddess, Marai, the ghost god Vetal and a host of others.

Their one place of inclusion was the *varkari* cult centred in Pandharpur which was the Bhakti cult of Vithoba (Krishna). In the fourteenth century, about the time of Dyaneshwar, the saint poet of Maharashtra, a Mahar poet named Chokhamela joined the ranks of the cult's pantheon of saints. His poems and those of his wife and son are sung even today by devout *bhaktas*. Mahars went on pilgrimage to Pandharpur but they were prohibited from approaching the image closer than the *samadhi* of Chokhamela at the foot of the temple steps.

One of the traditional duties of the village Mahar was making decisions about boundaries in land dispute cases. His other job included repair of the village wall, assisting the police or government officials, being a watchman at the village gate, summoning villagers to hear announcements, carrying messages, bringing fuel to the burning *ghat* and dragging dead animals out of the village.

With modern times, this traditional work became less important and since the Mahars had no special skills and were not craftsmen, they moved easily into occupations like road building, railway work, dock work, menial jobs in factories and mills and into the army, etc. Mahars had served with Shivaji and the Peshwa's armies but it was service in the armies of the British that started the Mahar movement for attaining a higher status.

In the nineteenth century, perhaps a fourth of the Bombay armed forces was composed of Mahars and though recruitment of the Sudras stopped in the 1890s, by then the martial tradition had done its work. Many of the twentieth century leaders (including Dr. B.R. Ambedkar) came from military families.

In the late nineteenth and early twentieth centuries, the Mahars were already beginning to become organised. They petitioned (unsuccessfully) to re-enter the British Army, held conferences to protest against the practice of untouchability and started hostels and a few schools.

With the coming of education and political awakening in the twentieth century, there came a desire to participate more fully in Hinduism. In the 1920s Mahars tried to participate in the Ganapati festival in Bombay and they held *satyagraha* in Amravati and Poona for temple entry. From 1930 to 1935 a massive *satyagraha* was held at Nasik in a futile effort to get the famous Kalaram temple opened to the untouchable castes and Mahatma Gandhi began his temple entry campaigns in the 1930s.

After attempting to participate in the Ganapati festival and watching the failure of temple entry attempts, Ambedkar called a conference in 1936 to consider the question of religion.

The Mahar conference declared its intention of giving up Hinduism after an impassioned speech by Ambedkar who said "religion which regarded the recognition of man's self-respect as sin was not a religion but a sickness; which allowed one to touch a foul animal but not a man, was not a religion but a madness; which said that one class may not gain knowledge, may not acquire wealth, may not take up arms, was not a religion but a mockery of man's life, which taught that the unlearned should remain unlearned, that the poor should remain poor, was not a religion but a punishment."

Two months before his death, Ambedkar called his followers to Nagpur and was converted to Buddhism by the oldest Buddhist *bhikshu* in India, Mahasthaveer Chandramani. On 14 October, 1956, five lakh people, including many Mahars, joined Ambedkar.

In the following months, all over Maharashtra and in Hyderabad, Agra, Delhi, Ahmedabad and a few other places, untouchable groups became converted to Buddhism. By the time of the 1991 census, Buddhists numbered 6.3 million in India.

In appearance the ex-Mahars look much like the agriculturists of Maharashtra, the Marathas. In dress and manner an educated Mahar is indistinguishable from any middle-class Hindu. In many ways, the long struggle for a self respecting identity has finally led the Mahars into the mainstream of Indian life and Ambedkar's most profound wish is now coming true.

The Reddi Community

The Reddis (or Kapus) belong to a Telugu-speaking community that is split into numerous subsections. Their traditional occupation is agriculture. Though they are to be found in Tamil Nadu (where they are known as Reddiars) and Karnataka, they belong to Andhra Pradesh and constitute nearly one-fourth of the total population. Telangana, Rayalaseema and the districts of Nellore and Guntur are their chief places of residence.

The Reddis originally belong to the fourth and last caste — the Sudra. They have, through the ages, assumed the role of Kshatriyas. They represent the genus of the *kapus,* the Telugu word suggesting 'protectors.'

With the submergence of the Kshatriya rulers under the onslaught of the Muslim invaders, on whom they inflicted crushing defeats, the Reddis emerged as a power in the Deccan. The confrontation between Warangal, the Kakatiya capital and Delhi led the resourceful Reddis to make a drive in 1329 for the liberation of the Deccan from the Muslims.

The term Reddi was a title denoting temporal authority. The Kakatiyas had 72 Nayakas under them among whom were the Reddis and the Velamas, two sections antagonistic to each other. They were classified into three groups according to the regions where they flourished, the Kondaveeti Reddis, the Oruganti Reddis and the Painati Reddis.

Prominent among the leaders of liberation were Prolaya Nayaka and his cousin, Kapaya Nayaka and it is said about seventy-five lesser Nayakas (feudatory chieftains) assisted them in their enterprise, including the celebrated Prolaya Vema, founder of the Reddy kingdom of Addanki and Kondavidu. About 1331, the entire coastal region from the Mahanadi to the Gundlakamma in the Nellore District had been freed from the Muslims.

It was thus that the Reddi kingdoms came into being which retained their power for over a hundred years (1325 to 1448). Although the Reddi rulers inherited the responsibilities of their Kshatriya predecessors, they acquired none of the rights as they were Sudras and were debarred from participating in the Vedic rituals. Nevertheless the Kshatriya rulers of Warangal and their Reddi chieftains were associated through social interaction such as occasional intermarriage.

Of the many Reddi kingdoms that flourished for one hundred and twenty-five years after the end of the Kakatiya empire, the one at Kondaveedu, founded by Prolaya Vema in 1320, was the most important.

Most of the Reddi kings were enlightened patrons of learning, literature and the fine arts. Prolaya Vema's court was particularly distinguished because of the presence of the illustrious Sanskrit scholar, Mahadeva. The greatest poet of the Reddi age was Srinatha, a Brahmana whose patron was Peda Komati Vema.

King Veerabhadra Reddi of Rajamathendiravaram was another celebrated aesthete and scholar with a knowledge of music and literature.

Another major Telugu poet of the age of the Reddi kings, was Vemana who probably lived in the earlier part of the fifteenth century and is believed to have been a Reddy. His succinct, four thousand odd aphorisms in verse, constitute the Bible of the Andhras.

Though agriculture is their main occupation, vocational diversification is in evidence. They are in the mica business, undertake forest, timber and *abkari* contracts and deal in wholesale trade in *gur,* groundnut and onions. Many Reddis are also involved in the cinema.

They are also represented in government service, particularly in the police, forest, revenue and agriculture departments. They do not work as labourers because of the memories of the suzerainty of their forbears in the fourteenth and fifteenth centuries.

The Reddis have no *gotras* nor can they trace their lineage to any of the *rishis.* Those who were once famous as fighters are today no less great as farmers and are the backbone of the Andhra economy. Their community is cohesive and compact with a complex of rigid, built in, mutually exclusive ramifications with a rural bias. The subsections are best distinguished by the tools they use, the crops they raise, the methods of farming they favour, the wealth in terms of lands and cattle they own and the manner in which they utilise their leisure.

The Reddis are more influential than other communities in the villages. Because of their wealth and numbers, they dominate the affairs of all the *panchayats.* Most of the legislators from Telangana are Reddis. They constitute the ambitious, property-owing elite of the village. Their assets include acres and acres of arable land, flour mills, ginning institutions, vineyards, cinemas and real estate.

A practical, down-to-earth people, they make natural leaders. This community has produced many eminent people including: a president of India who was formerly Speaker of the Lok Sabha (Sanjiva Reddy).

Reddi women have held prominent positions in Indian society. Lakshmi Reddi who received the Padma Bhushan in 1956 was the first woman graduate in medicine and surgery from the University of Madras. This recipient of five gold medals was the founder of the Cancer Institute in Madras. She later went into politics, and represented India at several international conferences for women. Sarojini Pulla Reddi was the first woman mayor of the municipal corporation of Hyderabad and Secunderabad, assuming office in July 1965. Others such as Sudha Reddi and Yasoda Reddi have been educationists and members of Parliament.

The Yadava Community

The Yadavas are spread throughout India. They include the Abhiras or Ahirs of Northern India, Raos of Haryana, Gwallas of Uttar Pradesh, Mandals of Bihar, Pradhans of Orissa, Ghoshals of Bengal, Gopas and Reddis of Andhra Pradesh and Wodeyars of Karnataka. Some historians think that the Jats are Yadavas in origin, that the Gujars and the Marathas were also Yadavas and that they and the Gujars intermarried. The princely houses of Baroda, Bikaner and Alwar chose to align themselves with the Rajputs, though their roots were in Yadava stock.

The Yadavas are a dynamic people with a capacity for assimilation and absorption, a quality to which their survival after the fratricidal *Mahabharata* war may well be attributed. Tribe after tribe has mingled and separated from the main Yadava fold. Socially and economically they began to be classed as backward. High-caste Hindus often call them Sudras but the Yadavas call themselves Somavanshi Kshatriyas.

The Yadava contribution to the composite culture of India is immense: the nomadic art forms, the Abhira language (Apabhramsa), the *Raslila* and certain ragas like Ahir-Bhairav, Abhirika, Gopika and Kannadagula, and perhaps most of all, the Krishna cult.

The Yadavas who ruled southern India till the thirteenth century were the Mauryas, Shalivahanas, Chalukyas, Rashtrakutas, Yadavas of Devagiri and Mankhed, Haihayas of Chedidesh (near Jabalpur), Kalachuris of Kalyan in Hyderabad, Bhattis of Jaisalmer and Shelars and Shilahars of Southern Maharashtra. The Rashtrakutas, too, were Yadavas: the Kailash temple cut out of solid rock at Ellora, stands as a perpetual monument to the greatness of Krishna I (756-73). In their inscriptions from the ninth century onwards, the Rashtrakutas are spoken of as Yadavas.

After the fourteenth century, Yadava power declined. Some of them linked themselves with the Suryavanshi Kshatriyas.

The Ahirs

Although the Ahirs and Yadavas form one group, the former (the Ahiras or Abhiras) are an important community of Haryana, although numerically they constitute less than 10 per cent of the total population. Most of them live in the region around Rewari and Narnaul, which is therefore known as Ahirwal or the abode of Ahirs.

The Ahirs today claim descent from Krishna. Their origin, however, is controversial. Some historians hold that they were a powerful race of nomad cowherds from eastern or central Asia who entered India from the Punjab in large hordes about the same time as the Sakas and the Yuechis in the first or second century BC and gradually spread over large parts of Northern, Eastern and Central India. Other views are that they came from Syria or Asia Minor about the beginning of the Christian era; were Dravidians; sprang from the Aayars of Tamil Nadu; lived in India long before the Aryan invasion; were descendants of the Yadavas of the Lunar family of Pururavas Aila; and that their original habitat was the region between the Sutlej and the Yamuna from where they migrated beyond Mathura in the East and beyond Gujarat and Maharashtra in the South.

The name of the State of Haryana may have been derived from its ancient inhabitants: Abhirayana = Ahirayana = Hirayana = Haryana. The name 'Abhira' may stem from *a-bhira* — *a*, not; *bhira*, fear—fearless.

At the beginning of the Christian era, the invading Scythians and Kushans forced most of them out of their land to lower Rajasthan in the Arbuda (Aravali region). In Marubhumi (Marwar), Saurashtra and Maharashtra they served the local rulers and established their own rule. Ishwarsena, a great Ahir general, became master of Western Deccan in place of the famous Satavahanas. He took the title of Rajan and an era was named after him. His descendants continued to rule for nine generations.

For centuries the Ahirs were eclipsed as a political power in Haryana until the time of the Pratihara dynasty. In time they became independent rulers of Southwest Haryana.

In 1150, Vighararaja IV, a Chauhan from Rajasthan forced them to become his feudatories. In 1181 they were defeated by Prithviraj Chauhan but only after they had put up a tough resistance.

The assimilation of the Abhiras and the Yadavas was an accomplished fact by the twelfth century. The Ahirs preserve their associations with the country lying between the Sutlej and the Yamuna. In many districts like Badaun, Etah, Mainpuri, Hissar, Rohtak and Gurgaon, the Ahirs are still in a majority.

In medieval times the Ahirs gave up their arms and took to agriculture. In early British settlement reports they are spoken of highly as farmers.

They stand on an equal footing with the Jats, Rajputs, Gujars, Rors, Sainis, Sunnars and Barhis in the caste hierarchy and though they eat with them, they do not intermarry.

In appearance, they proclaim their Aryan descent. They are tall and wiry, have dark eyes, long noses, black hair and their complexion varies from wheatish to dark brown. Though mostly agriculturists, they also make good soldiers.

In the annals of Indian military history there is sufficient proof of Ahir bravery that is immortalised in the ballads of Alah and Udal of Bundelkhand.

In 1962, a company of 120 Ahir men laid down their lives fighting against the Chinese — the commander, (Major) Shaitan Singh was posthumously awarded the Param Vir Chakra. Equally meritorious was the Ahirs' record in the Indo-Pakistan war of 1965 and the heroes of Chushul (Ladakh) are famous.

The Tribals of Gujarat

There are over 5 million Adivasis in Gujarat, making up 13 per cent of the state's population. They mainly inhabit the rugged terrain adjoining the Aravalis, the western ridges of the Vindhya and Satpura mountains and the northern slopes of the Sahyadri Ranges. The Adivasis consist of numerous different tribal groups, the term 'Adivasi' meaning the 'original inhabitants'.

The tribal belt in Gujarat consists of the districts of Danga, Surat, Broach, Baroda, Panchmahals, Sabarkantha and Banaskantha. Various sects of adivasis, mainly of Bhil and Konkan origin live in this region.

Tribals such as the Siddhis, Rabaris, Padhars, Mers and Bharwads live in the coastal Saurashtra districts of Junagadh, Jamnagar and Kutch and work as casual labourers, cattle breeders and find employment in the ports.

The Siddhis are known to have come to India from East Africa and have distinct Negroid features. The Rabaris and the Mers seem to have come from the Mediterranean in early times.

The Australoid Adivasis (who have Australoid features) live in two tracts. Those living in the river valleys of the Surat, Broach and Bulsar Districts, are the Voknas, Varlis and Gambits who have Konkan features; and those living in the hill tracts along the state's eastern border, the Bhil Garasias, Dungri Bhils, Ratwas, Naikas, Dangi Bhils, etc., who have Bhil features. In the plains of the Surat, Broach and Bulsar Districts, there are also other tribals, such as the Dublas, who seem to have a foreign origin, the Dhodias, who might have migrated from the Dhulia region of Maharashtra and the Choudhuris, who may have come from Orissa or Bengal.

Tribals with Bhil features account for more than 50 per cent of the state's Adivasi population. Most of the Adivasi sects claim descent from clans such as the Rathod, Solanki, Chauhan, Parmar and Makwana. The colourful *ghagra*, the *jhulki*, the *sallo* and the jewellery worn by the Bhil Garasia women reveal Rajput influence.

The Bhils near Akkalkavu in West Khandesh and those living in Ratnapur, came under the influence of the Muslims and though they adopted the Muslim faith, their women neither accepted the practice of wearing veils nor could they get over the fear of the power of black magic.

In British times, British and Parsi contractors, forest officers and distillers, had liberal access to Bhil women in central Gujarat and the progeny of their illicit unions are to be found near the Alirajpur settlements bordering Madhya Pradesh. They often have light-coloured hair, fair skin, blue eyes and chiselled features.

The *Ramayana* and the *Mahabharata* make several references to the hill tribes. The reference to the Bhil hunter mistakenly slaying

Krishna at Prabhas Patan, shows that the tribe had freedom in this region. In the character of Shabri, the *Valmiki Ramayana* portrays the simple and hospitable nature of Bhil women.

Bhil tribes ruled over the Chhota Udaipur, Rajpipla and Sagbara region of Ratanmal in the Panchamahals district, the Danta region in the Banaskantha district and over principalities around Idar.

In the eleventh century, Karnadeo (son of Bhimadeo, the Chalukya king who ruled over North Gujarat) marched against Asha Bhil of Asha Palli and, vanquishing him, established Karnavati, a new kingdom near Palai, in the southern suburb of Ahmedabad. But the prominence of Asha Palli was affected seriously till Ahmad Shah established the city of Ahmedabad some centuries later.

Tribals are animistic in religion. They worship animals, such as the tiger (*wagh*), crocodile (*mogra*) and snake (*bathi*) as Gods and also worship some plant Gods and a hill God (Thumbi Dev). They also have many Gods in common with the Hindus such as Chamunda, Kalka, Amba, Hanuman and Guval Dev (Krishna). Their greatest festival is Holi.

It is said that this and other festivals such as Diwali, which it is said originally belonged to these aborigines, were in due course of time adopted by the Hindus. Scholars are also of the opinion that the concept of the Mother Goddess, Parvati (daughter of the hill king) and that of the Siva has been borrowed by the Hindus from the Adivasis. The tribals also worship their dead ancestors.

In olden days the Bhils depended on the slash-and-burn cultivation system under which they cleared thick forests by cutting trees or burning them and cultivated crops in the land so cleared for a few years until the natural fertility of the soil was exhausted. They then moved on to new forests, leaving the land fallow for it to recover its fertility. They also lived by gathering forest produce and hunting wild beasts or fishing.

Due to the restrictions imposed by the new forest laws against cutting trees and clearing for cultivation, their economy and way of life have been upset, resulting in large-scale unemployment.

Of the Adivasis, the Koknas, Gamits, Dhodias, Vasawas, Garasias and some other Bhils generally lived on agriculture. The figures show that 90 per cent of the Adivasis depend on agriculture either as landowners or as farm workers. Government measures to protect them from the clutches of usurious money-lenders have not made much headway.

Being primitive and ignorant, the Adivasis do not easily absorb the various benefits afforded to them. The most advanced sections among them, the Dhobias, are said to be reaping the maximum benefit of the government allocations made for Adivasis.

Marriage is secular for tribals while it is a sacrament for Hindus. A sex offence, such as adultery by a married adult, is viewed more as a breach of contract or a breach of faith than as the moral debasement of the person and the damage can always be undone by imposing an equitable penalty.

Tribal women mix freely with men in all spheres of life. They climb trees to pluck fruit, axe firewood and plough the fields. Though by custom the male takes precedence over the female, this disability of Adivasi women is insignificant when compared with that of their Hindu or Muslim sisters.

A tribal woman can resort to divorce and remarriage. The total surrender or submission to the husband, as in the case of Hindu women, is a phenomenon neither easily understood nor liked by tribals.

Though marriages arranged by parents are customary among the Adivasis, the more popular forms seem to be marriages of love preferably those made by elopement, with the eloped lovers returning home after a few days spent in hiding. Their parents then complete the formalities — fix the *dhej* (the bride price, which is usually prescribed by the tribal *panchas*) and celebrate the wedding.

The custom of levirate is common among the Bhils, the Dhankas and many other tribes in Gujarat. If the widow prefers another person, the prospective bridegroom is liable to pay only half the amount of the original bride price.

If there is a love affair between a Ratwa man and woman, she enters his kitchen and starts cooking for him. His erstwhile wife, taking her cue from this, leaves the house, making room for the new 'wife'.

The Adivasis also have a system by which a man and a woman may live together and have children but undergo the marriage rituals only before the marriages of their children or grandchildren. This is so because being very poor, they find the cost of celebrating a marriage prohibitive and prefer to postpone the rites till they have saved enough money.

Promiscuity among the unmarried is a common feature of tribal life. The isolated setting of tribal houses inviting no scrutiny by neighbours, a carefree life for both the boys and the girls in the privacy of thick forests, unrestricted indulgence in drinking liquor followed by all-night community dances, have all led the tribals to entertain no inhibitions about sex.

Literacy among the Adivasis has spread with the opening of hundreds of schools *(Ashram Shalas)* in the tribal belt by social reformers.

The influence of the Christian Missionaries activities in Broach, Surat and Bulsar and of the Arya Samajists in Surat have had a considerable impact on Adivasi thinking. The enactment of the prohibition law has, to a large extent, helped in improving the tribal way of life.

The Adivasis have produced ministers and legislators in Gujarat from among the Choudhury, Vasawa, Bhil, and Dhodia groups, as also members of parliament, doctors, professors, journalists, government officers, contractors, businessmen, lawyers and magistrates. The more advanced among them show an increasing tendency to not identify themselves with their tribal antecedents.

It is claimed that the Adivasis gave India her first civilisation. In the physical forms and physiognomical characteristics represented in the old sculpture of Bharhut, Sanchi, Bodhgaya, Karle, Ajanta, Khajuraho, etc., and also in their dress and coiffure, one can see the art prototypes of the present-day Adivasis: the Bhils, Murias, Gonds, Baigas and Santals who, from time immemorial, have inhabited the regions where these centres of artistic achievement are located. The affinity of the low-relief wood carvings (particularly in the funerary pillars and temple doors of the Marias) with the style of carvings of the gateways of Bharhut and the Sanchi stupas, is unmistakable.

Among Adivasi arts and crafts the most interesting are textiles, wood and ivory carving, horn, bamboo and cane work and the making of a variety of archetypal bronzes used for ritual and domestic purposes. It is surprising how the technique of bronze casting (known as cire perdue casting) practised in India from the proto-historic age, survives today in the Adivasi craftsman's method of bronze casting.

The cult of the totem is an important feature in the Adivasi culture, which has conditioned the life and thought of the people and their arts and crafts. The totem is deeply revered in each clan and many of the significant forms and colours used by them bear an intimate relationship with their life. Totems are propitiated through rituals and magic.

Dance, with all its intricacies, is a salient feature of the Adivasis social expression and constitutes an important part of ceremonies connected with marriage, harvesting and funeral rites. The aesthetic awareness is also revealed in their personal adornments and belongings.

The Bhotia Tribe of Kumaon

The Bhotias and Ban Rawats of Kumaon are hill tribals, scattered over the Uttarkashi and Garhwal regions. Although they come from the same stock, almost every village has its own customs and religious rites.

The Bhotias have Mongoloid features, are fair in complexion and of sturdy build. Their origin is uncertain. They differ in religion, physiognomy and customs both from the Tibetans and the Hindus. They are a hardy race, genial, cheerful and hospitable.

They are perhaps the best climbers in the country and reach high altitudes with little difficulty. They have a keen sense of direction and if this sense is at fault, as in a blinding blizzard, their dogs always come to the rescue. Whenever the Bhotias ascend steep mountains, they add a stone in thanksgiving to a heap (*kithburiyas*) which is already there.

The Nanda Devi, Pancha Chuli and Badri Kedar peaks are worshipped by them. There is a temple to the Goddess Nanda in Martoli, where an annual fair is held in September, when a large number of buffaloes and goats are sacrificed to propitiate the Goddess. Some Bhotias, who have come under the influence of Hinduism, worship Hindu Gods.

The most popular of their deities is perhaps Gabla, the weather god who, on entreaty, dispels both rain and snow and brings fine weather. The shepherd gods Runiya and Sain, protect their animals from disease and cure diseased animals. The eternal snows inspire reverence and the snow covered Pancha Chuli peaks, locally known as Miyula, are an object of worship.

They make a constant effort to exclude malevolent spirits. If a person dies away from home, his belongings are scattered where he died and along the path to his house so that his soul may come home.

Being a nomadic people with regular trade with Tibet, most of the men folk had to be away from home for long periods. As a result the Bhotia women are self-reliant, sturdy and independent. They are equals with their men in work and play and are useful wives and competent mothers. For the intermingling of the sexes, the Bhotias have a unique system. Unmarried boys and girls in the community and married girls who are childless have a club which is located in a house called *rangbang kuri* (club house). When they meet here, the whole night is passed in singing and dancing. The *rangbang* plays an important part in bringing young people together.

The Bhotias are not stringent about marriage and a woman can remain unmarried if she so chooses. In fact, many women prefer to remain unmarried if they cannot find a suitable match. Monday is considered inauspicious for weddings and none take place on this day. At a wedding, a pretence is always made that the bride will never go to her husband voluntarily and has to be carried by force.

As a part of the celebrations the bridegroom's father invites the bridegroom's friends for a feast at night. Later, the party proceeds to the bride's village and carries her away from the *rangbang* for a short distance. Here they call the bridesmaids to join them and then proceed to the bridegroom's house. On entering the house, the village elders produce their *dalangs* or cones of dough with liquor, which are given to the bride and bridegroom for consuming. This is followed by a feast. Drinking may last a fortnight. The next ceremony, the formal rite of *datu,* then follows. The bridegroom and the bride exchange the dough and fish given to them and by this they are bound in wedlock.

The semblance of a forcible removal is kept up, and envoys are now sent to the bride's father to make peace. They accept a small sum of money by him and all is well again.

Death ceremonies are more elaborate. Children who have not outgrown their milk teeth are buried, the head placed northwards. Those dying a bit older, are cremated. The dead body is placed in a white bag, with the knees touching the chin. The bag is then placed on a bier. A white cloth — cotton for a man and woollen for a woman — is tied to the front of the bier so that the spirit of the deceased can be guided in the next world.

The funeral procession is led by a young boy or girl holding burning faggots, followed by the women, then the bier and finally the villagers carrying fuel for the cremation, which is usually held by the side of a stream. The corpse is placed facing east and before it is burnt, the cloth bag is slit and a piece of precious metal is put into the mouth to purify the corpse. A bone of the deceased is collected on the next day and placed in a hole in the place in the village where the bones of dead persons are interred. The same night, a funeral feast is given and a special provision of food is made for the departed person: some rice and other food is put just outside the deceased's house, thrice daily until the *dhurung* ceremony is over.

In Garhwal, the Bhotias are known as Marchas and in Uttarkashi as Jads. They can be roughly classified as belonging to five groups — the Mana and Niti (in Garhwal) and the Johar, Darma and Byans (in Pithorgarh District). They live at very high altitudes and it is believed that Dwan in Johar is the highest inhabited spot in the world, at an altitude of over 3,050 metres.

Before the Chinese took over Tibet, the Bhotias, who are a shrewd and enterprising people, carried on wide-scale trade with Tibet in wool, women, fabrics and sheep-skins. Having lost their trade with Tibet, the present day Bhotia faces great difficulties. Their agriculture is primitive, their methods and implements, crude and the severe climate makes agriculture very precarious and so they produce jute enough to eke out a bare existence. Their sheep and goats are their mainstay which provide them with wool, hide and fur and whose meat is dried and eaten.

At Sera are the Ban Rajis. The Ban Manas (men of the forests) never leave their forest dwellings and even the local people have no contact with them. They have wheatish complexion and are short in stature. They trade in articles made of wood and leave them at the doorsteps of the houses of the villagers, who in turn leave, at the same place, rice, wheat, etc., which are taken away by the Ban Rajis.

Ethnologically, there is meagre information about the Rajis but a legend has it that when the world began, two Rajput brothers, the elder a hunter who lived in the forests, and the younger, a cultivator, had a fixed abode. The latter insisted that there could be only one raja there, the elder brother retired to the forests and the Ban Rajis are said to be his descendants.

Since the Rajis profess royal descent, they refuse to salute anybody and even speak of the *rajwar* of Askot as their younger brother. Nor, being of royal blood, do they expose their women to the view of strangers. The Gazetteer of the Almora district says that their language is like the twittering of birds and belongs to the Tibeto-Burman family.

Hinduism has influenced them and they worship Nanda Devi but they also worship their own gods.

Marriages are arranged by parents, who exercise complete control over their children and there are no priestly ceremonies or feasting. The bridegroom is normally given a present or goats. Polygamy is practised sometimes but child marriage and widow marriage are rare. They have hardly any property, excepting a few cattle. The inheritance goes to the sons.

The Gadaba Tribe of Koraput

A singularly attractive tribe is that of the friendly and hospitable Gadabas. Their villages with square or circular houses and conical roofs and gaily dressed women, present a picturesque sight.

The Gadabas can be divided into three groups: Bada Gadaba, Halar Gadaba and Parenga Gadaba. In appearance, they can be distinguished by their yellow-brown complexion, dark-brown eyes, prominent cheek-bones and broad flat nose. They are essentially an agricultural people, who cultivate low-lying areas, grow rice, maize and *ragi* the last being their staple food.

Their special drink, *salaps,* is very sweet and highly intoxicating. Prepared from the juice of the *salaps* tree, it is their community drink.

The Gadabas, unlike other tribals, appear to be enlightened in certain respects. A Gadaba woman usually wears a two-piece dress which is very colourful, often striped in red, blue and white, which is woven by the women themselves. The textile is made from the bark of the *kereng* plant. The ornaments they wear are not very different from those of other tribals. They wear beads of various colours in the hair, silver necklaces and very big brass earrings. The *kereng* is being slowly replaced by the sari.

Marriage in a Gadaba community takes place mostly by elopement, usually on the weekly market day or on days of festivals when people from different villages congregate. The boy and girl run away to a distant village, stay there for some nights and then return to their village when they are declared married.

The Gadabas regard cattle raising as the true source of their wealth. They believe in sacrificing pigs, cows and buffaloes at the altar of their *vanadevata* (god of the jungle). Almost every family rears pigs irrespective of its status and size and keep dogs to ward off evil spirits.

Their biggest festival is Chaitra Parba during which the women weave *kerengs* in their houses and the men go hunting. When they return, they have a community dinner irrespective of age and status and eat, drink and dance throughout the night.

The Toda Tribe of the Nilgiris (Blue Mountains)

The Todas are a pastoral tribe who herd buffaloes that roam the Nilgiri hills. Where they originally came from remains a mystery. Their way of living is pristine and with their flowing beards, long hair, fine bodies and tall sticks in hand, they resemble the prophets of the Old Testament.

The earliest record about them dates back to about 1117, when a ruler of Karnataka came to the Nilgiris and dedicated the highest peak in the area to the Goddess Lakshmi. They were still there in 1602 when a Portuguese Roman Catholic priest from Calcutta visited them. Interest in them was revived about two hundred years later, when the British reached the Nilgiris.

They live in *munds* that nestle in sleepy hollows high in these 'blue mountains' and judge time by the opening of the evening primrose, which they call the 'six o'clock flower'. Whether they have any connection with the cairns, cromlechs and victory towers that lie scattered over the Nilgiri Plateau is not known. The cairn builders were probably members of a Turanian tribe from Western Asia who brought with them their culture and customs.

The Todas believe that God created the sacred buffalo first out of the earth of the Nilgiris, then the Todas and then the domestic buffaloes. So to the Toda his buffalo, the land on which he lives and himself are inseparable. His religion centres around his herd of sacred buffaloes. His priest takes care of them and only he is allowed to graze and milk them. The sacred milk is kept in the temple where the priest churns it, makes curds and butter and ghee. With the ghee he lights a lamp every morning and evening, and prays for the welfare of the tribe.

The temple is a sacred place and the priest keeps himself pure and celibate for the purpose of entering it. The charge of the dairy, therefore, ranks amongst the most respected offices. The Todas also have a 'cathedral' which has a tall conical thatched roof crowned with a large flat stone. It is surrounded by a circular wall. Only three of these now exist in the Nilgiris.

The Todas were a polyandrous people and some historians suspect that the practice was introduced in some primeval epoch, when migrators left central Asia for new homes eastward of the Indus in circumstances that limited them to just a few women. This system was abolished many years ago. The Todas also practised female infanticide which ceased even earlier than polyandry.

The Toda lives in settlements consisting of a *mund* (a duster or beehive huts), a dairy temple, which is larger than the normal Toda hut and a cattle pen which consists of a circular enclosure surrounded by a loose stone wall with a single entrance guarded by powerful stakes. Their homes are on the tops of minor rounded eminences, studded with cairns raised for burying the dead. There is only one small entrance to a Toda hut and one has to get down on all fours to crawl in. These half-barrel-shaped constructions are built of bamboos closely laid together, fastened with rattan and covered with thatch.

Todas live in a sort of classless, caste-less society where everybody is equal. They have a sacred tree, the *thon,* which they venerate.

The Todas cremate their dead. In the past, according to the status of the dead man, a number of buffaloes were killed in the belief that the spirit of the buffalo would accompany the deceased to the next world, where he could live in much the same way as on earth. However, the buffalo sacrifice was stopped by government order in 1964.

When a Toda male is cremated, the fire has to be lit by wood friction by a stick taken from the "kedz tree" (*Litsaca wightiana* or 'scared firestick') but a female's pyre can be ignited with an ordinary stick or match. When a buffalo dies, it is not cremated.

Their language has no script but they are great poets and great singers. They have only one musical instrument, a flute, without finger stops which is made of hollow bamboo, called *pooheeri* but now it is almost a dead instrument and only a few Todas can play it.

When they reach puberty, Toda women are tattooed on the face with the dark purple juice of the fruit of the *Eugenia arnottiana.* They grease their raven-black hair with butter and twist it into glossy ringlets. They touch up their eye-brows with a charred stick and their sparkling eyes enhance their *cafe au lait* complexions. Their white mantles edged with red and blue lines make a splash of colour.

Then men have luxuriant beards and they let their long hair fall in curls about the neck.

A man can dispense with his wife but the compensation in buffaloes is so heavy that it acts as a deterrent. When a Toda wishes to divorce his wife, he is summoned to appear before the *panchayat,* who may ask him to hand over from three to eight buffaloes, according to his wealth. If a Toda marries outside his community, he is thrown out of the tribe and never taken back.

The Todas have one important festival in the year: the Modhweth, which is held in December or January in Norsh (where the Toda claims he was created). Todas from the twenty *munds* scattered all over the Nilgiris ʳrek to this place. Here they pray to their Goddess, Thekish. Coffee and puffed rice are served before the festival ends.

Slowly, the way of life of these people is changing. The Tamil Nadu government has started tribal residential schools for Toda children that provide education free and from where some have even gone on to college. Toda huts are fast being replaced with brick houses. Some consider that giving a Toda some education which brings him the job of an office peon or a taxi driver, is a pity since it is small recompense for the destruction of a whole beautiful way of life and that it is possible for the Toda to have a self-sustained economy with his buffalo. Attempts since 1952 to turn the Todas to agriculture have not been successful as they have a certain sentiment against cultivating land. But anything to do with buffaloes — the increase of milk, cheese production, butter or ghee-making — interests him, as he understands his buffalo thoroughly.

The Todas live in "reserved" forest land. Ever since the British arrived in India, they began a slow but deliberate encroachment on their grazing ground and today they have hardly any fallow land left for their use. The little that was their when the British left, is now being lost to eucalyptus plantations. Should their grazing ground disappear, it could spell the total collapse of Toda culture and tradition which would indeed be the greatest tragedy of all, for the Todas are unique.

The Todas have been linked with the lost tribes of Israel who are believed to have arrived in Muziris (Cranganore) in AD 69 and also with the Romans, the Christians, the Sakas and the Macedonians. Prince Peter of Greece saw possible Sumerian survivals in Toda rituals and found eleven names of deities of Sumerian origin in use among the Todas. According to him, Todas are the only living descendants of the expatriated buyers from Sumeria who were stranded in India and, being unable to return home, settled in the Nilgiris.

According to a learned foreign scholar writing in 1873, the Todas were probably immigrants from the Canarese region who had dwelt in the Nilgiris for about eight hundred years. Another, writing in 1875, thought their language had a distinct affinity with Finnish and those of the Ugrians of Siberia who overspread Europe before the arrival of the Celts and the Goths.

7

JAINISM

HE WORD 'JAINA' IS DERIVED FROM JINA — the conqueror, the victor or one who has conquered himself. The Jains believe that their religious system was evolved by twenty-four Tirthankaras who came to lead the people along the path of righteousness in this *yuga* when truth and goodness are steadily being superseded by evil. Three of these, Rishabha, Ajita and Arishtanemi, systematised the doctrine. Most of Jain hagiography is legendary but history records the existence of Parsvanath (812-772 BC), the twenty-third Tirthankara and Mahavira (599-527 BC) who is considered to be the founder of Jainism and was the twenty-fourth and last Tirthankara.

In its formative phases Jainism was not only a protest against Brahmanical Hinduism but was influenced by some external religion, possibly Zorastrianism which flourished in Persia. One feature of the Jain legends — the continuous struggle between good and evil is common to both.

Mahavira's religious theory was that everything, animate or inanimate, has *jiva* (life force) and the worst thing a human being can do is to take *jiva*. The goal of human endeavour should be to exhaust karma and the way of deliverance is in the three gems (*tri-ratnas*) or rules of behaviour: right faith, right knowledge and right conduct; the latter meaning non-violence (*ahimsa paramo dhar-mah*), adherence to truth, chastity and the renunciation of worldly possessions.

Jainism is, therefore, not a passive religion but one calling for exertion so that the soul's past experiences and unfulfilled desires are purged. Jains believe that the universe is infinite and eternal and was not created by any God. They worship the *Jinas* or the Conquerors "the enlightened ones", who by their pious deeds and acts of self-denial in past lives had overcome worldly passions, freed themselves from the unending cycle of rebirths and attained *moksha*. The Jains rejected the Vedas and ignored the priestly order of the Brahmanas and the caste system.

Philosophy and Sects

Jains soon came to be divided into two sects — Svetambaras (white clad) and the Digambaras (sky clad). The Digambaras, the more religious of the two, do not allow women to become nuns and recognise no canon.

Each school is further subdivided into two sects on the basis of ritual and worship. Of these four, the Svetambara Sthanakvasi is quite different from the others as its members do not worship images or idols or have any form of organised worship; their shrines being the Upashrayas (congregational halls) where the devout gather to listen to the preaching of the monks and to meditate.

The Jain doctrine is based on the fundamental principle of *ahimsa* (non-violence). Jains are strict vegetarians and do not eat even root vegetables as in digging them up many insects and organisms are killed. They filter their drinking water and prefer to eat before sunset to avoid the tiny insects that flock round the light from getting destroyed. It was because of their adherence to *ahimsa* that they never took to farming or agriculture and turned instead to commerce, trading and banking. Many Jains were prominent figures in the days of the Muslim rulers as they were often appointed bankers to the sultans and emperors.

According to Jainism, every material thing such as earth, water, fire, air and vegetable possesses a soul. The Digambara monks use a fan of peacock feathers to keep flying insects from harm. Svetambara monks use a hand broom to sweep tiny living creatures out of their way. They keep their mouths covered with a piece of cloth so as not to swallow invisible organisms. Like most other ascetics, they

take a vow of *aparigraha* (non-possession) reducing their require-
ments to the barest minimum of worldly goods.

For all Jains, fasting and austerity are considered essential for
self-purification. They lay stress on mental discipline to obtain self-
control, concentration in contemplation and purity of thought. An
idol before a worshipper, say the Jains, is like a flower before a
mirror. The mind reflects what is in front of it and takes on its
colour. The ideal Jain way of life includes discipline, purity of
thought, contemplation, confession, atonement and repentance.
Undertaking fasts and practising austerities for self-purification is
considered essential.

A Jain's contemplation is 'Let there be friendship with all living
beings, delight at the sight of the virtuous, compassion for the
afflicted and tolerance towards those who are ill-behaved.'

During Mahavira's time, many social and religious evils flourished in India — the caste system (which relegated the Sudras and
the untouchables to a life only a little better than animals), animal
sacrifice, slavery and the exploitation of women. Mahavira, the
protagonist of *ahimsa*, declared that all living beings had an equal
right to live and that no living creature should be killed, injured,
enslaved, tortured or exploited. The killing of any living creature
amounted to killing of oneself.

He permitted people of all castes to be initiated into his monastic order. He allowed women an equal right to practise religious
rites and to study the scriptures.

His philosophy is essentially based on the spirit. The soul is an
objective reality, characterised by consciousness and different from
matter which is devoid of consciousness. The bondage of karma
results in the transmigration of the soul (the cycle of birth and
death). To emancipate it from this cycle, one has to become free
from the bondage of karma, a state that can be attained only
through one's own endeavours by the practice of self-discipline,
vigilance and equanimity. For this he prescribed the path of fourfold *sadhana:* right knowledge, right faith, right conduct and right
penance which include the observance of non-violence, truth, non-
stealing, celibacy and non-possession, as well as the practice of
meditation, fasting, forbearance of hardship, etc.

Based on these principles, he established an order of monks, nuns and lay followers. At the time of his *nirvana,* there were fourteen thousand monks and thirty-six thousand nuns. These included great personalities and royal dignitaries, such as Abhaya Kumar (the son of King Bimbisara of Magadha) and king Udrayana of Sindh. The lay community at that time was a hundred thousand strong. Mahavira also wielded tremendous political influence.

His chief disciples, the Gandhara, collected his speeches and compiled them into the *Agamas,* a vast portion of which is now lost. Whatever was preserved in memory was written down in 454 (or 467) under the leadership of Deverdhi Gani at Vallabhpur in Gujarat and these texts constitute the authoritative scriptures of the Svetambara sect. The Digambara sect denies its authority and has a separate literature written by later *acharyas* but the main theme of the texts of both sects is almost the same.

The schism between the Digambara and Svetambara sects is believed to have taken place in the second century. It developed between the monks practising two types of asceticism — *jina-kalpa* (a stricter form) and *sthavirakalpa* (a more liberal form). They differ mainly in their views on the use of clothing to be used by monks and the possibility of salvation for women.

In 1451, Lunika Mehta, a Jain lay follower, started a campaign against the laxity of monks in the Svetambara sect. The revolt crystallised in about 1663 with the formation of a new sect, the Sthanakavasi. This sect was also against idol worship and therefore against the building of temples. Initially, the lay followers began building houses in which to perform religious activities. Later, monks began to reside in them and they came to be called *sthanakas* (abodes). In 1760, a Jain *acharya,* Bhikshu, brought about a revolution in this third sect against the building of *sthanakas* as abodes for monks. This led to a further subdivision and the Terapanth sect was formed. Bhikshu was also responsible for the reorganisation of the monastic order into a more disciplined one.

The Digambara sect was also subdivided into some subsects such as the Tairahpanth, Beespanth and Taranpanth and the original Svetambara sect (which became known as *Murti-pujak*) also became subdivided into several subjects such as the Tapagach-chha and the Khartaragachchha.

Buddhism spread all over Asia but Jainism remained confined to India, the main reason being that their religious laws did not permit Jain monks to travel abroad.

The Jains have played a large part in the enrichment of Indian painting, handicrafts and calligraphy. They have had an equally great share in developing Indian theatre through music, dance, drama and folklore. Jain literature, both canonical and non-canonical, is replete with discussions on these arts.

There is a large volume of original Jain literature written in the last 2,500 years in many languages, particularly in Prakrit, Ardha-magadhi, Sauraseni, Apabhramsa, Sanskrit, Hindi, Gujarati, Rajasthani, Kannada and Tamil. (Tiruvalluvar, author of the great Tamil classic, *Tiru Kural,* was probably a Jain).

For Digambaras, the canonical texts are mainly the texts known as *Shatkhandagama,* which were written by Bhutabali and Push-padanta. The books written by Kunda Kundacharya (first century BC) are also equally revered. The language of the Digambara texts is mainly Sauraseni.

The canonical texts believed to have been composed in Maha-vira's own time are in Prakrit. The most important among them and considered authoritative, are the eleven *Angas,* the twelve *Upangas,* the four *Malas,* the four *Chedas* and the *Avashyaka.* According to some sources there were eighty-four such texts.

Non-canonical literature mainly comprises the commentaries on the canonical texts. They were written by several *acharya* teacher-scholars from the second century to the present time. The oldest commentaries are the *Niruktis* written by Bhadrabahu Swami (the second) and are in Prakrit. Then follow the *Bhashya* and *Churnis* (between the sixth and fifth century) also mostly in Prakrit. Hindi translations of all the texts and English translations of some of them have also been published.

Among the later works on Jain philosophy, the *Tattvarthasura* by Umasvati (or Uma Swami) in the first century, is the most important because of its exhaustive nature. Its authority is ac-knowledged by both Digambaras and Svetambaras.

In the first decade of the Christian era, the logical explanation of Jain philosophy was the main theme of the Jain writers of both the sects.

Although most of the canonical texts deal with metaphysical and ethical discussions and are in ordinary prose, a few canonical works and other valuable literary material are in poetical form, the later Jain *acharyas* having composed some master pieces in both prose and poetry. The Puranic literature of the Digambara tradition in the Apabharamsa language and some poetic works of Jain poets (such as Sidhasondivakar, Hari Bhadra Suri and Hem Chandra) illustrate the Jain contribution to ancient Indian literature.

The sacred books of the Jains are equally important for their contribution to scientific concepts. They evolved their own theories about mathematics, physics, chemistry, biology, astronomy, alchemy, medicine, the atom, cosmology, the structure of matter and energy, the fundamental structure of living being, the concept of subjects and time and the theory of relativity.

Jain monks practise asceticism but also contribute to the welfare of society. Mahavira uttered his discourses in Prakrit because it was the language of the masses whom he wanted to benefit by his teachings. The rule that Jain monks and nuns must always travel on foot also helped the Jain ascetics to keep in touch with the people.

With the renaissance of Hinduism the Jain following dwindled. The Jains suffered because of the close affinity to Hinduism (frequently one-way) and intermarriage with the Hindus. Some attempts to organise themselves and retain their identity were made.

Jain influence in India is largely due to its higher standards of literacy and the comparative affluence of the community which is a small one comprising 3.4 million people (1991 census).

Some decades ago Jains were mostly traders, land-owners and shopkeepers but now some of them are big industrialists. Some of India's biggest industrial houses belong to Jains such as Sahu Jain and Sarabhai. Mahatma Gandhi was greatly influenced by the Jain principles of *ahimsa* and elevated it from a personal and ethical belief to a national and political creed of non-violence. Jains have also distinguished themselves in the arts and literature. The literary prize, the Jnanpith Award, instituted by the Sahu Jain Trust, has been acclaimed as a national award.

Impact of Jainism

During the lifetime of Mahavira, the Jain religion was confined to the region which included modern Bihar and Uttar Pradesh, where the teacher lived and preached. Later his followers spread the faith in many parts of India. Bihar remained the centre of Jainism. Mahavira was a Kshatriya and belonged to a royal family and many of his contemporary kings like Bimbisara and Ajatasatru of Magadha, Chetka of Vaisali, the heads of the Malla and Lichhavi republics, Satanika of Kausambi and his successor Udayana, Chand Pradyot of Ujjain, Udrayana of Sindh and Dadhivahana of Anga (Bhagalpur) became his followers or admirers and patronised his monastic order during his lifetime. Many of them and their families also became initiated into it. King Shranik (Bimbisara, 543-491 BC) and his queen, Chetana, find an important place in canonical literature. Their son, Ajatasatru (491-459 BC) is also believed to have been a follower of Mahavira. Both are claimed equally by Jains and Buddhists as followers of their respective faiths, which shows that some rulers in ancient Indian extended uniform courtesy towards religious leaders of different sects. King Samprati of Ujjain (220-211 BC), the grandson and successor of Asoka, is also referred to in early Jain literature with great respect. Gradually the state of Magadha acquired hegemony over most of North India. The Nandas who ruled in the fourth century BC were also staunch followers of Jainism. After them Chandragupta Maurya, who ruled over Magadha was also an ardent Jain and when old, joined the monastic order and journeyed to South India with his guru, Bhadrabahu. An inscription found at Chandragiri in Karnataka mentions that Chandragupta died through penance undertaken unto death for self-purification.

From the Kharvavela inscriptions at Khandagiri, it is evident that in the second century BC, Kalinga (Orissa) was the centre of a powerful empire ruled by Kharavela, one of the royal patrons of the Jain faith. Mathura, a very ancient city known for its jewelled *stupas,* was a stronghold of the Jains. According to the Mathura inscriptions (belonging to the reign of Kanishka and his successor) the Jain community was firmly established there in the first century. After the end of the Mauryan dynasty, Jainism and Buddhism not only lost political patronage but had to face strong opposition from Brahmanism and its supporter kings. The persecution by Pushyamitra of the Sunga dynasty (second century BC) compelled most of the Jains to leave Magadha and thus Bihar which was the birthplace of Jainism has virtually no Jains today. The seat of the Jain religious hierarchy shifted to Karnataka, Tamil Nadu, Gujarat and Rajasthan and the cities of Mathura and Ujjain now saw the growth of the religion. The third and the last council of Jain monks was held in 466 at Valabhi (modern Wala, near Bhavnagar in Gujarat) 993 years after the *nirvana* of Mahavira, when the Jain canon was put into writing. In the twelfth century the Jain religion gained ascendancy in Gujarat when the Chalukya king, Siddharaja, and his successor, Kumarapala, professed Jainism under the influence of the renowned *acharya,* Hemchandra and gave the Jains royal patronage under which they established their position in Western India.

Jainism has also played an important role in the history of South India. The Ganga dynasty (fourth to eleventh century) was virtually a creation of the famous Jain *acharya,* Simhanandi. The Kadamba rulers were responsible for the spread of Jainism in Karnataka. The period of the Rashtrakutas (750-1000) was most auspicious in the history of Jainism as it produced the renowned Digambara Jain teachers, Jinasena and Gunasena. The Hoysala monarchs also extended their patronage to Jainism. In the Tamil region, Madurai, Kaveriapatanam and other places were centres of Jainism. In Andhra, the Eastern Chalukyas patronised the Jains. Thus the whole of South India became a centre of Jainism for over a century. The Jains continued to maintain their political influence during Muslim rule. Akbar was greatly impressed by the Jain acharya, Hira Vijay Suri. In Gujarat, Nawab Mahamuda Beg once received financial help from the Jain community at the time of a severe drought.

Contribution

The Jains have made valuable contributions to almost every branch of learning. Jain literature is a treasure house of popular stories, fairy tales and narrative poetry with the help of which the writers illustrated religious ideas and ethics. Besides composing epics, plays and poetry, the writers produced works on grammar, lexicography, prosody, mathematics, politics, astronomy, medicine, yoga, etc. The Jains have also enriched the Kannada, Tamil and Telugu literatures. The Kannada poets, Pampa (or Adi Pampa), Ponna and Ranna, who wrote in Kannada and Sanskrit, were the followers of the Jain faith.

The most ancient piece of sculpture that is extant after Mahavira's time is probably his idol found at Mathura, which is said to have been made eighty-four years after his *nirvana,* in the fifth century BC. The inscription on it says that King Ajatasatru (Kunika) worshipped Mahavira.

The Jains have erected exquisite temples either on hill-tops or in secluded valleys. The fine torso of a Jain image found in Lohanipur (in Bihar) is said to have belonged to the Mauryan period. Stupas at Mathura with various accessories, stone railings, decorative gateways, stone umbrellas, elaborate carved pillars and statues, figure in the history of Jainism. The Indra Sabha (the council hall of Indra) in Ellora is the best known Jain cave temple of the medieval period.

The colossal statue of Gomateshwara Bahubali of Sravanabelagola in Karnataka is one of the wonders of the world. Almost seventeen metres high, it is carved out of solid rock and is visible within a radius of twenty-four kilometres. It was ordered by Chamundaraya, a renowned minister and a great general of Rachamalla, in the tenth century. A great festival, *abhisheka* (bathing ceremony), is held here by the Digambara Jains.

The shrine of Parsvanatha at Khajuraho is the largest and finest of all Jain temples situated there. The two marble temples at Mt. Abu, known for their delicacy of carving and richness of design, are considered the most notable achievements of the Jains in the domain of the arts. In Ranakpur is a unique example of the Chaumukha (four-faced) style of architecture which has doorways facing the four quarters with a Tirthankara in each.

Temple cities have been built on the Shatrunjaya Hills at Palitana and on 1,220 metres high Girnar in Gujarat. The largest
temple at Girnar is that of Neminatha, the twenty-third
Tirthankara, connected with the legend of Krishna, who attained
salvation on this hill. The Kirtistambbha (pillar of victory of glory)
at Chittor is a singularly elegant specimen.

Besides the wall paintings of the seventh century, there are
miniature paintings of the twelfth century in Gujarat and Rajasthan. The earliest Jain miniature paintings are decorative
roundels in the palm-leaf manuscript of the Nishithachurni dated
1100.

Festivals

Parjusana (staying at one place for four months during the rainy
season) or Dashlakshmi, as it is called by the Digambaras, which
falls in the month of Bhadrapada, is an important festival. It is
observed for eight days by the Svetambaras and for ten days by the
Digambaras. During the festival certain restraints in food are to be
observed and harsh language not used. Samvatsari, the last day of
Parjusana is the solemn occasion of forgiveness and introspection
when the Jains ask their relatives and friends to pardon them for
any offences they might have committed by deed, word or thought.

Shrutapanchami or Jnanapanchami is another important festival. On this day they worship their sacred lore and remove dust
and insects from their books and rearrange them. On this auspicious occasion, a number of *grantha bhandaras* or book stores were
established at Jaisalmer, Khambahat, Jaipur, Patna, Mudibidri,
Karanja and other places where thousands of valuable palm-leaf
and paper manuscripts have been preserved.

Mahavira Jayanti, the birth anniversary of Mahavira is celebrated with great pomp. The festival of Diwali and Rakshabandhan
or Shravani are observed by Jains in common with the Hindus.
According to the Jains, Mahavira attained salvation on Diwali at
Pavapuri, when the confederate kings of Kasi and Kosala observed
a fast in commemoration of this event.

Beliefs

Mahavira threw open the doors of his religion to all without any distinction of caste, creed or sex. Both men and women could enter the religious order on equal terms. Even the (so-called) untouchables were allowed to embrace the Jain religion. With the passage of time, however the Jain community came to be divided into various castes and creeds such a *upadhayaya* (priest), *chaturthi* (the fourth caste or *ast* or good Sudras), *panchama* (fifth or the lowest caste) and so on. Formerly, the Jains asserted the superiority of the Kshatriyas but gradually the Brahmanas gained a prominent place in their purview.

Jains, like Buddhists, denied the authority of the Vedas and did not consider them to be of divine origin. They have their own holy scriptures. They do not attribute the creation of the universe to a God or hold a God responsible for what is good or bad in life. These views are different from those of Hinduism; yet the followers of Mahavira adapted themselves to the Hindu way in religious practices, social customs and manners. There are intermarriages between Jains and Vaishnavas.

Monks and Nuns

Jainism allows full freedom to all human beings to observe vows and practice self-discipline but the vows for monks and nuns are stricter than those for lay votaries. For instance, the observance of the great vows is uniform for all the Jains but the vow of non-possession is followed in its fullest sense only by Digambara monks, who own nothing and remain unclad. Their only possessions are a peacock-feather whisk and a water-pot (*tumbdu*). They remain standing when they eat, holding the food in the hollow of the palm. Sthanakvasi and Terapanthi monks and nuns (of the Svetambara sect) tie a piece of cloth round the mouth, which distinguishes them from other monks and nuns. *Murtipujak* monks and nuns carry a *muhapatta* (mouth cloth) and hold it at a distance from the mouth while delivering religious discourses.

Clockwise from top left: Marta Abhishek of Bahubali on the occasion of the 1000th installation ceremony at Shravanbelagola. Interior view of the Ranakpur Temple. Devotees inside a Jain Temple at Calcutta. Carvings of Jain tirthankaras on the mountain sides at Palitana in Kathiawar.

Top: Temple at Girnar in Junagadh.
Above: Sculptured relief at the
Parasnath Temple in Ranakpur.
Left: The temple chariot at Palitana
Temple in which the images of
Gods are taken in procession on
festive occasions.

Top left: Gate to the Sanchi stupa;
Top right: The Buddha in Abhaya Mudra: the only such extant bronze from Nalanda.
Above left: The Damik Stupa at Sarnath where Buddha preached his first-sermon.
Above right: The Sanchi Stupa.

Top left: The Dalai Lama at the Buddhist Elephanta caves near Bombay.
Top right: A rock cut Buddhist Chapel at Karle.
Above: The entrance to a Chaitya at Baja.

Above left: A devotee at the Meenakshi Temple at Mudurai.
Above right: Ayyangar priests at a temple in Kerala.
Left: The Shore Temple (eighth century) of Mahabalipuram.

Above left: Lingraja Temple at Bhubneswar. *Above right:* Linga puja at the Sri Mangesh Temple in Goa. *Right:* The temple elephant at the Gurvayur Temple in Kerala.

Top left: Garhwali women at work in rice fields. *Top right:* A family in Ladakh.
Above left: A Manipuri wedding procession.
Above right: Coorgi women in their distinctive style of sari.

Top: A Toda priest outside the temple.
Above left: A Bhil village in Madhya Pradesh: in the foreground are tomb-stones erected in the memory of prominent Bhils.
Right: Bhil boys practising archery.

It is ordained that the monks and nuns should walk from place to place (except in the rainy season), thus working not only for their own elevation and spiritual enlightenment but also for those of the people. Their's is the spirit of bondlessness, non-possession and missionary zeal. As they move on foot through different parts of the country and among all sections of the people, they become aware of prevailing ills and shortcomings. They play a positive role in enriching the moral fibre of society and in helping to ameliorate the woes of its people.

The Jain order of nuns had its origin in the times of the first Tirthankara, Rishabha. They follow the same rules of conduct as the monks. The Digambara nuns do not practise nudity and therefore the Digambaras hold that nuns cannot attain liberation, as they do not observe the rule of non-possession. Well-versed in the Jain canons and other systems of Indian philosophy, some of the Jain nuns have done good work as preachers and are examples of simple living and high thinking.

8

BUDDHISM

ABOUT THE MIDDLE OF THE SIXTH CENTURY BC, India was divided into a number of warring kingdoms among which were Magadha, Kosala, Panchala, Kasi and Chedi. The Vedic religion had degenerated into ritual but the speculations of the Upanishadic seers still inspired thinking men. New systems of thought had also taken shape, theistic, atheistic and agnostic.

It was during this period that Siddhartha, a prince, was born in Lumbini (Rumindei), in 563 BC His father kept all knowledge of sorrow, decay and death from him. Siddhartha was a young man when he first learnt of sickness, grief and death. The experience so affected him that he became determined to seek the way, for all mankind, out of sorrow, despair, suffering and death. In renunciation of worldly pursuits he left his home, his young wife and infant son. For six years he underwent fasts and mortification of the body at Uruvela. Then he went to Bodhgaya where under a *bodhi* tree he attained supreme enlightenment and became the Buddha or the Enlightened One. He then moved on to Sarnath (near Varanasi) where he preached his first sermon to his five original companions.

Setting the Wheel of the Law in motion, he explained to them the four noble truths: that there is suffering, that it has a cause, that it can be overcome and that there is a way to accomplish this. He exhorted his followers to adjure the two extremes and follow the 'middle way' and the noble eight-fold path — of right view, right intention, right speech, right action, right livelihood, right effort, right mindfulness and right concentration. He taught that the cessation of pain comes with non-attachment. This sermon of his contains the essentials of Buddhism in a nutshell. He also accepted two earlier dogmas, karma and rebirth as cardinal.

But there are aspects to the teachings of Sakyamuni that make his religion unique. He dismisses all that is supernatural and lays no claim to "revealed" truths; he does not describe prayer to a supreme being or to any God; his path of liberation is that of mental discipline and psychological analysis; he does not promise a heaven nor the *ananda* of the Hindus.

The earliest Buddhism texts are the three *pitakas* or baskets — of *dharma,* discipline and fables. The *Dhammapada,* a celebrated work, is an anthology of the sayings of the Buddha. The *Milinda Panho* (Questions of Milinda) contains the dialogue between the Buddhist dialectician, Nagasena, and the Greek king, Menander, ruler of Northwest India in the first century BC The *Jatakas,* the most popular Buddhist texts, are mostly stories of the former incarnations of the Buddha.

In course of time, Buddhism branched out into two major schools, the Hinayana and the Mahayana. The word *yana* means a vehicle, a ferry-boat. The idea of a ferry-boat or crossing, occurs frequently in Indian thought. (The Jain Tirthankaras are 'creators of fords'). The Buddha's doctrine itself is simply called *yana.* To sail in the Buddhist boat is to go across from the shore of desire, ignorance and death to wisdom and liberation.

The Hinayana (inferior vehicle) doctrine is followed by people who are lights unto themselves, those who are on the voyage of individual release. "There is no thinker but only thoughts; no feeler but only feelings. It is a pure phenomenalism maintaining the non-existence of substances or individuals." It offers to all beings in all worlds, salvation by faith and love as well as by knowledge. Like the 'unknown way', it is exceedingly hard. In theory the Hinaya-nists were atheists but in practice they worshipped the Buddha and even developed a popular polytheism.

The Mahayana (superior vehicle) doctrine arose at a time when Buddhism had become something of a pan-Asian religion. It avails to convey over the rough sea of becoming, to the farther shore of *nibbana,* those few strong souls who require no external spiritual aid nor the consolation of worship and does not require that a man should immediately renounce the world and all the affection of humanity.

Lamaism, Tantrism and Zen are other developments of Buddhism. Zen is derived from the Sanskrit word *dhyana* (meditation) and the school is the contribution of Hodhidharma, a Kanchipuram priest, who settled down in China. The ultimate truth, according to Zen, cannot be found in writings. It has to be discovered through the "inner light" by awakening the "Buddha heart". To do this, one has to practise a special form of meditation.

Many kings are associated with Buddhism. Of these the Magadhan monarch, Bimbisara (543-491 BC) was a contemporary of the Buddha. His son, Ajatasatru, was first enemy of the Buddha, who later became a follower. But the most celebrated devotee and friend of Buddhism was the Emperor Asoka (273-238 BC). According to tradition, the great Mauryan monarch was converted to Buddhism by Upagupta after the Kalinga war. It was under his aegis that Buddhism spread all over India and to other countries in Asia. Kanishka, the Kushana king (first century) was another patron of the religion. The last great supporter of Buddhism in India was probably Harsha (606-648).

Buddhism flourished in India for over a thousand years and its followers were to be met with in areas as far apart as Kashmir and Kerala. Its contribution to the heritage of India led to an intellectual re-examination of Vedic thought. Sankara, regarded as the greatest opponent of Buddhism, was paradoxically very much influenced by it.

Shankara's monism is so impersonal as to be nearly Godless. Hindus had no monastic order and it is likely that Shankara borrowed the idea from Buddhism when he established his *pithas* with their monastic heads.

More than in religion, it was in art that the influence of Buddhism was felt. Indian architecture may be said to have begun with the Buddhists. The Buddhists built many stupas (funerary mounds), *chaityas* (chapels) and *viharas* (monasteries). Many were hewn out of rock, a practice later adopted by the Hindus. The frescoes of the Ajanta caves represent the most monumental achievement of Indian painting.

Buddhism, despite its disapproval of caste, hardly affected the social structure of India. It declined in India as it depended on official patronage, its fortunes fluctuating with those of the kings who supported it. In course of time, Buddhism included practices like worship and devotion which made it hardly distinguishable from Hinduism and eventually it was more or less absorbed by the earlier religion. The *Bhagavatapurana* elevated the Buddha to the status of an *avatar* of Vishnu.

It was a religion without a God, without mythology and without a liturgy yet it had rapid expansion far beyond the borders of its homeland and spread to the north and east of Asia, becoming there the religion of the masses and influencing the civilisation for centuries. Its hold in China was remarkable because it made itself felt in the face of the highly evolved philosophies of Confucianism and Taoism.

Buddhism is believed to have made its appearance there during the time of the Han emperor, Ming Ti (first century). Numerous Indian teachers propagated the message of the Sakyamuni, one of the earliest being Kumarajiva. Chinese scholars and monks also came to India, two of the most famous being Fa-Hien, who stayed here from 405 to 411, and Hiuen Tsang, who spent many years here leaving for China in 643, both of whom visited the important Buddhist sites and universities and collected many authentic Buddhist texts to take back to China.

Buddhism flourished in China during the Tang (sixth-tenth centuries) and Sung (late tenth to thirteenth centuries) dynasties. The 'Cultural Revolution' in China had wiped out most of the traditional values, including those of religion. But the temples of China remain as museums holding memories of nearly two thousand years — of a way of life that inspired and enriched the country's art and thought.

From China, Buddhism spread to Korea and Japan. In 369, a monk, Sundo, crossed the Yalu River and brought the texts of Buddhism with him to Korea. In a few centuries the new religion established itself all over the land. Monasteries were built that grew powerful with state patronage. Japan received the message of Siddhartha from Korea in the sixth century and it was under Shotoku Taishi, nephew of Empress Suiko (sixth century) that

Buddhism took firm roots in the islands. (The temple he built at Horyuji still survives). The Nara period was the golden age of Buddhism in Japan. It began during the reign of Emperor Shomu who made Nara his capital. The spread of Buddhism in Japan was made easy by the friendly attitude of the official Shinto religion towards it. Japanese life, art and literature were also profoundly changed by Buddhism.

The national chronicle of Sri Lanka, the *Mahavamsa,* claims that the Sakyamuni himself visited the island. It is commonly believed that Buddhism was introduced there by Asoka's son, Mahendra, in the fourth century BC who is said to have gained the conversion of King Tissa. Legend has it that Asoka also sent his daughter, Sanghamitra, to the Sinhala island with the gift of a sapling of the Bodhi tree. Sri Lanka was thus historically among the first nations in the world to receive Buddhism.

The introduction of Buddhism to Burma (Suvarnabhumi) is also ascribed to Asoka. The ancient capital, Pagan, developed into a religious centre and for two centuries numerous pagodas were built there.

In the early centuries of the Christian era Hinduism and Buddhism spread to many countries of Southeast Asia, including the Indonesian archipelago. Hinduism survives only in the island of Bali but Buddhism still flourishes in Indo-China and Thailand. The temples or *wats* of these two lands are world famous.

In Afghanistan (Gandhara) and Central Asia, Buddhism is remembered only by the ruins of a past civilisation and archaeological work in Central Asia has revealed sculpture that points to the pervasive influence of Buddhism in this region.

Buddhism in Tibet has been a combination of Mahayana Buddhism, magic and mystery. It was officially introduced in the seventh century when the Indian teacher, Padmasambhava, was brought to Tibet — his followers belonging to the Red Hat sect. In the fourteenth century a reformer emerged, Tsong-kha-pa, who enforced celibacy among the monks and founded the Yellow Hat sect.

His nephew, Dge-hdum-grub-pa, was probably the first Dalai Lama. The origin of the institution of the Tashi or Panchen Lama is also obscure. The present Buddhist Dalai Lama lives in exile in India.

The lion capital of the Asoka pillar and the wheel of the law are Indian State symbols today — one way in which homage has been paid to the gentle *bhikku* whose 'kingdom' once extended to most of Asia. In 1956 India celebrated his 2,500th *mahaparinirvana* anniversary.

The neo-Buddhist sect came into being when a large number of Scheduled Caste people, following the lead of the late (Dr.) Ambedkar, embraced Buddhism at a meeting in Nagpur in 1956, leaving the Hindu fold in disgust at its caste-conscious mentality.

Ambedkar had a dream of drawing the whole of India towards Buddhism. In this faith born on Indian soil, he felt, lay the strength to give the nation, and perhaps even the world, an integrated identity. According to the 1991 census, the population of Buddhists in India is 6.4 million.

9

SIKHISM

IKHISM IS A MONOTHEISTIC RELIGION opposed to idol worship and is against the practice of asceticism, the caste system and ritualism. The founder of Sikhism was Guru Nanak (1469-1539) who proclaimed that there was no Hindu and no Mussulman. Accompanied by an aged Muslim musician, Mardana, and a Hindu peasant Bala, Guru Nanak went from village to village preaching his message. He taught that there was one God, and that caste, ritual and form were evils that must be abolished. Within a few years his disciples became a homogeneous group called the Sikhs, the term originating from the Sanskrit word *shishya* for disciple. He travelled all over India, and to Ceylon (Sri Lanka), Mecca and Medina.

He sang his hymns wherever he went, spreading his message of love, purity and universal brotherhood.

Arjun, the fifth guru, in the line of ten gurus who followed, compiled the *Granth* (holy book of the Sikhs) from the hymns composed by Hindu and Muslim saints as well as the writings of the other Sikh gurus, the body of the work and its inspiration being the verses (*Japji*) of Guru Nanak.

Arjun infused great vigour into Sikhism. He made Amritsar his headquarters where he built a gurdwara (temple of the guru). He incurred the displeasure of Jahangir, the Muslim emperor, and was tortured to death in 1606. His martyrdom created a rift between the Sikhs and the Mughals and started the process by which Sikhism gradually became a militant organisation.

Govind Singh, the tenth guru (1675-1708) converted the Sikhs into a militant fraternity called the Khalsa (the pure). He gave the Sikhs a distinct individuality in 1699 by baptising five of his followers (who had risen to his call to sacrifice themselves for the guru and the faith) at a small ceremony of cleansing; he poured water into an iron vessel and stirred it with a two-edged dagger and his wife put in a particular sweetmeat (*batasa*) making it *amrit* (water of immortality) and the five drank out of the same bowl and were given new names with the suffix 'Singh' (lion).

As the outward sign of this discipline he enjoined them, among other admonitions, never to cut their hair, always to wear a comb, a pair of short drawers, a bangle and a *kirpan* (dagger). Not content with this, he had himself baptised by them — emphasising through the ritual that the Guru and the disciples were knit together in a common brotherhood — an initiation that was unique. Since then all Sikhs append this 'family' name of Singh to their own names.

The Sikhs rose to power under Ranjit Singh (1710-1839) whose kingdom extended from the Khyber Pass to the Sutlej and from Kashmir to the deserts of Sind. They were defeated by the British who annexed their kingdom in 1849. They recruited them into the army and gave them lands in areas opened up by canals. As part of the Punjab went to Pakistan in 1947, many of the Punjab's biggest landholders had to abandon their homes and estates and settle down in India.

They number about 16.3 million (1991 census) and most of them live in the state of Punjab. Before the partition of the country in 1947, about half lived in that portion of the Punjab which is now in Pakistan. They form less than 2 per cent of the population of India.

Next to the Parsis, they are the most prosperous community in India. Industrious and energetic, they make the best farmers, fine soldiers (Sikhs constitute a substantial portion of the country's army, navy and air force) and sportsmen. Good at nearly all the sports, they excel in field hockey. In 1965, of the nine who successfully climbed the world's highest peak, Everest, three were Sikhs.

They are good technicians, mechanics, carpenters, artisans and engineers. They control the transport system of many of the bigger cities of India. The percentage of literacy among this community (particularly among the women) is higher than amongst either the Hindus or Muslims and they have produced a large number of writers, artists, scholars, scientists and eminent people in law and medicine.

The language of the Sikhs, Punjabi, is written in the Gurmukhi script. Their greatest works of literature are the *Granth* and the compositions of Gurus Nanak and Govind Singh. A great figure in recent Punjabi literature was Bhai Vir Singh (1872-1957), other well-known contemporary writers being Mohan Singh, Amrita Pritam, Prabhjot Kaur, Gurbaksh Singh, Dalip Kaur Tiwana and Kartar Singh Duggal.

Of the famous Sikh painters, three have been outstanding in their contribution to modern art: Amrita Shergil (1913-41), S.G. Thakur Singh and Sobha Singh. The Sikhs have a rich tradition of folk music and their repertory consists of songs for every occasion: lullabies (*lori*), songs sung at weddings (*ghori*) and songs of love and separation. *Bolis* and *tappas* are two other lively typical Punjabi forms that are sung on festive occasions. The most popular folk song is the balled of Heer-Ranjha, two legendary lovers, rendered into beautiful verse by Warris Shah and Damodar.

The most popular dance form of this community, the *Bhangra* is famed for its vitality and vigorous movement. After the wheat crop has been harvested, the men with bells on their ankles, dressed in white shirts, brightly coloured *lungis* and fancy waistcoats with large mother-of-pearl buttons, perform this dance moving round in a circle to the deafening beat of drums, stamping their feet and clapping their hands, turning and twisting their bodies in gay abandon. The dancing is interspersed with singing and ends in a frenzied whirl. The *Giddha,* the feminine counterpart of the *Bhangra,* is equally lively and is also performed on various festive occasions.

Most of the Sikhs are peasants living in scattered villages. being reasonably prosperous, by Indian standards, most of them have comfortable homes with courtyards where their cattle are tethered. The families of all the sons of a father live jointly under the governance of the mother until the land is divided. Every village has a *gurdwara,* which has a flag pole draped in a yellow sock and the triangular yellow flag with the Sikh symbol a dagger in the centre of a quoit and two crossed swords beneath.

Sikh peasants eat nutritious and strengthening food. Though not vegetarian by conviction, few can afford to eat meat, except on special occasions. The Sikh's staple diet is wheat, buffalo milk and milk products like curds, cottage cheese and buttermilk. In winter, it is spinach (usually the mashed mustard plant) with blobs of butter and corn *chapatis*, a diet that is responsible for Sikh's almost proverbial stamina, physique and virility.

A Sikh temple is called *gurdwara* (gateway or temple of the guru). The central object of worship in the *gurdwara* is the *Granth* which is placed on a low *divan* and is usually draped in embroidered silks. It is opened ceremonially every morning and wrapped up and put away in the evening. Both men and women read it while a fly whisk made of white yak hair is waved over it.

Four gurdwaras, known as the four *takhts* (thrones) of the guru, associated with Guru Govind Singh, are marked with special sanctity. One is at Patna (his birthplace), one at Anandpur where he performed the first ceremony of 'baptism'. The third, the Akal Takht (the throne of the timeless one) is in the Golden Temple at Amritsar, from where all important edicts issue to the community and the fourth is at Nanded in Maharashtra, where he died.

There are over two hundred historic *gurdwaras* to which Sikhs go on pilgrimages. Of those associated with Guru Nanak the ones at his birthplace at Nankana Sahib, at the site of his encounter with a Muslim divine at Hasan Abdal and at the site of the martyrdom of the fifth guru, Arjun, at Lahore, are all in Pakistan. In India the place of the execution of the two younger sons of Govind Singh at Fatehgarh (in Patiala) and the site of the imprisonment and martyrdom of the ninth guru, Teg Bahadur, at Chandni Chowk, Delhi, are among the most frequented.

Festivals and Ceremonies

Sikhs participate in some of the festivals celebrated by the Hindus of northern India; they celebrate Basant Panchmi, Holi, Baisakhi and also Diwali, when they light lamps although the religious part of the ceremonial takes place in the *gurdwara*. Of their own festivals, six are important: the birthdays of Guru Nanak and Govind Singh, the martyrdom of Arjun, Teg Bahadur, and the two sons of Govind Singh, and the day of the founding of the Khalsa and Hola Mohalla. On these occasions, the *Granth,* placed on top of a flower-bedecked van, is taken out in procession through the city. On either side two men carry the Sikh ensigns (Nishan Sahib) and five men (*panj piaras*), representing the first five converts, march in front of the van with drawn swords. While the women walk behind it, the men, in groups of singers walk in front. Mass feeding of worshippers at the *guru ka langar* (the kitchen of the Guru), sometimes as many as one lakh is also arranged on these occasions.

Some sections of Sikhs recite the first five verses of the morning prayers in the ears of a new-born child. At the name-giving ceremony, the *Granth* is opened at random and the child is given a name beginning with the first letter of the first word at the top of the page opened.

The Sikhs of North-western Punjab perform certain ceremonies and festivities when the child's hair is plaited for the first time (*gundana*). Among some families, a child's initiation into reading the *Granth* is a matter of elaborate ceremonial at the *gurdwara,* followed by feeding of the poor.

When boys and girls attain puberty, a baptism (*pahul*) ceremony takes place in the same way that adopted by Guru Govind Singh at the first baptismal ceremony (in 1699) and five orthodox Sikhs are chosen to initiate the new convert in the presence of a congregation. *Amrit* is also prepared in the same way. Passages from the scriptures including Guru Govind Singh's compositions (the *Jap Sahib*) are recited. The initiate then takes the vows of the Khalsa. Each vow is read out aloud and the novice signifies his or her acceptance by bowing before the *Granth. Amrit* is then splashed in the face with the cry, *Sri Wah Guru Ji Ka Khalsa, Sri Wah Guru Ji Ki Fateh.*

The baptised also takes on another name. The *pahul* imposes all the obligations of the faith but also confers some rights on the initiate. Once baptised, a person has the right of access to the holiest shrines — like the Akal Takht in the Golden Temple at Amritsar — and that of entering into matrimony.

The Sikh marriage is much like the Hindus but religious texts used are from the *Granth*. The wedding is called *Anand Karaj* (ceremony of bliss). The bridegroom leaves his home on horseback accompanied by his friends and relations and music and is received by the male relatives of the bride (*milni*) at her home. The wedding itself takes place before noon. Professional singers (*ragis*) sing hymns prescribed for morning worship (*asa-di-war*)). The couple then sits in front of the *Granth*. A priest tells them of the obligations of married life and then reads the hymns on marriage from the *Granth*. The couple circumambulates (*lawan*) the *Granth* four times and the man and woman are pronounced husband and wife.

Among the peasants, the custom of taking women — usually widows — under 'protection' simply by 'casting the mantle' (*chaddar*) obtains. The children of such unions are recognised as legitimate.

Some hymns are recited when death occurs. The corpse is bathed and dressed in the emblems of the faith. The only strict injunction is against lamentation and the beating of breasts. The mourners sit round the deceased and recite the mourning prayers. The Sikhs cremate their dead and, as with Hindus, the funeral pyre is lit by the son or nearest male relative. The ashes are thrown into a river, if possible into the Beas at Kiratpur. Sikhs are forbidden to erect memorials to the dead or to celebrate death anniversaries. A period of mourning, varying from four to ten days, depending on the age of the deceased, is prescribed during which people visit the bereaved to condole with them. It is customary to remove all furniture from the house and to sit and sleep on the floor. On the last day of mourning, friends and relatives assemble in the house to participate in the singing of hymns and the recitation of the *Granth*. If the occasion is the death of the head of the household, his eldest son is officially recognised as the new head by having a turban tied on his head before the assembled friends and relatives.

Sikh Communities

The Jat Sikh Community

The Jat Sikhs are of the same stock as the Hindu Jats of Haryana and western Uttar Pradesh and the Muslim Jats of Pakistani Punjab. A large majority of those baptised by Guru Govind Singh were Jats and it was they who became the instruments of the Sikh rise to power and the land-owning group during the rule of Maharaja Ranjit Singh, maintaining their position as the premier section of Sikhs under British rule as well.

The Jat Sikh is characterised by a spirit of enterprise, zest for life, a sturdy independence and a love for the soil. The words 'Jat' and 'farmer' are synonymous in Punjabi. The Jat Sikhs are excellent farmers and in the early decades of this century, they transformed the barren lands now in Pakistani Punjab and after the partition of India, the thick jungles of the *terai* into green fields of wheat and sugar-cane. The men of this community are also soldiers *par excellence.* Essentially they are fighting men, their qualities being best exhibited in the army.

The most important Jat Sikh clans are Atwal, Aulak, Bains, Bajwa, Bal, Chima, Chung, Deol, Dhaliwal or Dhariwal, Dhillon, Dhindsa, Garewal, Ghuman, Gill, Goraya, Hor, Hinjra, Hundal, Kahlon, Kang, Khaira, Khosa, Mahal, Malhi, Man, Mangat, Pannu, Randhawa, Sohi, Sahota, Sandhu, Sara, Sekhon, Sindhu, Sohal, Variach and Virk. All claim Rajput origin except the Hor, Bhullar and Man which claim to be the original Jat clans which sprang from the *jata* or matted hair of Siva.

The Namdhari Community

The Namdhari movement was started by Baba Balak Singh of village Hazro in the North-West Frontier Province. He chose a disciple, Ram Singh, a carpenter of the Ramgarhia caste as his successor, whom the Namdharis believe to be the twelfth incarnation of the Sikh gurus in accordance with Guru Govind Singh's prophesy that there would be a carpenter from Bhaini with spiritual powers unsurpassed by any other.

Ram Singh introduced certain changes in the Sikh canon. He forbade the spending of more than thirteen rupees on a wedding which makes the Namdhari mass wedding the simplest, quickest and least expensive. The ceremony comprises both Hindu and Sikh rites.

He introduced changes in the forms of worship, address and in the appearance of his followers to distinguish them from orthodox Sikhs and became an ardent cow protector. His disciples chanted hymns endlessly and like 'dancing dervishes', worked themselves up into a state of frenzy, emitting *kuks* (loud shrieks) from which they came to be known as the Kukas.

His disciples come mostly from the poorer classes — Ramgarhias, cobblers, Mazhabis and, later, Jat peasants. He had separate *gurdwaras* built for them. The Kukas became trained in the use of weapons and established a para-military organisation.

Due to their anti-British activities, Ram Singh and eleven of his followers were deported to Burma. He died there in 1885.

The Pothohar Community

In 1947, when India and Pakistan were partitioned, thousands of homeless and destitute Hindus and Sikhs came into an independent but truncated India among whom were the Pothohari Sikhs, who today have become synonymous with ingenuity and hard work.

The plateau of Pothohar or Potwar, covers 6,400-8,000 square kilometres of the Sind-Sagar *Doab* including the districts of Rawalpindi, the eastern part of the Jhelum District converging on the salt range, a major portion of the Attock District and the Haripur Tehsil in the Hazara District. The Murree Hills (altitude 684 metres) provide scenic beauty to the lowland plateau.

It was probably here that the *Rig Veda* was "revealed" to the sages. Panini is said to have lived here. In this area are the ruins of Takshasila, the great Buddhist university of ancient times.

At the beginning of the sixteenth century, Guru Nanak undertook a mission to Hasan Abdal in this tract. A number of tribes are said to have settled here during the many invasions from the Northwest till the reign of Ranjit Singh (1780-1839). Hindus and Sikhs became prosperous here. Forced to migrate to India when the country was partitioned, they settled down in India.

The Pothohari Khatris are subdivided mainly into the Dhai Gharas (two-and-a-half) who include the Kapurs, Khannas and Malhotras; the Khukrains (Sethis, Suris, Sahnis, Sabharwals, Anands, Chaddhas, Bhasins and Kohlis); the Bahris who have twelve subcastes such as Kakkar and Chopra; and the Bowanjiwee Khatris who constitute a fraternity of fifty-two subcastes.

Starting with nothing except their business acumen and adaptability in 1947, the Pothoharis captured the markets of east Punjab and Delhi and now dominate the bicycle, motor parts and radio parts industries and the cloth markets of Punjab, Haryana, Delhi and Bombay. They have reached Singapore where they are shopkeepers and Africa and Indonesia, where they deal in the bicycle trade.

The Pothoharis started several educational institutions and their organisations like the Sikh Educational Conference and the Arya Samaj have created a new social awareness. Many eminent political leaders, dedicated educationists, legal luminaries, scholars, writers, artists, journalists, workers in industry and employees in the civil service and other professions, belong to this community.

Optimistic and dynamic, the Pothoharis possess an innate common sense for making the best of what comes their way and the community has a prime place in the commercial world of India.

The Ramgarhia Community

The original caste name of the Ramgarhias was Thoka (carpenter) from their occupation. Their ancestors had become Sikhs and were raised from their lowly status to become the high priests of Sikhs. Their skill and their strong right arm brought them power. When Sikhs became the dominant force in Punjab and captured Amritsar, their leader Jassa Singh Thoka (b. 1723), built a fort (named Ram Rauni) and changed the name of the clan to Ramgarhia. He, his brothers and their father, Bhagwan Singh, helped Zakariya Khan in a number of battles and were rewarded with several *jagirs*.

About the middle of the eighteenth century, the Sikhs took advantage of the conflict between the Afghans and the Mughals and spread out in the Baro Doab, the Jullunder Doab and across the Sutlej as far as Jind and Thanesar.

Clockwise from top left: Guru Nanak. A Gurdwara dedicated to Guru Amar Das. Guru Ram Singh. Guru Gobind Singh, the 10th Guru.

Top: The Golden Temple at Amritsar.
Above: A procession on the birth anniversary of Guru Nanak.
Left: The bride and groom perform the *lawan* ceremony at a Sikh wedding.

Top: Wall Paintings at the thirteenth century
Orthodox Syrian Church in Cheppad.
Above left: An ancient church on the
West Coast of India.
Right: The Armenian Church at Madras.

Clockwise from top left: Mother Teressa.
The Sacred Heart's Cathedral in
New Delhi. A congregation at the
Solemn High Mass in Bombay.
St. Paul's Cathedral in Calcutta.

Mir Mannu (the Mughal governor of Punjab) found that most of his domains were in the hands of the Sikhs. Adina Beg Khan's territory was also affected by Sikh incursions. In March 1753, he fell upon Sikh pilgrims at Anandpur. When the Sikhs retaliated by plundering the villages in the Jullunder and Bari Doabs, Adina came to terms and assigned to them some of his revenue and took many Ramgarhias, including Jassa Singh, into his employ.

Mir Mannu now marched to Amritsar and blew up Ram Rauni, killing the entire garrison of nine hundred Sikhs, mostly Ramgarhias. Reprisals went on till Mir Mannu's death in November 1753, when the administration in the Punjab collapsed. The Dal Khalsa Sikh leaders offered the people *rakhi* (protection) which was readily accepted and the Sikh military command retained its headquarters at Amritsar, the Ramgarhias protecting the land between Amritsar and the Himalayas. They levied tribute on Kangra, Nurpur, Chamba, Basohli and Mandi.

After Jassa Singh's death they became practically leaderless and were soon overpowered by Ranjit Singh. When he died in 1839, much of India, with the exception of the Punjab was under British domination.

The Sikh soldiers did not share all the grievances of Hindustani sepoys which gave rise to the 1857 struggle and with a few exceptions, the Sikhs expressed unreserved support for the British for which they were duly rewarded. They received from the British a tract of land (known as *nili bar*), irrigated by the 683-kilometre long Chenab canal. But there were no artisans among these Sikhs.

In the latter half of the nineteenth century, the artisans in Punjab ranked just above the untouchables but below the Jats and Rajput zamindars. They performed menial duties for the landowners. With the turn of the century the Sikh artisans of *tarkhan* (carpenter) and *lohar* (blacksmith) origin began to add Ramgarhia at the end of their names. In the 1921 census, a new caste, 'Ramgarhia' was added.

By the 1930s the term had come into general use because of the growing involvement of Ramgarhias with work in Eastern India, East Africa and other parts of the world and their entry into roles of relatively higher status as contractors and industrial entrepreneurs in the Punjab. When the Punjab Land Alienation Act was passed in 1900, the Tarkhans and Lohars, among others, were debarred from buying agricultural land. With time, they started to initiate against this injustice through preachers, literature, congregations and educational institutions, etc.

The first All India Ramgarhia Conference was held in Phillaur which led to the formation of the Ramgarhia Central Federation. The main objective was to get the Land Alienation Act of 1900 amended in which the Central Federation was ultimately successful. In later conferences various social issues were tackled.

Rules were framed by the Ramgarhia conferences to make marriage less expensive, the barriers of endogamy being removed. Efforts were also made to establish schools, technical institutes and a postgraduate college.

The largest concentration of Ramgarhias is in Ludhiana which also houses the central secretariat of the Ramgarhia Central Federation.

Through gurdwara elections held in Delhi, Ramgarhias have also entered the field of gurdwara management. On the political side, one of them became chief minister of Punjab in 1972. Others have been cabinet ministers in Uttar Pradesh and West Bengal (the first Sikh ministers outside Punjab). They are also represented in Parliament and the Punjab Legislature.

Ramgarhias made a considerable contribution to India's struggle for freedom. Munsha Singh 'Dukhi' was an active member of the Ghadr Party. On his return from the USA, he was arrested and imprisoned for life, and all his properties were confiscated. Karan Singh Soi and Madan Singh Gagga suffered the same fate. Nand Singh Bharaj was one of the six Babbar Akali leaders and was hanged in Lahore central jail. Amar Singh took part in the Kisan Movement of 1907. In 1912, he threw a bomb on Lord Hardinge's retinue and managed to escape to South Africa.

Sardul Singh Kaveeshar is perhaps the best known Ramgarhia freedom fighter. A member of the All-India Congress Working Committee, he co-ordinated the Civil Disobedience Movement started by Mahatma Gandhi. A close friend of Subhas Chandra Bose, he was instrumental in helping him to escape to Afghanistan.

The Ramgarhias have not lagged behind in other fields. Major General Sahib Singh Sokhey, a renowned scientist, was director of the Haffkine Institute, Bombay, and regional director of the World Health Organisation. Paramjit Singh Sehra was the first Indian scientist to reach the South Pole in 1971 for research in the upper atmosphere. Other Ramgarhia scientists are doing atomic and space research in different centres in India. Gurbachan Singh Marwaha, a mining engineer, is the director of the Indian School of Mines, Dhanbad. Inderjit Kaur Sandhu, Vice-Chancellor, Punjabi University, Patiala, was the first Ramgarhia woman to hold such a position.

10

ISLAM

HE FOLLOWERS OF ISLAM, THE MUSLIMS, form the largest religious minority in India of 101.6 million (1991 census) or more than 12 per cent of the total population.

The word 'Islam' is Arabic and has two meanings: 'compliance' implying submission to the will of God and 'resignation' which implies performance of special duties leaving the results to God.

Muhammad, the founder of Islam, was born in 570 and was the posthumous child of Abdulla, of the noble family of Quraish of Mecca, where he grew up. His mother died when he was hardly six years old and when his grandfather died after two years, he came under the care of his uncle, Abu Talib, who took him to Syria with trading caravans. He was honest and forthright in his dealings and a signatory to a pact promising help to the victims of oppression and persecution.

His employer, Khadija, a wealthy Meccan tradeswoman, found him so trustworthy that she let him manage her business and though fifteen years his senior, married him when he was twenty-five.

Disgusted with the degenerate life lived by the people around him, and the superstitions and debased beliefs and practices they indulged in, he sought seclusion in a cave on Mount Hira (about 3 miles from Mecca) where he spent months in meditation and in reflecting on the abominable conditions which prevailed amongst his countrymen. One day he felt that an angel (Gabriel) was standing before him who made him recite certain verses which, according to the Muslims, were the first revealed verses of the *Quran*, their holy book.

He came out and recited the verses of the message before the Meccans: that there was only one God and that the worship of idols was not necessary. They were extremely annoyed but were amazed that an unlettered person could produce such splendid and inimitable poetry. But they opposed him, and even resorted to physical torture in order to dissuade him and his handful of followers from following the new path. They ostracised him and his family and demanded that he be handed over to them for being put to death.

Muhammad bore this persecution patiently for twelve years and then left for Medina on 20 June 622, the year which marks the beginning of the Hijra, the Muslim era. In Medina he was acknowledged the leader of the new community of Muslims and it was here that the social and personal laws of Islam were promulgated, community life was organised, total prohibition enforced on drinking and the practice of usury administration was set in order and a militia raised.

Then one day, the small and ill-equipped army of Muhammad clashed with the mighty force collected by the Meccan chiefs and defeated it. Finally the victorious army of Islam marched into Mecca. The Ka'aba was purged of all traces of idolatry and was dedicated to the worship of Allah. Certain traditional practices like circumambulation in a counterclockwise direction and kissing the meteorite set there by Ismail, were retained.

In 632, with an enormous throng of his followers, Muhammad went on *haj* to Mecca. It was during this pilgrimage that he delivered his last sermon, the fragments of which are preserved in the *Hadith*. The purport of the sermon was that the Creator was One; no Arab had a preference over a non-Arab; Muslims were like brothers to each other; a slave had to be treated as oneself; women had the right of divorce and to inherit and own property; men had their rights over their women and their women had rights over them.

The first Muslims arrived on the coast of India in the eighth century and settled down as traders and proselytisers. Punjab was conquered by the Turks in the eleventh century. The Ghaznavi and

Ghuri governors imported into their territories the etiquette of the courts of Ghazni and Herat which had been influenced by the manners of Abbasid Baghdad and of pre-Islamic imperial Iran. The majority of Indian Muslims of today are descendants of the early Hindu, Jain and Buddhist converts.

When the Turks established the first sultanate in Delhi in the thirteenth century, the Persianised Tartar influence became predominant. Babur, who founded the Mughal Empire in India in 1526 was from Central Asia. The Mughal kings were patrons of learning, art and architecture. During their times many architects, craftsmen and painters came to India from Iran and worked with their Hindu counterparts and evolved the Indo-Mughal style of architecture, etc.

The style, manners, and etiquette of the Mughal court were followed by the provincial governors and later by the independent rulers. Rajput princes as well as the Maratha Peshwas adopted Mughal dress and many Mughal-Persian traditions in their courts.

The Mughals had a passion for gardens, flowing water, fountains, canals, pavilions, etc. Their flowers and trees had their own symbolism and poetic allusions which were also depicted in the layout of their gardens in Delhi, Srinagar (Kashmir) and elsewhere, in carpet designs, textiles, buildings, courtyards, mosaic and decorative motifs and formed part of the imagery of classical Persian poetry. Many of these designs and motifs survive in Indian handicrafts.

The Muslims brought about various changes in dress in many parts of India many of which were adopted by large numbers and thus became integrated with the Indian life-style. The style of liveries worn by the Mughal servants was retained by the British for peons and bearers and is still seen in the garb of some grades of servants.

To cover the head is a religious injunction for a Muslim and is a mark of respect for others. A large variety of caps and turbans were thus introduced into India. The Tartar *kulah* was four-cornered and continued to be worn by the gentry of old Delhi till recent times. The nineteenth century Lucknow of the nawabs became a centre of high fashion and they created many varieties of caps, including embroidered caps of muslin called *dopallis*.

The *gharara* or full, shirt-like *pyjama* (created by King Nasiruddin Hyder of Avadh in the early nineteenth century) and a long shirt with a *dupatta* was worn by most well-to-do women. Later the *salwar* was also adopted by them and the *sari* is now commonly worn. The aristocrats mostly followed Mughal fashions. The women wore *pyjamas* of dark colours with a muslin *kurta* and a *duppata* of a pastel shade. The muslin *dupattas* were often decorated with *kamdani* and gold or silver borders and crinkled.

Islam has no order of clergy or priests. A Muslim offers his prayer five times a day alone or in congregation with others when an *imam, mullah* or *maulvi* (a theologian who looks after the mosque as well as the religious affairs of the community) leads the prayer.

The cultural contribution of the Muslims has been great. Since the time of Amir Khusrau (fourteenth century) the Muslims have produced some of the most outstanding exponents of Hindustani classical music.

There is also a class of musicians which has become a 'caste' called *meerasi* (Arabic *meeras,* inheritance) which continues a tradition of music. The beautiful chikan embroidery done in muslin (a speciality of Lucknow) and certain other handicrafts are produced by Muslim craftsmen who have preserved the traditions of these exquisite crafts from Mughal times.

The Prophet Mohammad enjoined the Muslims to eat together as well as to share their food with strangers in order to foster the sense of brotherhood and equality, a teaching that has also influenced the Muslims' food habits and their traditions of hospitality.

Before the introduction of dining-tables and chairs, food was served on a cloth (*dastarkhwan*) spread on the floor or a *takht* (a low wooden table). Religious feasts and wedding dinners, etc., are also still served in this way.

Muslims, who are meat eaters, have always been fond of good food. The variety of dishes runs into thousands, most being of middle eastern origin. The Muslim cooks of Delhi, Hyderabad, Lucknow, Kashmir, Patna and other places have been famous for their culinary art. The eating of pork is forbidden to them.

The basic religious rites of Mulims are simple, do not involve priest-craft and mainly consist of recitations from the *Quran.*

When a child is born, the Islamic credo, the call to prayer, is intoned in its ear. The ceremony is called the *aqiqa* and is performed on the seventh day. The barber shaves the infant's head and the equivalent of its weight in silver is to be distributed to the poor. A he-goat is sacrificed. Circumcision, a few days after birth, during infancy or early childhood, is obligatory for every Muslim male.

Marriage (*nikah*) is not a sacrament but a civil contract that is signed in the presence of the *qazi* (registrar of marriages) and two adult witnesses. In India, from the fourteenth century onwards, this simple procedure has been accompanied by many colourful customs, mostly of Hindu origin. Mulsims in India have also adopted the dowry system. Under Hindu influence, widow marriage, allowed by Islam, was sometimes frowned upon till the end of the last century when various social reform movements were launched.

On the whole, however the main Islamic tenets and traditions are maintained. The proposal is always made from the boy's side. No horoscopes are matched.

In a traditional North Indian Muslim wedding, as the *barat* arrives at the bride's house, her women relatives tap the *samdhins* (the women of the bridegroom's party) with floral sticks. After the *nikah* is solemnised in the presence of the men guests, rose-water is sprinkled and *choharas* (dried dates) scattered among the guests.

At the bridegroom's house, his sisters stop him at the door and demand the *neg* (gift of money). When the bride is taken inside, the bridegroom washes her feet with milk and water and *seharas* or poems of felicitation are recited.

The next day the bride's younger brothers take her home. In the evening the two families play *chauthi*, a mock battle, in which the two 'factions' pelt each other with vegetables and fruit.

A dying person recites the credo, "I testify that there is no god but God and that Mohammad is His Prophet." Yasin, a *surah* of the *Quran*, is recited and the face of the deceased is turned towards the Ka'aba. The body is washed with warm water in the prescribed manner. Once the 'traveller' is shrouded, the corpse becomes sacred. A brief prayer is said by the grave. Permission is asked formally of the next-of-kin to lower the corpse into the grave. After the burial the mourners throw a handful of dust on the grave.

Soyam is held on the third day. The *Quran* has thirty parts called *paras* and one *para* each is distributed to the mourners and visitors gathered at the deceased's house which are read at home and in the mosque. New cloth, a prayer rug, etc., are given to the poor and food is sent to an orphanage. The same simple rites are performed on the fortieth day.

The *Quran* is recited at the grave for forty days. The departed ones are always referred to as 'the blessed'.

Festivals and Calendar

The lunar *Hijra* calendar is followed by the Muslims for all religious matters, weddings and celebrations. The Muslim new year starts as a period of mourning with the month of *Moharram*. On *Ashra,* the tenth of the month, the Prophet's grandson, Hussain, some of his family and followers were killed at Karbala, Iraq, by the army of Caliph. The martyrs are commemorated with mourning and beating of breasts by the Shias and, with more restraint, by the Sunnis. *Tazias* (models of the martyrs' tombs at Karbala) are taken out and elegies recited.

The Moharram rituals were introduced from Iran by the Qutub Shahi sultans of Golconda. The Moharram celebrations of Lucknow, Hyderabad and some former princely states have been famous. Many Hindus also take part in the event. No marriage takes place during this month.

The next month is *Safar*. In the third, *Rabi-ul-Awwal,* the Prophet's birthday falls on the twelfth day and is duly celebrated. The fourth, fifth and sixth months are *Rabi-us-sani, Jamadi-ul-Awwal,* and *Jamadi-us-sani,* respectively. On the eleventh day of the last mentioned is held the feast of Ghausaul Azam Sheikh Abdul Qadir Jeelani, the great Sufi saint of eleventh century Baghdad, which is celebrated by the Sunnis.

On the sixth day of *Rajab,* the seventh month, the Urs of Moinuddin Chisti, a Muslim saint, is held at his tomb at Ajmer. The thirteenth day is the birthday of Ali, the Prophet's cousin and son-in-law, whose aid is invoked by Shias and Sunnis alike. On the twenty-second day is the feast of the sixth apostolic Imam, Jafar

Sadiq, which is celebrated by both Shias and Sunnis. The night of the twenty-seventh is *Shab-i-Miraj*, when the Prophet is believed to have made his spiritual journey from the mosque of Al-Aqsa, Jerusalem, to the highest heaven. Mosques are illuminated and prayers offered all through the night. Between the fourteenth and fifteenth days of the eighth month of *Shaban,* falls *Shab-i-Barat*, the night of liberation or the night of the angels when the souls of the departed are believed to visit their earthly homes. *Fatiha* for the dead is recited over especially prepared *halwa*. People visit cemeteries and light candles on the graves of their loved ones.

Ramazan, the ninth month, is the holiest of all the months. From dusk to dawn, for thirty days, men and women fast during the hours of daylight as a means of self-purification. When the fast is broken, prayers are offered in illuminated mosques. From midnight *Sehri* is cooked and eaten before sunrise. The night of the twenty-sixth of *Ramazan* commemorates the martyrdom of Ali. Between the twenty-sixth and the twenty-seventh falls *Shab-i-Qadr* or the night of majesty. It is the holiest of all nights of the year, when during certain moment one's prayers are believed to be accepted by God. On the twenty-ninth day of *Ramazan* and when the new moon is sighted in the evening, it heralds the festival of *Id-ul-Fitr.* Men go to the *Idgah* for congregational prayers after which people visit and embrace one another.

The tenth and eleventh months are *Shauwal* and *Zilqada,* the twelfth Zilhajja when all men and women are enjoined to perform the pilgrimage to Mecca if they can do so. On the tenth day, when the *haj* rituals are over, animals are sacrificed by the *haj* pilgrims and by Muslims all over the world, commemorating Abraham's intended sacrifice of his son Ismail in their *Id-ul-Azaha* (or *Baqr-Id*) which is the most important festival of Islam.

Law

The personal law of the Muslims, the *Shariat* (the way) is based on the *Quran,* the practice and the injunctions of the Prophet, *ijma* (consensus) of specially qualified persons and *quiyas* or analogical deductions by eminent jurists. The four main schools of Sunni law were formed in the eighth century by the great doctors of law, the Imams Abu Hanifa, Malik Shafi and Hanbal. Isna Ashari and Fatimid laws are followed by the Shias.

The law of inheritance is aimed at avoiding concentration of wealth. The property (movable and immovable, realty and personal) of a deceased male is divided among his nearest male and female blood relatives (the principal heirs) according to what is irrevocably fixed by the law. Daughters get one-third of the property or one-half of the male share and widows one-eighth.

A woman is absolute mistress of her property. Both husband and wife are heirs to the spouse's estate. After the principal heirs, the residue goes to male and female relatives of various degrees, ascendants as well as descendants. Under Shia law, persons related through the women are on par with persons in the male line. Women, however remote, inherit on the analogy of the daughter and sister.

In the *mehr* marriages (or dower) fixed by mutual agreement, it is not a bride price but a bridal gift which the husband must give the wife. In case the husband has not paid the *mehr* during his lifetime, the widow is entitled to get it from his estate and she can retain the possession of the estate till the *mehr* is paid to her. The widow as well as the divorcee can marry after a period of *iddat* which lasts a few months. Marriages between the different Muslim sects are valid and common and the wife is not compelled to join the husband's sect.

A woman is entitled to lay down various conditions at the time of marriage and even to get them enforced later through a court of law. The wife is entitled to maintenance even if she can support herself and can also claim separate maintenance if the husband marries again. Legally, the individuality of the wife is not merged in that of her husband. She owns property and is expected to pay the annual, compulsory poor tax called *zakat*.

The *Quran* restricted the number of wives at any one time to four under special circumstances and strict conditions. In the past the sanction was often exploited mostly by the well-to-do.

Every Muslim is enjoined to observe five duties: *kalima*, confession of faith; *namaz*, the recitation of the daily prayers; *asum* (roza), observance of fast in the month of Ramzan; *zakat,* giving a poor tax; and *haj,* undertaking the pilgrimage to Mecca.

Muslim Sects and Communities

The Shia, Sunni, Wahabi, etc. are not castes but sects which follow different schools of law and theology. There are seventy-two Muslim sects in all that are not strictly hereditary and there is no hierarchy among them.

The members can change over from one set of beliefs to another. For instance a Sunni can become a Shia and *vice versa* and intermarriages among them are not uncommon. However, over the centuries, many sects have become hereditary. There are also regional groups that follow one or the other of the various sects.

Sheikh, Saiyyad (Arabic), Beg, Khan (Turki-Tartar) and Malik were originally respectful honorifics in Arabic, Turki and Persian. Later they came to denote the racial groups of the countries concerned. Only the descendants of Mohammad came to be called Saiyyads.

Most Saiyyad families keep well-documented genealogies. They have caste names like Zaidi, Jafri, Kazmi, Rizvi and Naqvi which denotes that their ancestors were *imams,* Zaid Jafer, Sadiq, Musa Kasmi, Reza and Naqi, etc., the successive descendants of Ali and Fatima (the Prophet's daughter). The Saiyyads are both Sunnis and Shias.

Mirza and Beg were Mughal titles, and Khans were Pathans or Afghans. Some Muslims in India retain their original Rajput names. Muslims continue to call themselves Rao and Rana.

All neo-Muslims in India are called Sheikhs. Most of the 'lower caste' artisans who were converted *en masse* were given Arab clan names like Quraishi, in adherence to the words of the Prophet: "whoever becomes a Muslim belongs to my clan Al-Quraish". After their conversion, north Indian weavers came to be called Ansaris and Momins, groups which have tended to follow their ancestral occupations and have married within their own clans although there has never been any restrictions on their eating with or marrying other Muslims. In the mosques all Muslims, high or low, stand side by side to offer their daily prayers. Often the poorest becomes the *imam* and leads the prayer.

There are two major sects of Islam, the Shia and the Sunni. A brief account of these and a few other major ones is given below.

The Shia Sect

The Shias form 20 per cent of the country's Muslim population. In the second half of the seventh century, when Muawia contended against the fourth caliph, Ali, Muslims became divided into two sects, the Shias of Muawia and the Shias of Ali. The former ceased to count by 745 but the latter continued. The word 'shi'ah' generally meaning group or sect, occurs about ten times in the *Quran*.

The Shias render exclusive devotion to the Hashimite section of the Prophet Mohammad's survivors. Fatima was his only surviving child; Ali, her husband, was his first cousin; and Hasan and Hussain, his two well-loved grandsons. They regard these four (and the twelve *imams* that followed) as infallible and the only group worthy of love and reverence after the Prophet. All other associates of the Prophet they ignore to an extent that arouses resentment in the Sunni majority.

The Shias refuse to acknowledge the senior-most companions of Mohammed, Abu Bakr, Omar and Osman, as Imams and hold that only Ali, who belonged to Mohammad's family, should have been made the caliph immediately after the Prophet and that he was the ordained spiritual successor. They regard their dissociation from the three earlier successors as a part of their creed. They also regard public eulogy by Sunnis of these first three caliphs as sacrilegious.

Shias reject the Sunni belief that the divine being will be seen by the pious on the day of judgement. They hold that Ali had compiled the *Quran* in chronological order which enables the Muslims to set the development of Islam in its evolutionary aspect. According to them in the present version, compiled in the caliphate of Osman, several passages have been placed out of order and context. Sunnis believe that the existing arrangement of the *Suras* was ordained by Allah and actually completed by the Prophet himself in his lifetime. Each sect has its own translation and commentaries.

Economically the Shias are today the most vulnerable among the Muslim groups. Communities allied to them such as the Bohras, the Khojas and the Aga Khanis, are all well organised, each having a living and recognised spiritual head and a distinct *jama'at* (community) that can combine and help its members.

Shias have no such religious organisation and believe that the last of the twelve *imams,* their real spiritual guide, is still living and guides them unseen, which leaves them without any visible nucleus except for a *naib imam* or a representative of the absent *imam,* elected by a college of *mujtahids* (theologians) in Iraq or Iran. Generally these persons can serve only as the final authority on questions of Shia jurisprudence and not in other matters.

Throughout Indian history Shia liberalism and Sunni orthodoxy have together kept Muslim culture alive and virile. Noor Jahan, the Shia consort of the Sunni Jahangir, was the ruler after Akbar. Sirhindi, the Sunni revivalist, had to contend against the Shia brothers, Abul Fazl and Abul Faizi. The Shia kingdoms of the Deccan have left a legacy of Hindu-Muslim accord. Hyder Ali and Tipu Sultan, who are still remembered with affection in South India, are regarded by many as having been Shias.

Three great Urdu poets, Mir Taqi Mir, Anis and Ghalib, have been Shias.

The nawabs of Rampur were Shias. For generations the Sunni nizams of Hyderabad had Shia prime ministers and no less than three generations of Salar Jungs were Shias.

The Shias are found all over India but mostly in Avadh, Rampur and Muzaffarnagar in Uttar Pradesh and Hyderabad in Andhra Pradesh.

The Sunni Sect

After Mohammad (570-632), the founder of Islam, had spread his message of the one God in Mecca and Medina in his lifetime. Islam was also preached to the scattered tribes of Western and North-western Arabia after his death.

The Sunnis were the orthodox Muslims and came into existence as a sect before the Shia sect in a more northerly part of Arabia. They accept the *Sunnah* (Arabic *sunna,* tradition) or corpus of Muslim law and doctrine based on tradition and not on the direct statements of the *Quran*. Most of them call themselves "*ahi-i-Sunnah w'al Jama'at*" that is, believers in the example, acts and sayings of the Prophet Mohammad and the integrity of the community. Those who do not accept this stand are regarded as heretics. They also believe that the *Suras* were ordained by God and completed by Mohammad and do not agree with the Shias that there was a logical and chronological order of the *Suras*.

They acknowledge the first four caliphs, Abu Bakr, Osman, Omar and Ali.

The majority of Indian Muslims have been Sunnis and differences between them and the Shias are on adherence to the Sunni Hanafi code of jurisprudence, the rejection of the *taqlid,* emphasis on the *Sunnah* and the *Quran* as the real source of guidance, the contention that all Mohammad's companions are worthy of honour and that there was nothing wrong in the election of his *Khalifas* and in giving pre-eminence to Ali without minimising the place and status of the other three *Khalifas.* These differences led to conflicts between the two sects which have gone on for centuries.

Sunnis have many *silsilahas* or orders of spiritual successors (something like brotherhoods or fraternities) which have come down from generation with recognised *murshids,* each having a group of *murids* who form the centre of truly religious life they attribute miraculous powers to their *pirs* and saints who are supposed to help them in worldly matters and alleviate their sufferings.

The Sunnis in India constitute the conservative group, most of whom hold that the Hanafi code is the correct and final expression of the Shari'ah (Muslim religious law) and that innovation and heresy are to be condemned.

There is no restriction of trade, employment or social intercourse among the Sunnis and marriage between them and the Shias is not uncommon.

The Ahmadiyya Sect

Ahmadiyyas are the proselytising Muslims of whom there are ten million spread all over the world today. The founder of the sect, Mirza Ghulam Ahmad of Qadian claimed that Jesus Christ did not ascend to heaven and will not come back to earth as believed by the

Muslims but that he himself was the promised messiah who had come to carry forward Mohammad's mission in the world. Orthodox *mullahs* called Ahmadiyyas heretics.

Mirza Ghulam Ahmad (1835-1915) founded the movement at his birth place at Qadian (district Gurdaspur, Punjab) in 1889. Ahmadiyyat (which is a synonym for Islam — renascent and resurgent) is a dynamic proselytising force and holds that Islam is not the heritage of Muslims alone but of the whole of mankind. Among the Ahmadiyyas are converts from Christianity, Hinduism, Sikhism, Jainism, Judaism, Confucianism and Communism in Asia, Africa, Europe and America. One of the chief achievements of the movement in its early stages was the revival of Muslim missionary activities, which had died out some centuries before.

Mirza Ghulam Ahmed belonged to a family which traced its pedigree to Haji Barlas, an uncle of Taimur. His great-grandfather founded Islampur Qazi, which later came to be called Qazian and then Qadian. His father (Mirza Ghulam Murtaza Sahib) held a *jagir* restored by Maharaja Ranjit Singh. From his boyhood he came to be acknowledged as 'God-intoxicated.'

The first revelation came to him at the age of 40 and it warned him of the imminent death of his father which occurred in 1876. The grieved son was consoled by the revelation : that 'God is sufficient for His servant', an assurance which is inscribed on a ring worn by all Ahmadies. In 1891, he declared himself to be the promised Mahdi and messiah which led to his condemnation and persecution as well as of his disciples by the orthodox *ulema* and *mullahs*. They declared him a *kafir* (disbeliever) although he never actually compared himself to Mohammad nor claimed the least superiority over him. He wrote some eighty books in Urdu, Arabic and Persian in defence of Islam and his claims.

Undeterred by the severe criticism of the *ulema*, he continued his missionary work. The stories of the fulfilment of the prophesies of the promised messiah and many cases of miraculous healing effected through his prayers drew thousands of persons to his village. The number of his followers rose to more than three lakh during his lifetime and Qadian became an international shrine. In 1901 when the opposition to Ahmadiyyat reached frightening proportions, he urged his followers to form a separate community and call themselves Ahmadi Muslims.

After his death, the movement came under a *khilafat* and Hakim Nuruddin (1908-1914) became the first and Mirza Bashiruddin Mahmud Ahmad (1914-1956) the second *khalifa*. The latter launched an extensive missionary programme in 1914 to which the followers dedicated their lives and the movement became powerful in Africa, Europe and Indonesia.

In 1947 the headquarters of the *Jamaat* was shifted to Rabwah. Qadian continued to be the headquarters for the Indian missions. Mirza Wazim Ahmad, a grandson of the founder, has been in charge of the missionary work in India. The secular outlook and preaching of the *Jamaat* have endeared Qadian especially to the people of Punjab.

Though the teachings and doctrines of Ahmaddiyyat — *Kalima, gibla, namaz, zakat, haj, roza* — are all based on the *Quran,* most non-Ahmadis (such as Wahabis, Maududis, etc.) have called the Ahmadis heretics. Here the differences centre on the two great prophets: Mohammad and Jesus.

The Prophet of Islam, Mohammad, is described in the *Quran* as *Rahtannir-nabiyin,* the word *Khatun* meaning both last and seal. The Ahmadis interpret this as not last but seal. *Khatum* denotes the consummation, authenticity and completion of a thing as when a seal is put on a letter, it becomes authentic and complete. Therefore the term means the thrust and the most perfect of prophets and not the last in point of time.

Some Muslim theologians (among whom has been the founder of the Deoband theological school) support this interpretation. The Ahmadis assert that *Khatme nabuwat* precludes not the appearance of a prophet in future but the advent of any law-bearing prophet with an independent mission and that a new prophet of God can serve Islam only if he will not change, add to or detract from the holy *Quran* or from what Mohammad taught, as to them those precepts are eternal and immutable. They also believe that in the present time, God sent Mirza Ghulam Ahmad as a non-law-bearing prophet to regenerate errant man so that the forgetful may be reminded and the erring corrected.

Another basic difference between Ahmadis and non-Ahmadis is that the latter hold that when the Jews tried to lay hold of Jesus Christ to crucify him, God changed the appearance of another man to look like Jesus which deceived the Jews and they crucified this person while God lifted Jesus to heaven where he has lived since then, his physical body remaining immune from the ravages of time. He will come down to earth before the day of reckoning to destroy Dajjal (anti-Christ) and will establish the final supremacy of Islam.

The Christian church teaches that Jesus died on the cross. According to the Ahmadiyyas, when Jesus was brought down from the cross he was still alive, as when his side was pierced with a spear, he bled and a dead body does not bleed. They believe he was rescued and ministered unto by his friends, travelled to the east and died in Kashmir at the age of 120. The Ahmadis maintain that Jesus will not come back in person but in the form of another man with the same power and spirit.

Unlike non-Ahmadis, Ahmadis believe in the continuation of the divine revelation even after Mohammad as God has spoken to man through His prophets from the inception of the universe and will continue to do so till the end of time.

The *Jamaat* is not politically motivated and has not harboured any political ambitions and enjoins strict abstinence on the part of its followers from all political disruptive and subversive activities. The movement inculcates in its followers obedience to the law of the land and loyalty to the government of the country in which they live.

The movement has a positive social development programme for Ahmadiyya communities all over the world. It has established 135 active missions in over forty foreign countries and a chain of educational and medical institutions in many countries, seventy-one educational institutions being in Africa and the Middle East. It publishes nineteen newspapers and a score of periodicals in addition to numerous publications for *tabligh*.

The *Jamaat*, which has a network of over 200 branches in India, is controlled by the Sadr Anjuman Ahmadiyya, Qadian. The activities of its institutions are financed from a central fund, which is raised through regular voluntary subscriptions from the members of the community, every Ahmadi generally subscribing to the extent of one-tenth of his income.

The Dawoodi Bohra Community

A small but close-knit merchant community of Muslims, the Shia Ismaili Tayabji Dawoodi community practises an Islam tinged with Hinduism. In common with other Ismailis like the Khojas, the Bohras believe in an esoteric interpretation of the *Quran* behind the manifest meaning. Since they lost political rule in Egypt in the twelfth century and Yemen in the sixteenth century, they have kept their esoteric faith intact from persecuting Sunni rulers by practising the doctrine of *Taqqiya* which permits them to deny their identity to outsiders when under extreme pressure.

These Muslims like other Shias, recognise the hereditary rights of Ali over the first three elected caliphs; assert the claims of Ismail as the seventh Imani; accept Musta'li as the rightful Fatimid Caliph of Egypt; believe that the Imam Tayyib went into seclusion about 1130, leaving as his vice-regent on earth a *Dai'l-Mutlaq* (supreme summoner) pending the return of the *Imam;* and hold that Dawoodis are those who acknowledge the legal succession of the Dai Dawood ibn Qutb Shah in 1589 as against the rival claimant, Suleiman ibn Hasan, who founded the Sulaimani Bohras.

The Bohras offer prayers three times a day instead of five by combining the afternoon and evening prayers; have no sermon (*khutba*) on Friday; use the astronomical lunar calendar to determine the beginning of each month; and place a special paper (*raqqa*) in the hands of the dead.

It is said that the first Ismaili missionary arrived probably in Gujarat, in 1067, two-and-a-half centuries before the Muslim conquest, and practised *jihad* by persuasion, not by force. The seat of the Dai Tyyabi was shifted from Yemen to India in 1539. Subsequently the sectarian split between the Khojas and Bohras (both Ismailis originally) took place. Probably, it was the Vaisya caste which supplied the bulk of the converts (since the word *vohra* means trader in Gujarati). Some Hindu customs, particularly those associated with marriage, were adopted by them, such as the breaking of a coconut at the wedding reception by the bridegroom.

With good business skills and aptitudes, they took advantage of the new opportunities offered in foreign trade and contracting which appeared in the nineteenth century with the establishment of British rule. They had no inhibitions against overseas travel and had the virtues of thrift, sobriety, the ability to do hard work and a traditional desire to remain self-employed.

From their places of origin in Gujarat (Surat, Cambay, Broach, Ahmedabad, Kapadwanj, etc.) the Dawoodis and Sulaimanis both began to migrate to Bombay early in the nineteenth century. Surtis soon achieved a dominant position in the ship-chandling business. Others followed the Parsis into the lucrative import-export trade and travelled to far ports of the Indian Ocean, the Persian Gulf, East Africa, Sri Lanka, Burma, Thailand, Hong Kong, and Japan. Later migrants to Bombay plied the more traditional Bohra trades in hardware, glass, paints, soap, leather, plumbing, stationery and soda water, callings avoided by caste Hindus for fear of ritual pollution. Often their occupation and business is reflected in the Dawoodi 'walla' suffix of the surname. Estimates of the number of Dawoodis in India and overseas range from three lakhs in each category to a million in all.

Organisation is the important characteristic of Bohras and Khojas compared to other Muslims. Salvation for them is obtainable only through the intercession of a hierarchy which reaches down from Allah to Mohammad to Ali to the *imams* to the Hujjats (all in seclusion with the *imam*) to the Dai'-Mutlaq. Next to the Dai (called Syedna or Mullaji) are the Mazoon (usually his heir apparent), the Mukasir, the Shaikhs and the Mullas. Amils or representatives of the Syedna in various cities are chosen from the ranks of the Shaikhs. They officiate at ceremonies and collect taxes. Loyalty is assured by a *mishaq* or ritual bath which has to be taken by all Bohras at puberty in contravention of which fines and ultimately boycott (*ba'arat*) and excommunication have to be faced. There are positive rewards and psychological benefits for continued membership of the community : advice and consolation, business credit, a system of titles, Anjuman Shiat-e-Ali, social, educational and business organisations, scholarships, student hostels, hospitals, *musafirkhanas* (traveller's rest houses), a co-operative bank, etc., and various forms of patronage, all financially supported by a system of private taxation or tithes, which is somewhat heavier than the usual Muslim *zakat*.

The Bohras of the present day, who live mostly in Maharashtra and Gujarat, were once all Hindu Brahmanas and were converted to Islam about nine hundred years ago. During the time of the eighteenth *dai* in Yemen, two missionaries, Maulai Ahmad and Maulai Abdullah were sent to India and landed at Cambay. It is said Abdullah gained the confidence of the local inhabitants by his miracles.

The tombs of these two missionaries in Cambay and of their first converts, the owner of the well, Kaka Akela and his wife Kama Akeli, are revered and visited by the Bohras of India.

The gravest vulnerability of the community has been its disputes over the legitimacy of succession to the daiship. The *imamat* is hereditary but the lesser offices are not although the same family has supplied all of the *dais* since 1840 when the controversies that arose around the succession of the forty-seventh *dai* plagued the community for a century.

More recently, the dissident progressives, who call themselves the Pragati Mandal, have abandoned this issue and have concentrated their efforts on democratising the organisation and obtaining popular control over its expenditure so that more of the income from endowments, charities and tithes will be spent on the welfare and education of the poorer members.

The Sulaimani Bohra Community

The Sulaimani Bohras belong mainly to Yemen and form only a small minority in India, about 10 percent of the Bohras in India. After the death of the twenty-sixth *dai*, Dawood Bin Adjab Shah, in 1591, most of the Bohras in India accepted Dawood Bin Qutb Shah as their twenty-seventh *dai* (hence the name Dawoodis). The majority of Yemenites supported his rival Sulaiman Bin Hasan and they form the Sulaimani Bohra Community.

The *dais* of the Sulaimanis always came from Yemen. It was only when the forty-fifth *dai* of the Sulaimanis, Ali Bin Mohsin, died in 1936, that an Indian, Gulam Hussain of Bombay, succeeded him. Their present *dai* is again an Arab, residing in Yemen.

He appoints his representatives in places where a large number of Sulaimanis live.

These twin communities of Bohras follow the same religious tenets and practices.

Sulaimani Bohras are an enterprising people and are mainly traders and businessmen. Some have distinguished themselves in several other fields such as law, medicine and education. The most well-known among them belong to the progressive Tyabji family, many of the members of which took to western education very early and also intermarried into other communities — Hindu, Christian and Jew. Among them the most prominent name is that of Badruddin Tyabji, an eminent judge, who became the third president of the Indian National Congress in 1887.

The Ismaili Khoja Community

Indian Khojas are mostly descendants of early converts. Their spiritual head (Prince) Karim Aga Khan, is a descendant of Ali. His *firmans* or directives are obeyed by the entire community.

The Ismailis are followers of *Imam* Ismail, one of the sons of *Imam* Jafar Sadiq, the sixth apostolic *imam*. Pir Sadruddin was a missionary or *dai*, who came to India from Khorasan at the time of Islam Shah, the nineteenth in the ascending line from the present Aga Khan. He first preached in Sind. In Gujarat, the new faith was accepted mostly by the Lohanas.

Khojas, being originally mercantile Hindus of Upper Sind speak Sindhi as well as Cutchee, a cognate dialect, and Gujarati.

The Kashmiri Muslim Community

About two thousand years or more ago, Kashmir was a great centre of Buddhism and some famous Buddhist councils were held there. From then onwards it continued to be one of the principal centres of Sanskrit learning. Arab and Persian influences first affected Kashmir nearly a thousand years ago and later, Persian became the official language.

The influence and teachings of Islam had penetrated the valley long before a Muslim king ascended the throne in the fourteenth century.

Missionaries and adventurers professing Islam came to Kashmir when it was still governed by Hindu kings and queens. The people had been groaning under the misrule of the later Hindu rulers, when trade languished and agriculture was at a standstill. As the shackles of caste had been broken by the teachings of Buddhism, the general mass of the people did not find it difficult to embrace the new egalitarian faith and Islam's social and religious humanism which was projected by a band of Sufi dervishes. By the time the last Hindu king ascended the throne of Kashmir, a fair proportion of the people had already accepted Islam.

The name associated with its earliest propagation in Kashmir is that of Bulbul Shah, who is said to have visited the tract first about 1310. He was a widely travelled Syed from Turkistan who had a long stay at Baghdad and was a disciple of Shah Nizamatullah Farsi of the Suhrawardy school of Sufis. He had an enormous influence on the people among whom he worked and lived.

When Sahadeva, the last Hindu king fled the kingdom following the invasion of Gaddi tribesmen from across the Banihal Pass, his army commander, Ramchandra, defeated the marauding tribesmen but was assassinated by Rinchin, another adventurer from Ladakh who, seizing power, married Ramchandra's daughter, Kota Rani.

Rinchin was Lamist in religion but wanted to strengthen his position by adopting the religion of his new subjects and requested the religious head of the Saivas to let him be submitted to the Hindu fold but he was curtly refused as the caste of his birth was not known.

In the early hours of the morning he heard the call of the muezzins: "There is no other god but God and Mohammad is His Prophet." and saw the devout Bulbul Shah at prayer. He asked to be admitted to his religion which was readily done and it was in this way that Rinchin became the first Muslim king of Kashmir and Islam became the state religion of Kashmir. But this hardly changed its political and cultural conditions, the administration remaining in the hands of the traditional official class (the Brahmanas) and Sanskrit continuing to be the court language for about two centuries after the advent of Muslim rule and the medium of official communication.

Sultan Shahab-ud-din (1345-73) refused to melt the silver and copper idols of a Hindu temple for coinage. He held that as past generations had set up idols to obtain fame and earn merit, to demolish them would be a great crime. But there were religious zealots like Sultan Sikandar, Yaqub Shah Chak and a number of Mughal and Afghan governors, though their persecution of non-Muslims was resented by many local Muslims, who protected their compatriots.

Mughal rule, which brought peace and prosperity to Kashmir, completely crushed the martial qualities of the Kashmiris. The brief Afghan rule from 1753 to 1819 brought suppression and tyranny. The Sikhs, who succeeded were also hard and rough masters so were the Dogras who followed.

The advent of Islam changed the social structure of the people but they retained some of their old customs. Many continue to bear their old surnames — Kaul, Bhatta Mantu, Raina and Pandit, are converts from the Brahmana caste, and Dhar, Magrey, Rathor, Lone and Chak from the Kshatriya. The name Syed indicates descent from the Prophet Mohammad's family and Pirzada descent from sufi saints. Every village has a *mullah* to minister to the religious needs of the people.

Kashmiri Muslims, who are in an overwhelming majority in Kashmir, are physically a fine stock, tall and well built, with complexions varying from olive to very light, almost fair. The women are beautiful lively and intelligent and the people are full of fun and fond of amusement.

Kashmiri Muslims are as noted for their hospitality as for their hard work. Theft in the villages is uncommon and personal crime negligible.

Kashmiri dress consists of a long loose smock worn over a *shalwar*, by both men and women. Women wear a skull-cap surrounded by a fillet of red and a shawl or white *chudder* thrown over the head and shoulders. Men wear turbans as a sign of status and affluence. The ordinary peasant is content with wearing a long pointed skull-cap. The peasant has a unique way of fighting the Himalayan cold. In winter a *kangri,* a little earthen brazier in a casing of wickerwork, in which charcoal cinders of a special type are lit to give constant warmth, is placed against the chest and under the *pheran* (gown).

The staple food of the Kashmiri Muslims is rice with which they eat vegetables, the favourite being the spinach *hak* or *karam*.

Kashmiri dishes are famous for their variety and taste. In spite of living in a cold region, Kashmiri Muslims do not like liquor. They drink large quantities of green tea to which salt is added instead of sugar. The Kashmiri *samovar* is always steaming with boiling tea.

Kashmiris, both Hindu and Muslim, have many points of resemblance in dress, social customs and ceremonies. The sacred shrines of both the communities are situated close together and celebrations and fairs are held at these shrines simultaneously. Hindus and Muslims join each other's important social functions.

Many of the ceremonies connected with the birth of a Muslim child are akin to those followed by the Kashmiri Brahmanas, such as visiting of shrines, requisitioning the aid of saints and *pirs* and the keeping of religious fasts by childless parents in order to be blessed with children.

When a child is born, the *mullah* intones the *azan*, welcoming the new arrival into the world of faith. Then he whispers into the child's left ear the *takbir* (God is Great, God is Great, God is Great) and adds the warning that death is the end of all things. A boy is circumcised at the age of four or five. His feet are dyed with henna and the relatives and friends invited to a feast. For seven days before the ceremony, there is continuous singing and feasting.

For a week before a wedding, festivities are held in the homes of the couple. The day before the marriage, a quantity of henna dye is sent to the bride, who paints her hands and feet with it. On the wedding day, the relatives give the bridegroom presents of money. First he and his party visit some neighbouring shrine and say their prayers and then visit the graves of his ancestors. Then they move in a procession to the bride's house. When they are near the bride's house, they are welcomed with songs sung by the women of the family. The *nikah* (wedding ceremony) follows the usual Muslim order. After the *nikah*, the bride is carried by her brothers or maternal uncles into the palanquin and, followed by a party of singing women, she departs with her husband.

Fairs at Astan Sharifs or the tombs of Sufi saints, that are spread all over the State, are very popular.

Perhaps the best example of the synthesis of the Sufi and Bhakti cults is provided by the emergence of the Islamic *rishis*. The founder of the order, Sheikh Nur-ud-din *alias* Nand Rishi (fifteenth century) is the patron saint of Kashmir and is venerated by both Hindus and Muslims. His teachings were conveyed through the Kashmiri language and have been collected and preserved in two volumes, the *Rishinama* and *Nurnama*.

A large number of Persian and Arabic works were produced by Kashmir Muslims during the medieval period. With the increasing patronage extended to the Persian language and scholarship by the later sultans, Kashmir's poets and writers produced works of beauty, style and depth of thought, the best known of whom were Sarif, Ghani, Faani and Hubbi. Considering the abundance of Persian scholars in this region, it is little wonder that Kashmir was known as *Iran-i-Saghir* (little Iran).

The earliest of the Persian scholars was Mullah Ahmad Kashmiri, a distinguished poet and historian (c. 1420). He was followed by a long line of eminent historians. Hyder Malik (also an architect who rebuilt the famous Jama Masjid of Srinagar which had been destroyed by fire), Chaudura, Mohammad Azam Didamari, Mohammed Aslam, Maulvi Hasan Shah and Mohammed-ud-din Fauq.

Two outstanding Kashmiri poets and scholars of the time of Akbar were Sheikh Yaqub Sarfi and Baba Daud Khaki. The former was also the author of several works on Sufism, Islamic traditions and travel. The greatest name associated with Persian poetry is that of Ghani Kashmiri who won fame in his lifetime within India and Iran.

A notable contribution to the study of comparative religion and philosophy was made by Mullah Muhsin Fanni, the celebrated author of *Dabistan-i-Mazahib*.

The Kashmiri language is indebted to several Kashmiri Muslim writers and poets. Nand Rishi's sayings are the jewels of Kashmiri literature. The lyrics of the great woman poet, Habba Khatoon, written towards the end of the sixteenth century, are beautiful and much loved. During the last century, they were the prolific productions of Mahmood Gami, followed by those of Maqbool Shah Kralawari, Rasool Mir, Abdul Wahab Para and others.

The modern period in Kashmiri poetry was ushered in by Ghulam Ahmad Mahjur, a votary of Hindu-Muslim accord, and Abdul Ahad Azad who longed for a socialistic pattern of society.

Among the new writers in Kashmiri may be mentioned Mohi-ud-din Akhtar, Ghulam Hassan Beg Arif, Mohammad Amin Kamil, Ghulam Nabi Khayal, Ali Mohammad Lone, Rehman Rahi and Abdul Khaliq Tak.

Kashmiri Muslims excelled in producing book illustrations. Numerous Persian manuscripts are copiously illustrated with miniature paintings of exquisite beauty.

Sufism, which predominated during this period, was partial to dance and music, believed to be essential in bringing about a state of spiritual ecstasy. The Kashmiri *hafizas* (danseuses) belonged to a class, of professional dancers who had to undergo a long and exacting training under competent masters. Their style of dance was popular till the beginning of the present century. The *rauf,* a folk dance, is performed at marriages and festivals.

A distinctive form of classical music known as Sufiana Kalam (mystical lyrics) developed with its style borrowed from Persian music and its 54 *magams* (modes) corresponding to the Indian *ragas,* some of which have Indian names (like Bhairavi, Lalit and Kalyan) and others Persian (like Isfahani, Dugah, Rasti and Farsi). Sufiana Kalam is always sung in chorus.

The santoor is the most distinctive musical instrument in use. It has a hundred strings, stretched over a hollow wooden frame of mulberry wood, which are struck with two delicate little sticks, beautifully carved and slightly curved at the end. Some other instruments are the *saz-i-Kashmir, sitar* and *durka.*

The Kashmiri craftsmen, among whom are many Muslims, are fine and artistic and have a great sense of the aesthetic, colour and design. Kashmiri weavers produce beautifully embroidered woollen shawls which have been famous in many countries, particularly those of Europe.

Their other cottage industries are carpet weaving, introduced by Sultan Zain-ul-Abidin, the carpets being beautiful and famous; hand embroidery done on silk saris, table ware, bags, etc.; making of leather goods; making of patterned silver ware; of exquisitely carved objects in wood; making of hand painted articles of papier mache; weaving of silk, fine and ordinary woollen fabrics and the cultivation of saffron.

The Memon Community

The Cutch Memons are one of the most important mercantile communities of the west coast. They number over five thousand many having migrated to Pakistan in 1947. Originally they were Brahmanas and Lohanas of Kutch and Sind having been converted by a Sufi saint, Pir Yusufuddin, in about the year 1400. As they sought asylum with the Baluch chieftains they came to be called Mamoon (Arabic: safe at peace) which, in common usage, became Memon. Groups of them sprang up in Makran, Sindh and Kutch. Due to famine and social unacceptability they began to emigrate to the port towns of West and South India. There was a mass exodus of the Memons to Bombay in about 1600, who became engaged in trade and commerce there.

About the same time some Memons from Jamnagar (old Kathiawar) emigrated to Sind (now in Pakistan) and settled down at Halai. They form the other group called the Hala Memons.

The Memons are a prosperous and advanced community. In Bombay and other places they run their own well-organised and wealthy trusts, hospitals, schools and polytechnics. Apart from industrialists, they have also produced distinguished persons in other fields.

The Moplah Community

The Moplahs are Malayalam-speaking Muslims of Kerala and have the same culture and outlook as the rest of the Malayalis. Muslims form some 15 per cent of the total population of Kerala which is more than 20 million. In the three districts of Cannanore, Kozhikode and Palghat (which form the Malabar region) the Moplah population numbers about two million. They are not a separate ethnic or linguistic entity but have, by their tradition and religion, a certain group individuality of their own. The word 'Moplah' comes from *Mapillai,* supposed to be derived from *Maha*

Pillai the great or respected person, indicating the honoured status in society of the early Muslim settlers.

Mapilla also means son-in-law in Tamil and husband in colloquial Malayalam. The early Muslim immigrants (Arab and others) who married into the local families and settled down in the region, would have been addressed as *'Mapillai'* by the local inhabitants. Even today the word *'Mapilla'* is used for Christians (Nazarene Mapilla) and Jonaka Mapilla for Muslims.

The Malabar coast, noted for its spices and other products from time immemorial, had a regular trade with the Greeks, Romans, Mesopotamians and Arabs long before the advent of Islam. Foreigners, traders and scholars were all welcomed and treated with hospitality in Kerala. Islam first came to India through Malabar. A party of Muslims, under Malik Ibn Dinar, reached Kodungalloor where they were most hospitably welcomed and the first Muslim mosque was established there with Malik Ibn Dinar, as the *Kazi*, which still exists. Intermarriages with the local families were frequent and it was thus that the small band of Muslim settlers grew into the Moplah community of today.

The Moplahs grew in numbers and influence, the main accretions to their community being from the agricultural, labouring and fisher folk classes. The lower castes had an inducement to become Muslims as they were treated as equals by their new co-religionists irrespective of wealth and influence.

Vasco da Gama's landing at Kapat near Calicut in 1498 marked a significant turning point in India's history as apart from objectives of trade, the Portuguese wanted to establish a political hegemony which they set about by playing one chieftain off against another.

The Moplahs and the Arab traders waged a relentless and bitter struggle against the Europeans. The Moplahs manned the navy of the Zamorins of Calicut which, under Kunjali Marakkar I and II, the Mopllah admirals, inflicted many defeats on the Portuguese, sometimes pursuing them far out into the ocean.

During British rule, Malabar became a single administrative unit under a British collector but Travancore and Cochin continued to remain under Indian rulers. The old feudalism on which the system of land tenures and the landlord-tenant relationship rested, became disrupted, the worst sufferers becoming the Moplahs, the majority of whom were cultivators and whom the big land-holding families had looked after as their feudal overlords. But as the landlords (mostly high-caste Hindus) began to enforce their rights without fulfilling their corresponding obligations, relations became strained and a series of agrarian riots broke out, the earliest on record being in 1836.

The last of these uprisings took place in 1921 and is generally known as the Moplah rebellion. When Mahatma Gandhi linked the civil disobedience movement with the *khilafat* agitation, the Moplahs took the opportunity to settle old scores with their landlords. Between July 1921 and February 1922 hardly any administration existed in central Malabar. One of the heroes of the rebellion was Variamkunnath Kunhamed Hajee who proclaimed himself king. The reprisals were total and satanic, about four thousand Moplahs being killed and wounded and thirty-eight thousand captured.

The Moplahs are strict in adherence to their faith but follow the customs and manners of the local people of whom they are a part. A number of Moplah families, especially in north Malbar, conform to the Hindu *marumakkathayam* (matrilineal) system.

The Moplahs have never had a language of their own. They speak Malayalam and are ignorant of Urdu but all Moplah children are taught to learn the *Quran* by rote. Islamic religious and social tenets were also taught in the same manner. This gave rise to a class of priests who specialised in Islamic theology and were called Musaliyars. The Moplahs are Sunni Muslims and mainly follow the Shafe'i school of thought, though there is a Shia shrine at Kondotti (thirty-two kilometres from Calicut) which is looked after by a family of Thangals who migrated from Iran.

The Moplahs did not take kindly to modern education. They developed a form of writing known as Arabi Malayalam in which Malayalam is written in the Arabic script. They also composed songs and ballads which are essentially based on Malayalam, but borrow freely from Arabic, Persian, Urdu and Tamil. This literature is known as *Mapilla Patu*.

Because of religious inhibitions, the only dance form developed by the Moplahs is the vigorous *Kolkali*. Twelve muscular men, with sticks and tiny cymbals attached to them, dance in a circle with the leader in the middle who sings, the players joining in the refrain. Some very intricate steps and a great deal of acrobatics are involved and the training generally takes place in *Kalaris* (local gymnasia). The women also have a sort of dance called *Kaikotti Kali*, which is accompanied with songs and hand clapping and is generally performed at the time of weddings.

The average Moplah is independent, self-respecting and upright. Some of the finest delineation of Moplah character are to be found in the novels *Uroob* by K.C. Kuttikrishnan and *Asura Vittu* by M.T.V. The study of the Moplahs has been done with originality and lyrical beauty by Vaikom Muhammed Basheer in the milieu of his own village in central Travancore. Dalya Kala Sakhi's *Childhood Friend* and Kunhipathumaayude Adu's *Kunhipathumma's Goat* are other Moplah stories and N.P. Mohammed has written some fine stories built around Moplah life and character.

The Moplahs are hardworking and adventurous. The peasantry fishermen and traders are industrious and thrifty. A large number of them plied lucrative trades in Burma (till they were sent away), Singapore, Malaysia, Indonesia, in the Gulf Sheikhdoms and the Arabian mainland.

Many have married and settled down in these countries though they keep up their contacts with India. They are some of the best lumberjacks in the country and are also very good at bridge and pier construction in underwater conditions. There are influential trading people in the higher strata, especially in Calicut and Cannanore, particularly in the timber and timber-based industries. Some are large land owners and planters as well.

The Sufis

The advent of Islam in India led to the rise of various movements which either tried to bring the two major communities — Hindus and Muslims — nearer each other or tried to reform Islam which had deviated considerably from the tenets of *Shariat* due to the conversion of a large number of lower class people in India, who brought with them their own customs and superstititions and continued to practise them. In this connection a number of mystic orders or *silsilas* emerged. Abul Fazl has referred to fourteen such *silsilas* in *Ain-i-Akbari.* But most of them were mystic groups and even sub-branches of the *silsilas.*

The most important of these orders were the Chishti, the Suhrawardi, the Qadiri, the Shattari and the Naqshbandi.

Chishti Order

Khwajah Muinud-din Chishti, a native of Sajistan, introduced the Chishti order in India. He reached Delhi in 1193 and shifted to Ajmer which was a place of considerable political and religious importance. He was highly sympathetic and humane, his approach being a pantheistic one which made a great impact on Hindus and he was able to attract a large number of followers. His important disciples were Shaikh Qutub-ud-din Bakhtiyar Kaki (died 1235) and Shaikh Hamid-ud-din (died 1276). The former popularised the order in Delhi and the latter in Rajasthan. Hamidud-din had completely adapted himself to the life of a farmer and like other villagers of his town, Nagaur, was a strict vegetarian. Kaki refused the post of *Shaikh ul Islam* offered to him by Sultan Iltutmish. He, however, extended all support to the sultan in the execution of works of public utility, such as *madrasas* and *sarais.* His most eminent disciple was Farid-ud-din Masud Ganj-i-Shakar who was able to spread the order to Hansi, Ajodhan and other places. He left a large number of Khalifahs, the most outstanding of whom was Shaikh Nizam-ud-din Auliya. Under him, the *silsila* prospered and spread to various parts of the country. The Shaikh himself stayed in Delhi and worked untiringly to 'create religious and moral consciousness of great intensity' among his followers. He died in 1325. He was able to create a sort of spiritual empire which was kept together by his successor Shaikh Nasir-ud-din for over thirty years. Another disciple of his, Shaikh Siraj-ud-din, took this movement to Bengal where it spread due to the ceaseless efforts of his followers, Shaikh Ala-ud-din and Syed Ashraf Jahangir. The leader of this movement in the Deccan was Burhan-ud-din, while it was popularised in Gujarat and Malwa by Husam-ud-din Multani and Wajih-ud-din Yusuf respectively.

Earlier Chishti centres were at Ajmer, Narrnaul, Suwal, Nagaur and Mandal in Rajasthan, Hansi and Ajodhan in Punjab and some towns of Uttar Pradesh. The missionary zeal of the *Khalifahs* led to

Clockwise from top left: A Muslim wedding or Nikah. A Kashmiri Muslim artisan. Nemaz or congregational prayer at the Jama Masjid, Delhi. Id celebrations.

Clockwise from top left: Toli
Masjid at Hyderabad (1671).
Entrance to the Kalan Masjid in
Delhi with Old Delhi's Turkman
Gate (1387). Jamaat Kaana Mosque
behind the tomb of Nizamuddin
Auliya in Delhi. Jami Masjid in
Fatehpur Sikri near Agra.

Left: Jamshedji Tata
(1839-1904),
Parsi industrialist.
Below: A Parsi wedding

Top left: Adoration of the Magi, a mural at St. Mary's Church in Bombay.
Top right: The Casket at the Church of Bom Jesus in Old Goa, where the
Body of St. Francis Xavier lies miraculously preserved.
Above: The exterior of the Church of Bom Jesus.

the establishment of centres in Bengal, Bihar, Orissa, Gujarat, Malwa and even in far off places in the Deccan.

The popularity and success of the Chishti saints in India, as rightly pointed out by Khaliq Ahmed Nizami in his book *Some Aspects of Religion and Politics in India During the 13th Century,* was due to their understanding of the Indian conditions and the religious attitudes and aspirations of the Indian people. They adopted many Hindu customs and ceremonies in the initial stages of the development of their *silsila* in India.

The Chishtis were liberal in outlook and recognised that there were many paths to God. Their insistence on following *Shariat* was in reality an emphasis on the necessity of conforming to a code of discipline and a system. Love of God and service to mankind were their most important principles. They were believers in pantheistic monism, the earliest exposition of which is to be found in the *Upanishads.* It was, therefore, no wonder that Hindus felt closer to this *silsila* and many of them became its followers. The life of abject poverty in which the saints of this order lived made a great impact on the Hindus whose religion held in high esteem all those who followed the path of renunciation.

Chishtis gave priority to social service over all other forms of devotion. They rendered help to the needy, alleviated the suffering of the distressed, etc. Prayers, fasting, *haj* or pilgrimage to Mecca, etc., were obligatory for every follower. Most of the Chishti saints lived in starvation and refused to accept any grants from the State. They were of the view that possession of any kind of private property is an obstacle to spiritual advancement.

Suhrawardi Order

Suhrawardi's was the only other *silsila* which had a considerable following in medieval India. Shihab-ud-din Suhrawardi (died 1234), a teacher in Baghdad, was the founder of this *silsila* which was introduced in India by his disciple Jalal-ud-din Tabrizi and Baha-ud-din Zakariya (1183-1262). The former took his abode in Bengal where he converted a large number of Hindus and established a *Khanqah.* However, Zakariya was mainly responsible for organising the Suhrawardi *silsila* in India. His *Khanqah* at Multan became one of the important centres of religious learning in India.

Yet another disciple, Jalal-ud-din Surkh Bukhari (died 1291), settled in Ucheh and set up a *Khanqah* there. His grandson and successor Sayyid Jalal-ud-din organised and strengthened this centre. He converted a large number of tribes. He played an important part in the political and religious life of Sind. Shaikh Rukn-ud-din Abul Fath (died 1335), grandson of Shaikh Bahaud-din Zakariya, was the most important Khalifah of this order. He occupies the same high position in the Suhrawardi *silsila* as Shaikh Nizam-ud-din does in the Chishti order. The whole population of Sind held him in high esteem.

Unlike the Chishtis, the saints of this order led a comfortable life. They made ample provisions for their families and even employed teachers on handsome salaries for the education of their sons. Suhrawardis believed that there was no harm 'in possessing and dispensing of wealth, if the heart was detached'.

Suhrawardis actively associated themselves with the government and accepted the posts of *Shaikh-ul-Islam* and *Sadr-i-Wilayat.* They exhorted their followers to be nearer to the kings who 'are the chosen of God, the Almighty. Under no conditions, showing disrespect to them or disobeying their orders is permitted or proper in *Shariat'.* One of the Suhrawardi saints Shaikh Rukn-ud-din Multani was of the view that it was essential for a shaikh to have money, learning or scholarship besides spiritual attainments to satisfy the variety of people who visited him.

Qadiri Silsila

The earliest mystic order in Islam was founded by Shaikh Abdul Qadir Gilani (1077-1166). In fact, he was responsible for the propagation of their beliefs. This *silsila* was introduced in India by Sayyid Muhammad Gilani (died 1517) who migrated to India and settled in Uchch near Multan in 1482. He was succeeded by his son Abdul Qadir (1459-1533). They had enough wealth and enjoyed a great deal of influence at the court. They were able to attract a number of Hindu followers, some of whom were even converted to Islam. The most famous saint of this order was Shaikh Mir Muhammad or Miyan Mir who died in Lahore in 1635. Some of the saints of this order were very orthodox in their outlook, such as Shaikh Daud and Abu Malli. Others, Miyan Mir and Mulla

Shah were quite liberal. This *silsila*, however, did not have much following in India.

Shattari Silsila

The Shattari *silsila* was introduced into India during the Sultanate period, but they did not make much impact. Shah Abdullah (died 1485) brought the Shattari order during the Lodhi period. This order produced a number of saints, the most important of whom was Muhammad Ghauth (1485-1562) of Gwalior. He was a disciple of Haji Hamid Husur. His two well-known works are *Jawahir-i-Khamsah* and *Khalid-i-Makhazin* which deal with Sufi doctrines and practices. His other work *Bahr-al-Hayat* or *Ocean of Life* describes the practices of the Yogis.

He was respectful to all religions and in fact he stood up even when receiving non-Muslims much to the great annoyance of his co-religionists. The famous musician Tan Sen and even Humayun seemed to have been attracted towards it. The Shattari saints tried to bring Hindus and Muslims closer by laying emphasis on the similarity of their spiritual thoughts and practices. Some of them such as Shaikh Qadiri learnt Sanskrit to enable him to delve deep into the scriptures of the Hindu religion. Wajih-al-Din Gujarati (1599) and Shah Pir of Meerut were other prominent saints of this order.

The Shattaris regarded the shaikh or *pir* as being in direct communication with all the saints, prophets and even God. It was not necessary for a Shattari to undergo the rigours of self-discipline. The very fact of his being a member of the order absolved him of this penance. The Sufis of this order led a spiritual life in comfortable worldly surroundings. It did not make much headway and the number of its followers was not very large.

Naqshabandi Order

This *silsila* gained momentum in the last years of Akbar's reign, with the arrival in Delhi of its prominent leader, Khwaja Baqi Billah (1563-1603) from Kabul. Of all the Sufi orders, it was the nearest to orthodoxy and tried to counteract the liberal religious policies of Akbar whom they considered a heretic. The death of Abul Fazl provided Baqi Billah with the desired opportunity and he was able to bring under their influence some powerful nobles such as Akbar's foster brother, Mirza Aziz Koka, Shaikh Farid, the bakshi, Qilich Khan, Governor of Lahore, and even the liberal-minded Abdur Rahim Khan-i-Khanan. The movement reached its climax under the leadership of Shaikh Ahmad Sirhindi (1564-1624), the most distinguished disciple of Baqi Billah. He was equally opposed to Shias and Hindus. In fact, his first pamphlet *Radd-i-Rawfid* was written against the Shia creed. He criticised the pantheistic philosophy of the Sufis and instead propagated his own theory of the 'unity of the phenomena'. He was strongly in favour of following the *Shariat* in practice and spirit. He did not agree with the Chishtis that the saints should keep aloof from the court and the king. He wanted to utilise them for the propagation of Islam.

For him Islam and *Kufr* (or Hinduism in the Indian context) were the antithesis of each other and no reconciliation was possible. His views led to bitter conflict between his followers Khwaja Masum Saif-ud-din and those who believed in the pantheistic doctrine of *Wahadah-al-Wujud* such as Miyan Mir of Lahore, Mulla Shah of Kashmir, Samad of Delhi and even Dara Shikoh who wrote *Majma ul Bahrain* to emphasise 'the basic unity of Muslim and Hindu religious thought'. Sirhindi's doctrines served as a great set-back to the process of Hindu-Muslim reconciliation particularly on a spiritual level. It reasserted the orthodoxy of Islam and not only alienated the Hindus, but also put Sunnis against Shias. And as Aziz Ahmad concludes in his *Studies in Islamic Civilization,* 'he was the pioneer of what modern Islam is today in the Indo-Pakistan subcontinent — isolationist, self-confident, conservative, deeply conscious of the need of a reformation but distrustful of innovations, accepting speculation in theory but dreading it in practice and insular in its contact with other civilisations.'

Organisation of the Khanqah

Nizami has given a good description of the *khanqah* in his *Religion and Politics in India.* A Chishti *khanqah* or *dargah* usually consisted of a long hall which was known as *jamaat khanah*. Its roof was supported by a number of pillars. At the foot of each of these pillars was accommodated a *murid* or a disciple with all his belongings. A senior person was appointed to look after the management of the *khanqah*.

An open kitchen or *langar* was provided. However, enough food was not there in some of the Chishti *khanqahs* and the disciples partook of what was available. All of them helped in the cooking and serving of the food. The rest of the time, the inmates spent either in prayer or in the service of the shaikh who was the central pivot around whom the organisation moved. Besides prayers in congregation and meditation, the shaikh received hundreds of visitors from dervishes to the nobles, scholars, politicians and soldiers who came to him with all sorts of problems — both material and spiritual. They found spiritual solace in him.

The Suhrawardi *khanqah*, however, was based on a different pattern. As the shaikhs of this order freely mixed with the sultan and nobles and even accepted jobs and *jagirs*, they were able to amass huge wealth. There was a regular income from *jagirs* to support the *khanqahs*. Shaikh Baha-ud-din Zakariya was perhaps the richest saint of medieval India. Unlike the Chishtis, the Suhrawardis did not distribute the money, as and when it was received, among the needy. On the other hand, they kept it with great care and used it sparingly. Moreover, the Suhrawardi *khanqahs* were not open to all and sundry. Only selected persons were allowed to seek the blessings of the shaikh.

Contribution to Indian Culture

These Sufi mystics were responsible for the spread of Muslim culture among the masses in the various parts of the country. The Islamic concept of equality and brotherhood of man greatly attracted the lower classes of the Hindus who had no access to temples and were even forbidden to read the scriptures. In the *khanqahs* set up by these mystics, the atmosphere was quite different. There was no discrimination between the high and the low. All worked together and dined and slept together. The mystics laid emphasis on the brotherhood and equality of mankind. Many of the mystics particularly of the Chishti order showed a spirit of toleration towards other religions and creeds. They stressed that there was essential unity between different religions. The great mystic poet Amir Khusrau for example says: "Though Hindu is not faithful like me, he often believes in the same God as I do". Muslim mystics were not particularly interested in the theoretical aspects of Hindu philosophy and thought. They were more concerned with the actual practices and the psychological and emotional content of the Hindu religion.

It alone would help them to make a direct and effective appeal to the Indian masses. The common medium of expression or dialogue was important for communication. It led to the use of Hindi words and the ultimate birth of the Urdu language. The idea of the brotherhood of Islam and equality among its adherent powerfully appealed to the low castes among the Hindus.

The mystics re-emphasised the unity of Godhead and superiority of the path of devotion over rituals and ceremonial pilgrimages and fast. It made a great impression on the minds of the Indian reformers and thinkers who became the pioneers of the Bhakti Movement which tried to harmonise Hinduism and Islam. These mystics raised their voice against all vices such as drinking, gambling, slavery, etc. which did influence the general Indian population and were thus instrumental in 'maintaining the social equilibrium of the medieval society'.

11

CHRISTIANITY

HRISTIANITY IS A RELIGIOUS MOVEMENT LAUNCHED about AD 30 in Palestine, on the western seaboard of Asia, by a Jewish spiritual master called Jesus. He proclaimed that he was the messiah or Christ, the son of God, promised by the prophets and awaited by many as a saviour. During his short-lived public life, he gathered followers from whom an important group of disciples emerged under the name of 'apostles' who were the active messengers entrusted by Jesus, their Master, to carry out his instructions. The little band of apostles, disciples and such other adherents soon became organised into a dynamic community which from its beginning was known as the church and quite early received the name 'Christians'. In the course of time Christianity spread far and wide.

The Christians believe that Christ was an incarnation of God, conceived by the holy spirit of God and born of the virgin Mary, who was espoused to Joseph, a carpenter. Jesus was born in Bethlehem when Herod was king and grew up to become a carpenter. When he was twelve, his parents took him for the feast of the Passover to the temple in Jerusalem. Here he sat down with the doctors and learned men, asked them questions and debated with them. They were all astonished at the child's understanding of issues that had puzzled them so long. After this incident nothing is known about his life for nearly eighteen years.

At the age of thirty he was baptised by John the Baptist in the Jordan river. From then on he began preaching the word of God, exhorting people not to sin, to help and succour one another, to be morally upright and forgiving and to desire the things of the spirit and not worldly power and wealth.

At all times he prayed and declared the glory of God. He spoke in parables on many occasions and performed many miracles bringing the dead back to life, healing the sick and lepers and casting out evil spirits. Jesus lived among the ordinary people, leading a life that was simple and exemplary. Some of his sayings like his Sermon on the Mount, form the bedrock of his teachings. Multitudes began to follow him and believe in his word. He aroused the antagonism of the ruling powers of Rome and of the Jews with his proclamation that he was the son of God and had come to save sinners and to establish the kingdom of God on earth of which he was the head. He was crucified at the age of thirty-three.

According to his own teaching, the Christians believe that he did not die on the cross but rose again on the third day after his burial to be received back into heaven.

From this originate the Christian concepts of resurrection and life eternal after death and also the belief that Christ will come again and his kingdom will have no end. The commandment he left for people to follow was to love God with all one's heart, soul, mind and strength and to love one's neighbour as oneself.

India's connection with Christianity is one of the oldest in the world. According to traditional accounts in *The Acts of Judas Thomas* in the *Apocrypha,* St. Thomas, one of Jesus's twelve disciple, came to India about AD 46.

With the merchant Abbanes, St. Thomas came to the court of King Gondopharnes of Takshasila, and was said to be one of the three wise men who went to pay homage to the Christ child at his birth.

It is assumed that St. Thomas left India but he is believed to have returned to India, landing at Muziris (Cranganore) about AD 52. and founded seven churches along the western coast. The altar of the Roman Catholic church of St. Thomas at Parur, near Cochin, depicts the death of the apostle who, it is believed, founded the church. He is said to have gone to the east coast where he carried out his missionary work but was assassinated by a

Brahmana lance. The site of his martyrdom is said to be at My-lapore in Madras.

One of the earliest references to Christianity in India mentions the visit of Alexandria's leading theologian, Pantaenus, to the Indian Christians at their invitation in AD 180. An Alexandrian merchant, Cosmos (the 'Indian voyager'), writes in 522, "Even in Taprobane (Ceylon) is a church of the Christians and such is also the case in Male (Malabar) ... and in Kalliana (Quilon or Kalyan)."

It is from these early 'St Thomas Christians' that the Syrian Christian community in India traces its descent. The name 'Syrian' evolved mainly because the liturgy and scriptures used had been in Aramaic or Syriac and also because of the influx of Syrians about 330 seeking refuge from religious persecution in Persia.

The St. Thomas Christians belong to the Eastern Church which includes all those Christians and their later derivatives who were originally found in the lands of West Asia and North East Africa, east of the Mediterranean. Today, the St. Thomas Christians are divided among themselves. The majority is united with the Roman Catholic Church but keep their autonomy and originality. The rest are either Orthodox or Mar-Thomites or are simply called Christians of the East.

By the sixteenth century, the Indian Christian had become a person of consequence commanding the respect and esteem of his Hindu neighbours. "They are second in rank only to Brahmanas", writes a Portuguese of the period.

As Akbar, the Mughal emperor, wanted to become acquainted with the 'new' religion, he invited some Jesuit fathers to his court and gave them permission to baptise all who wished to become Christian and the very first church (at Lahore) was built with his sanction.

The close of the sixteenth century saw a struggle between the Portuguese power as represented by the Roman Catholic Church and the Syrian Christian Church which ended in the vast majority of Indian Christians becoming Roman Catholics in response to the pressure exerted on them by the forceful Archbishop Aleixo De Menezes.

From the eighteenth century onwards, Christians clergymen of the Protestant denomination from the eastern provinces of Germany came to India. They worked first in the coastal belt of Tamil Nadu, south of Pondicherry and after some years moved into the interior, including Tanjavur, Tiruchirapalli and Madras. They not only founded congregations of devout followers of Christ but were the first to begin translating the Bible into the Indian languages, starting with Tamil.

When, early in the twentieth century, with individual baptisms of educated Indians, mass conversions of the depressed classes and untouchables took place, the work of the missionaries and the evangelists was looked on with utmost suspicion by the non-Christian communities in India. What appealed to 'outcaste' persons was the self-respect they could command as 'casteless' Christians which would free them from the disabilities and degradations they had suffered for centuries.

As the European missionary considered his way of life the most progressive, he often tried to superimpose Western civilisation on the newly-converted Indians which sometimes had the effect of alienating them from their natural cultural moorings. On the other hand for some of the northeastern tribals, who seek to preserve their distinctiveness, Christianity became synonymous with modernisation. Therefore, for the young tribal, conversion to it became a natural process.

Today, however, steady Indianisation is going on in many aspects of Christian life. Church architecture no longer follows the old Western pattern. Hymns and *bhajans* set to Indian tunes are often sung in churches. Many of today's missionaries are knowledgeable or even specialists in the fields of agriculture, technology, medicine and education.

There are several Christian organisations working in India today: Mother Teresa's home for the dying destitute in Calcutta and Lucknow; the Christian Agency for Social Action (CASA) which was begun after the holocaust of 1947 to help suffering refugees; Catholic Charities (CARITAS), the Indian head office which was established in 1962; the Young Men's Christian Association (YMCA); the Young Women's Christian Association (YWCA), the National Christian Council and other church and philanthropic Indian and world organisations, all of which have worked for many years for the underprivileged.

Nearly half the number of Indian Christians in India (19.6 million according to 1991 census) belong to Tamil Nadu and Kerala. Owing to a constant migration of South Indians to some of the most industrialised regions in the North many Christians from the South have also come to the North in quest of work. They are spread in Bengal, Bihar, Uttar Pradesh, Delhi area, and Madhya Pradesh, with particularly high numbers in the regions of Jamshedpur, Calcutta, Secunderabad and the industrial belt of Bombay-Pune. Large communities of Christians are also to be found in the hill districts of Assam and adjacent states, the Ahmednagar and Nasik Districts of Maharashtra, Punjab and parts of Gujarat. The cities of Bombay and Calcutta have many churches and various Christian institutions.

India has the three main branches of Christianity, the Catholic, the Orthodox and the Protestant.

With respect to the long years of struggle for national independence, many personalities among Christians were involved, either directly or indirectly (not excluding the role played in final liberation of Goa). To mention but a few they were: C.F. Andrews (d. 1940), the personal friend and ardent supporter of Mahatma Gandhi, Upadhyaya, Brahmabandhav (d. 1907), a prominent nationalist, educationist and thinker; M. Madhusudan Dutt (d. 1934), one of the people's leaders in Orissa; K.T. Paul (d. 1931) who instilled nationalist ideas into the YMCA; Amrit Kaur (d. 1969), daughter of (Raja) Harnam Singh of Kapurthala, who was one of the earliest women to be a minister in the central cabinet; Susil Rudra (d. 1925) a friend of C.F. Andrews and the first Indian principal of St. Stephen's College, Delhi; Roche Victoria (d. 1962), a modern Christian leader in Tamil Nadu; Father Jerome D'Souza (d. 1977) a Jesuit priest, one of the most articulate Christian representatives at the Constituent Assembly; M. Ruthnaswamy (d. 1977) former M.P. and great political thinker and writer.

Centres of Pilgrimage

Whereas Protestant Christians, with the exception of the Anglicans, do not go on pilgrimages, Catholics and the Orthodox visit places of pilgrimage, particularly on the occasion of some important festivals. Among the all-India centres of Christian pilgrimage are St. Thomas' Cathedral at Mylapore, Madras, where the grave of St. Thomas, the apostle, is venerated; St. Xavier's shrine at the Bom Jesus' Church (in old Goa); the church of Our Lady of the Mount at Bandra, Bombay; and the church of Our Lady of Health at Velankanni (on the east coast of Tanjavur) as well as many places of pilgrimage of a more local or regional character such as the church of Our Lady at Sardhana near Meerut (in western Uttar Pradesh), the church of Our Lady of the Rosary at Bandel (north of Calcutta), St. Thomas Mount at Malayattoor, Kerala; the shrine of St. Xavier at Kottar (just north of Kanya Kumari); the shrine of St. Theresa of Avila at Mahe (close to Tellicherry in north Kerala); the shrine of St. John de Britto at Oriyur in Ramnad district (Tamil Nadu). Christians come to venerate the relics of and pray to St. John de Britto who was martyred there in 1693. In the Orthodox church of Manarkad located a few kilometres east of Kottayam in central Kerala, the feast of the birthday of Mary, the mother of Jesus, is celebrated on 8 September each year by the St. Thomas Christians. Owing to their greater Christian population places like Goa, Kerala and Tamil Nadu and cities like Madras, Bombay and Calcutta, have many places of pilgrimage.

The Roman Catholic Denomination

Jesus Christ had told Peter, the leader among the apostles, that he was the "rock" on which He would build His Church, and he thus became the first Bishop of Rome. In course of time the Roman Church came to occupy a special place among the other churches in Europe which began to consult it regarding important decisions.

In the Roman Catholic priestly hierarchy, the pope (who is the bishop of Rome) as God's representative on earth, is the supreme authority in matters of faith and morals for Catholics all over the world. Christ's authority, which was given to St. Peter (the first Bishop of Rome), according to them, has descended in an unbroken line through the popes. He has been called pope (father, Greek, 'papas') since the fourth century. Important and senior helpers who carry out the executive functions of the pope are the cardinals and since the eleventh century a college of cardinals elects the pope. They are about 106 in number. In the college of cardinals, which sits in Rome, India is represented by two cardinals (of Bombay and Ernakulam). Next are the bishops who are appointed by the pope on the recommendation of senior priests. They are in charge of a group of churches known as the diocese. They ordain priests and other bishops. There are 120 bishops in India. The priest forms the broad base of the pyramid. His rights and duties are strictly regulated by canon law.

Ceremonies

Seven sacraments of the Roman Catholic Church have to be administered by a priest or bishop. Baptism is performed when a child is a few days old. It is dressed in white, signifying purity, the head is washed with water and anointed with holy oil symbolising the washing away of original sin and the sign of the cross is made on the forehead. Confirmation is performed when a child is seven among Catholics and fifteen among Protestants. He or she is taught the main tenets and obligations of the Christian faith for several months by the priest. After this instruction he is ready to be confirmed by the bishop.

Penance, which is a rite of the Roman Catholic Church, is the act of confessing one's sins to the priest, who in the name of God forgives the offender whom he reinstates in the eyes of God. He prescribes a penance also which now usually takes the form of saying various prayers. Marriage rites have to be solemnised by a priest in church. Ordination is the conferment of holy orders, consecration of an ordinee as a priest. Extreme unction is administered by a priest when a sick person is dying by anointing his body and giving him holy communion.

Priests

There are thirty-five religious orders of priests in India. Jesuits are primarily teachers, Dominicans are preachers, Franciscans lay stress on a life of poverty and simplicity and Redemptorists specialise in preaching retreats. Catholic schools and colleges are run by religious orders of priests and nuns. There are 5,789 (secular) priests in India, the majority being from rural backgrounds.

Religious priests have no personal allowance. All their expenses are provided by the Order to which they belong. There are over several thousand (religious) priests in India and more than sixty-five seminaries where training is imparted. Some of them live in cloisters and are called monks. In India there are three contemplative orders of monks — the Benedictine, Augustinians and Norbertines.

The Catholic as also the Protestant Church, is entirely dependent on donations, monthly subscriptions and the offerings on Sunday mass or service. Sometimes there is income from lands and estates.

All Roman Catholic priests are celibates, though the Vatican Council has declared that "celibacy is not demanded by the nature of the priesthood" and the "married priests are fully deserving of the Kingdom of God", nevertheless the law of celibacy has not been abrogated by the Roman Catholic Church.

Fasting is an important part of the religious life of the priest and five fasts are undertaken during the year — at Christmas, Repentance (Nineva), Lent, Apostles' fast and Assumption of Mary.

The Protestant Denomination

There are more than 5 million Protestants in India, most of whom live in the northern and eastern regions. In 1706 Frederick IV of Denmark sent out two Germans, Bartholomew Ziegenbalg and Henry Pluetschau, who established the first Protestant mission in Tranquebar in Tamil Nadu.

In India, the Protestant missionaries had also to contend with Catholics, who had been doing the work of proselytisation for many centuries and south of the Godavari had made Catholicism more or less an indigenous creed.

Among the Protestants themselves there were several divisions. After the Reformation had spread all over Europe hundreds of sects developed from the Protestant matrix. Some of these that are active in India, are the Presbyterian, Methodist, Baptist, Anglican, Mar

Thoma Syrian Church, Assembly of God and the Seventh Day Adventist.

Martin Luther had declared that the Bible, and not the Pope, was the infallible authority, and that it should be taught to the people in their own language rather than Latin. Liberated from its linguistic shackles, the Protestants took it upon themselves to spread the word of God all over the world. The Society for the Propagation of the Gospel was founded in America in 1701. A few years later, the first Protestant Mission was established in India.

The former Anglicans and most of the Protestants are now united into two great Churches, the Church of South India formed in 1847, and the Church of North India formed in 1970. The Church of North India is a union of Anglicans, British Methodists, the United Church of Northern India (Congregationalists and Presbyterians), Church of the Brethren, Disciples of Christ and Baptists. Its central body is called the Synod. The Church of South India is a union of several Protestant groups in the south and is organised along the lines of the Church of North India. These united churches are engaged in a move towards creating only one Church for India. Much has been achieved already in developing a better understanding among the Catholics, the Orthodox and the Protestants and the result is a growing spirit of co-operation and increased spiritual fellowship between these groups.

Christian missionary activity actually came to northern India with the British but the early British were indifferent and at times even hostile to the missions. They being practical business minded people and traders and having established their entrepots in India were more interested in profit than proselytisation. Consequently they adopted a policy of remaining neutral in matters of religion. On the other hand, the Spanish and the Portuguese were Roman Catholics and were committed to winning heathen souls for the pope. Their forcible conversions of the natives and their Inquisition in Goa made the Indians hate and fear them.

The missionaries, however, found a great supporter in Charles Grant, who served in Bengal as an official of East India Company. Later, despite the ban which the East India Company had placed on the entry of missionaries, William Carey arrived in India in 1799 to set up his Baptist Mission and printing press at Serampore, a Danish settlement near Calcutta. With financial help received from America, his Serampore press translated the Bible into thirty-six Indian languages. He also started a newspaper in Bengali and a magazine (which later became *The Statesman*) and established a leper asylum.

In England, more missionaries agitated against the ban which was removed in 1813 enabling many religious organisations to send missionaries out to India for evangelical and social work.

By the end of the nineteenth century many changes had occurred in outlook abroad. Churches had become more active and missionaries were extending the spiritual frontier to the East.

The Serampore Baptist Mission was largely responsible for propagating the gospel in the north-east of the country. By 1818 it was running 127 vernacular schools where ten thousand people received "simple instruction in Christian religion." The famous Serampore College was opened in 1821.

In 1833 the American Baptists went into the tribal part of Assam and central India and converted the Adivasis *en masse*. In 1846 the German Lutherans began work among the tribals in Bihar. The American Presbyterians spread out in the rural areas of north India and set up their mission in Ludhiana in 1834 and also established some missions in South India. During the 1850s the American Methodists started work in the region now called Uttar Pradesh and the American Quakers began work in Jabalpur in 1869.

The missionaries' relief work during the terrible famines and epidemics which ravaged India in the last century also caused great bitterness among other religionists. The destitute and orphans converted by them during the famines were nicknamed "Rice Christians."

There were ninety thousand Protestants in India in 1851 and by 1871 the number had doubled. More than half had been converted by American missionaries. During the famine of 1891, the Methodists converted fifteen thousand people.

In the second decade of this century, many Protestant missionaries realised that Hindu religious ideas (such as that of *bhakti*) should be utilised to present the gospel. The study of Hindu religion was thus made essential for missionaries.

The National Christian Council consists of 19 Indian Churches which include most of the Protestant Churches, the Mar Thoma Church, the Chaldean Syrian Church of the East, as well as the Bible Society of India, the YMCA, etc. Its service agencies "enjoy partnership with churches overseas." The National Christian Council's Christian Service Agency has provided massive aid and relief to the Bangladesh and Tibetan refugees.

The Methodist Church

The Methodist Church in Southern Asia (the name assumed by the Methodist Church in India in 1939) has three hundred churches and more than half-a-million members. The Methodists in India have four bishops, one each at Delhi, Bombay, Lucknow and Hyderabad. The Church has eleven conferences which send delegates to the Central Conference which is the legislative body of the Church and elects the bishops. District Superintendents preside at the quarterly conferences which are the governing bodies of the local churches.

The Anglo-Indian Community

There are over nearly half-a-million Anglo-Indians spread all over the country. The story of the birth and growth of the Anglo-Indian community begins from the founding of the British settlement at Fort St. George, Madras, in 1639, but the community actually traces its ancestry to the Eurasian and Anglo-Indian Association which was inaugurated on 16 December, 1876. The years that followed were of affluence and prosperity. Anglo-Indians, sons of British fathers, were accepted willingly into the covenanted ranks of the British services and they gave a good account of themselves in the armed forces.

From 1857 to 1919 was a period of building and development. The Anglo-Indians played an outstanding role in serving and maintaining the posts and telegraphs, customs and police services, and specially the national asset, the railways.

From 1919 to 1942, Henry Gidney, an ophthalmic surgeon, was the leader of this small community and at this critical time of political unrest, he chose to lead it to the side of the rulers. But he must have seen the writing on the wall, for he exhorted his community at Bangalore, "You have a right to live in this country and you are first and last sons of India."

In 1942, Frank Anthony was elected to succeed Henry Gidney as the president of what was then the All-India Anglo-Indian and Domiciled Europeans Association. He had the expression "Domiciled European" deleted. He began with an open letter to the community in which he spelled out the truth for the first time, "We must realise that we are of this country, we are here, for better or for worse." The die was cast.

On the eve of independence, the request for a single seat in India's Constituent Assembly was refused by the British. Frank Anthony then appealed to the generosity of the Indian leaders and his astute and convincing appeal ensured a place for his community in the Constituent Assembly as also a special position in republican India's constitution.

The Kanara Catholic Community

Soon after the capture of Goa in 1510, the Portuguese established factories at Honore, Barcelore and Mangalore in pursuance of their treaties with the chiefs of Sonda, the kings of Vijayanagar and the local chiefs. In a short period Christian (Catholic) settlements sprang up in these towns and several other places in the interior of Kanara.

To prevent the newly-converted Catholics from practising Hindu customs, the Portuguese introduced the Inquisition in Goa in 1560. Rather than be declared heretics and be condemned to death, they left Goa to settle down outside the Portuguese dominion. Large numbers went to Kanara where they were welcomed by the Bendore kings of Kanara (1565-1760), given grants of land and recruited to their regiments. There they formed a large and important community as is clear from the clauses guaranteeing their interests incorporated in the treaties concluded between the Portuguese and the Bendore Kings in 1671, 1678, 1707 and 1714.

The grants the kings made to the churches testify to the respect the Catholics commanded at the court of Bendore. Hyder Ali also confirmed these privileges. Living under the rule of these Hindu rajas, these Catholics lived on friendly terms with their Hindu neighbours whose dress, food, habits and ways of living they soon made their own.

In the last quarter of the eighteenth century Tipu Sultan of Mysore, suspecting that the Catholics were supporting the British against him, placed almost the entire population (about sixty to eighty thousand) in captivity at Seringapatnam till 1792, when those who had survived went back to Kanara where they had to start afresh as their property had been appropriated by others.

Brought up as Christians from infancy, they are characterised by their honourable principles and exemplary conduct and enjoy a high reputation among the Hindus and Muslims with whom they live. In the past they were land-holders, merchants and tradesmen and for their superior-intelligence and fidelity were employed in offices of trust under government in preference to others.

They are governed by a caste system which is akin to that of the Hindus which came from Goa with the early immigrants. The castes are Bamon (Brahmana), Charodi (Kshatriya and Vaishya), Sudra (artisan) and Gaudi (comprising local converts from the original fisher caste). Superimposed on this is another artificial division — that of the 'refined' and the 'rustic'. The members of the former, consisting of about two hundred families, live in the city, speak English and have adopted western dress and customs.

In the rural areas, they are deeply attached to farming either as tenant farmers or labourers. They have hardly any social life. Except for some parochial functions and weddings, christenings, Christmas, Easter and the parish feast are the only occasions when they have celebrations.

They eke out a frugal living on their farms and often have to supplement their income by petty trading and by sending their family members to cities for employment.

The urban members of the community are concentrated in Mangalore and are often called Mangalorean by outsiders. With the establishment of British rule, many claimed and got their property rights in the city and the district confirmed.

The prosperity of the dominant Catholic families of Mangalore since the latter half of the nineteenth century owed itself to the tile industry, coffee plantations and trade in plantation products. The tile industry was first introduced in Mangalore by German missionaries who kept their technology a secret and bought an entire village which had suitable clay for the manufacture of tiles. In course of time the Mangaloreans learnt the secret and so was born the famous Kanara tile industry. The tiles were so much in demand that the Portuguese from Goa would exchange gold for them.

Mangaloreans have helped set up colleges, schools, hospitals, leprosoria, T.B. sanitoria, asylums and so on. An expansion of education without a corresponding expansion of employment opportunities combined with pressure on land in the rural areas led to the emigration of many Kanara Catholics to cities like Bombay.

Many have been successful as trade unionists, taxi drivers, domestic servants, writers, caterers, and managers in different spheres, etc.

The record of Kanara Catholics in the freedom movement is creditable. Those who did not participate directly in the struggle helped the cause by sheltering the fighters and giving them moral and material support. Catholics have played a leading role over several decades at the village *panchayat* level and in the Mangalore municipality.

To enrich their language, Konkani, through drama, journalism and literature have been the work of a band of dedicated men and women from among uprivileged some of whom have been Alix Pais, Louis Mascarenhas, J.J. Rego, G. Rodrigues, V. Saldanha, Mark D'Souza, C.F. D'Costa, J.S. Alvares, D.P. Pai, S.S. Resquinha, M.P. D'sa, A.T. Labo, G. D'Souza, R. Miranda, J. D'Souza, Francis Fernandes, B. Mendonca, Eulalia, Alvares, Monthi Lasrado, Mabel Baretto, Betty Mazareth and Rose Kanwarstreet.

The Syrian Christian Community

The Syrian Christians of Kerala trace their origin from the time of St. Thomas, the apostle, who first came to India about AD 46 and then again to Malabar in AD 51-52 where he founded seven churches. They form about one-fifth of the country's total Christian population (over nineteen million) and theirs is one of the most ancient Christian communities in the world.

Before the coming of the Europeans, their chief vocation, apart from agriculture, was trade and commerce and a large part of Kerala's trade in pepper and other commodities was probably in the hands of Syrian Christian merchants.

There is a strong conservative streak in these Christians and some traditional practices and patterns of behaviour are still adhered to by many. A typical Syrian Christian wedding is an elaborate affair and is arranged by the elders, the girl's people making the proposal to the boy's.

The most important holy days are Good Friday and Easter Sunday. The former in Malayalam, means the 'Friday of Sorrow' and the church service held is a symbolic representation of the entire drama of Christ's suffering and crucifixion. The Easter service, which ritually tells the story of the resurrection, is more important than Christmas.

Syrian Christians have taken a leading part in the educational, medical and industrial development of Kerala. A large proportion of the schools and colleges in Kerala are run by them. The women have been among the earliest Indian nurses. Their teachers and professors have distinguished themselves all over India and they have also served in a significant way in the armed forces.

Syrian Christian Church

The Syrian Christian (orthodox) clergy have Catholics at the apex, with ten bishops (called metropolitans) for ten diocese. There may be as many as a hundred churches in one diocese, the total number of priests being about one thousand. Entrance is after the pre-university level. The training is given at the M.D. Seminary, Kottayam, where the course lasts for four years. A B.D. degree has to be obtained from the Serampore University.

The bishop is usually chosen from among the celibate priests or monks but a layman can be elected provided he obtains the B.D. degree and goes through the state mentioned earlier. The Patriarch of Syria generally consecrates the Catholics though he has no jurisdiction over the Church, which is Indian and independent.

12

ZOROASTRIANISM

ARATHUSHTRA, THE PROPHET OF ANCIENT IRAN, was born in the city of Rai on the bank of the River Darej (exact site not determinable). It is not possible to fix the date of his birth but Greek classical writers, including Zanthus, Pliny, Aristotle and Hermipus, have recorded that he lived more than six thousand years before their time. Plutarch places him at about 1700 BC Some modern Western scholars, relying on Pahlavi writers, say he lived about 600-700 BC Others relying on philological evidence, say he lived between 1,500 to 2,000 BC The language of the *Gathas,* the earliest Zoroastrian scriptures, is almost identical with Vedic Sanskrit in respect of vocabulary, grammar and syntax. Internal evidence points to the conclusion that they were composed by Zarathushtra himself.

Not many facts are known about his early life. He was born in his father, Pourushaspa's house. He was descended from the family of Spitama and, according to Pahlavi and Persian writers, his ancestry is traceable to Minocheher and Faridoon, kings of the legendary Pishdadyan dynasty of Iran.

He was brought up in the practices and traditions of the Mazdayasni faith, the followers of which were the worshippers of Mazda, the lord of creation, then the religion of the Iranians. From his childhood he had thirsted after the divine and when fifteen years old he went away in quest of the infinite and lived in jungles and mountains for fifteen years. During this period he also served the people and comforted the sick and suffering.

After this he often went into a trance to commune with the Creator. Sraosha, God's messenger, brought him the message from God (Ahura Mazda) that he had attained the stage in spiritual development where he could receive divine revelation and it was through Vohu Mano or Good Mind, the noblest archangel, that he had the vision of the Almighty.

He received all the answers to his questions from the Supreme Creator and came to know what the source and purpose of the universe was and what man's part was in the divine creation and how he could play it so as to have bliss and peace in this life and in the life to follow.

In his closest moments of communion with Ahura Mazda, he realised that the supreme attributes of Ahura Mazda are Vohu Mano or (the good mind), Asha Vahishta (the eternal principle of righteousness), Kshatra Vairya (the divine sovereignty), Spenta Armaiti (bountifulness), Haurvatat (eternal bliss) and Ameratat (immortality), which man must strive to cultivate in himself.

He pondered deeply over the problem of evil — that when Ahura Mazda was the source of all good and all bliss, where could evil and suffering come from. The answer came to him from on high that there are two bitterly warring principles : Spenta Mairyo, the good and creative, and Angre Mairyo, the evil and destructive, and that man must ally himself with the one and fight against the other, for good to triumph over evil ultimately.

After the revelation of this holy Deena or religion, he became an enlightened and realised soul. But when he started preaching the new gospel, no one heeded him and he was subjected to persecution.

After ten years, his cousin Maidhyomah became his first disciple and several other persons embraced the new religion, including his wife and daughters who became his disciples.

He says in the *Gathas* that whosoever acquires fully the knowledge of the Deena and, showing affection towards all people, performs righteous deeds and announces to the people the laws of Ahura Mazda, is a person who helps the cause.

Ahura Mazda Himself says that He has created bliss and suffering so that in the scheme of evolution man may carry on the good fight and strive after perfection. It is the consciousness of pain and misery which should make man keep to the right path, the path of Asha. They are strong deterrents without which humanity would sink into *tamas,* inertia and sin.

Angre Mainyo, the evil spirit, became angry and told him to shun the Deena and that if he worshipped him, he would be made the ruler of the material world. Zarathushtra replied that even if his bones and intellect became separate from his body and even if he lost his life, he would not forsake the holy religion.

After this he went to the court of Gusthasp of Balkh (Bactria, Central Asia) to preach the message, who received him with great honour and listened to his preaching. But the courtiers became jealous of his growing influence and popularity and as a result of conspiracies and the accusation that he was a sorcerer, he was imprisoned and persecuted. But the conspirators were exposed and he was vindicated.

He passed the rest of his life preaching his religion. When he was seventy-seven years old, Balkh was invaded by Arjasp, the ruler of the neighbouring kingdom, who hated the good religion and one of his soldiers assassinated Zarathushtra while he was praying in the fire temple. But eventually the enemies were repulsed and Zarathushtrianism continued to spread.

Today there are about 2,00,000 adherents of the faith in India, Iran, Pakistan, Britain and North America. The *Avesta,* the holy book compiled by Zarathushtra, presents an ideal belief in the resurrection of the body, the life hereafter, the coming of a saviour and the rewards and punishments for the immortal soul. The divine law of *karma* prescribes that good will come unto the good and evil unto the evil. If man makes a wrong choice, he will invite suffering on himself. He must practise benevolence and kindness to all beings, be industrious and active in the performance of his duties and be just and truthful in all his dealings.

Zarathushtra says that man should become righteous for the sake of righteousness, for righteousness is its own reward. He constantly reminds his fellow men that there is a spark of immortality in man and life will continue after death.

Zoroastrians have often been called fire-worshippers but this term is a misnomer. The Zoroastrian scriptures make it clear that

Ahura Mazda, the supreme lord of creation has created fire, just as He has created the entire universe, so they venerate fire.

The Parsi Community

When the Parsi followers of Zoroastrianism fled to India from religious persecution in Iran, they approached the Hindu king, Jaddi Rana, for shelter who, in his graciousness, gave them land for building the first fire temple at Sanjan (in Gujarat) and placed them and their successors under an everlasting debt. By contributing to the progress of the land of their adoption, the Parsis may be said to have repaid that debt in ample measure.

About three hundred years ago the Parsi settlers migrated from the towns and villages of Gujarat to Bombay and from a predominantly agricultural community, it became a highly urbanised one. The Parsis came to play a leading role in transforming Bombay into a busy and prosperous port. Among the several Parsis employed in the East India Company's dockyard at Surat was Lowjee Jusserwanjee who was so efficient in supervising the building of a ship, the *Queen*, that he was called to Bombay to establish a building yard there where he laid the foundation of an establishment which came to be considered "the finest naval arsenal in India."

His sons and grandsons continued the hard work, building over a period of 150 years, several trading ships as well as man-of-war ships which distinguished themselves in countless sea battles, so much so that the shipbuilding industry in Britain, which had monopolised the trade, became alarmed that if the policy of using India-built ships were to be continued, the families of the shipwrights in England would be reduced to starvation. But the policy was continued by the level-headed authorities of the day. A frigate, the *HMS Cornwallis*, built by the Wadias and launched from the Bombay dockyard in 1800, was purchased for the (British) Royal Navy and, as a supreme tribute to the Indian master builders, was renamed *Akbar* by the lords of admiralty.

A scion of the Wadia family, master builder Nowrojee, built the *Hugh Lindsay*, the first steamer in Bombay to make the voyage to

Suez and back in record time. On the day he died after fifty-two years of meritorious service the British Commodore ordered the dockyard to be closed and flags to be flown at half-mast on all vessels in the harbour, the only recorded instance when a private individual was so honoured.

The Parsis were also among the first to open up extensive trade in their own Indian ships with China, making and sharing large fortunes. Nearer home the Parsis took a decisive lead in industry by establishing cotton spinning and weaving mills in the latter half of the nineteenth century, several cotton and ginning factories and the earliest import and export firms. They were in the vanguard of the fight for the amelioration of the lot of mill labour and the control of child labour. Sorabji Pochkhanawala conceived the idea in 1811 of a banking institution, wholly Indian in outlook and approach, with the development of indigenous enterprise as its main objective. The well-known doctor, Temulji Nariman, founded the first maternity home in Bombay.

The Parsis played a notable part in building Bombay where many institutions, statues and roads bear Parsi names. Under the inspiration of men like Pherozeshah Mehta (recognised as the uncrowned king of Bombay), the growing city directed its energies to those primary tasks of civic administration which, when fulfilled, made it India's first city. R.P. Masani was the first Indian mayor and the first municipal commissioner to establish the supremacy of the civic body by clearly defining and demonstrating the commissioner's constitutional position as government's agent vis-a-vis that of the municipal corporation.

Rustomji Cawasji Banaji migrated to Calcutta with his family in 1838 and grew to be a merchant prince of that city. He bought the Calcutta Docking Company and together with his sons came to own twenty-seven ships in all, fifteen of which were chartered by the British government during the Chinese wars. He also founded an agiari at Calcutta and was one of the twelve justices of peace appointed by the Calcutta government in 1835. Another scion of the Banaji family, Maneckshaw Rustomji Banaji, became the first Indian sheriff of Calcutta in 1873. Prior to that he had been appointed Persian consul in Calcutta in 1870.

From Dadabhai Naoroji, thrice president of the Indian National Congress, to K.F. Nariman, who was president of the Bombay Provincial Congress Committee and led the civil disobedience movement in Bombay in 1930, to (Dr.) M.D. Gilder, one time mayor of Bombay Municipal Corporation who was the first Parsi minister in the Provincial Assembly in 1937-1939 to M.R. Masani, former leader of the Swatantra Party, the Parsis have been politically conscious and active.

India's first atomic energy establishment, located in Bombay, is named after Homi Bhabha, the great Parsi scientist who was its inspiration and head. The Tata Memorial Hospital, founded in 1931 for the systematic study and treatment of cancer, another Parsi contribution, has at its helm one of the country's best known cancer specialists (Dr) Jal C. Paymaster. Two other eminent Parsis, Jalbhai Bharda and Kaikobad Marzban were pioneers in the field of high school education, far ahead of the time.

The Bombay Samachar was started by Faredoonji Marzbanji in 1923. The first Indian-owned English newspaper, *The Bombay Chronicle* was launched by Pherozeshah Mehta. The tradition of a frank and fearless press has been kept alive by R. K. Karanjia who launched *Blitz* news magazine and later, by D. F. Karaka with *Current.*

Jamshetjee Framji Madan founded a film producing, distributing and exhibiting empire. Ardeshir M. Irani made India's first talking picture, *Alam Ara,* in Hindi. Adi Marzban has given to the stage in Maharashta a Parsi impetus.

Brilliant Parsi advocates from (Sir) Jamesetjee Kanga to N.A. Palkhivala have lent lustre to the bar and several eminent Parsi judges to the bench of the Bombay High Court.

Parsis have served with distinction in the army, navy and air force. (Field Marshal) S.H.F.J. Manekshaw (retired) played a decisive part in India's resounding victory over Pakistan in the fourteen-day war in 1971.

Today Tata and Godrej (the names of two industrial concerns) are household words. Jamesetjee N. Tata laid the foundation, at the low initial cost of twenty-one thousand rupees, of the steel industry in Bihar and conceived the hydro-electric industry. Since then Tatas have grown into a vast industrial complex, comprising a multiplicity of heavy, ancillary and consumer industries. In planning the steel city of Jamshedpur, Jamsetjee Tata gave specific instructions for laying "wide streets planted with shady trees", keeping "space for lawns and gardens" and for "football, hockey and parks" and, above all, earmarking areas for "Hindu temples, Muslim mosques and Christian churches". Ardeshir B. Godrej's decision in 1897 to make fine locks led to far-reaching consequences as Godrej steel equipment (of many varieties) has over the years become a synonym for security in the country. From safes to soaps may appear to be a far cry but it was he who also expanded the industry by adding the production of soap made purely from vegetable oils.

Godrej also was deeply concerned with the problem of industrial slums and the degradation to which they lead. The Godrej garden township at Vikhroli in Greater Bombay is the outcome of that concern. Considering human relations the first principle of management, Godrej was practically the first concern to provide such benefits as holidays with pay, provident fund, bonus, gratuity, medical and canteen facilities.

The many sided and characteristic philanthropy of the Parsis has established, through their *panchayat* system, a remarkable social security system for the community. Its members make their contributions to the local *anjuman* fund or community chest which constitutes the base of the system. At the apex is the Parsi panchayat of Bombay which attends, as far as possible, to the community's needs in the relief of poverty, assistance in education, provision for medical relief, etc.

The community has many trusts and foundations, benefiting non-Parsis as well. The earliest was the monumental N.M. Wadia Charitable Trust constituted in 1909, under a clause in Wadia's will by which the proceeds of the trust property, valued at eighty-eight lakh rupees at the time of his death, was ear-marked for the benefit of such institutions, persons, objects and purposes without distinction of place, nationality or creed, as the trustees deemed fit.

The Parsis have laid claim to no territory and to no special rights for themselves. Their sense of fair play and their philosophy of life to live and let live, which they have always practised, make them look at human relationships with a dispassionate eye.

The qualities of the community that are significant are its vitality, which enabled it to withstand history's vicissitudes, its adaptability to changing circumstances, its industry and civic sense and its philanthropy, qualities which have been inducted by its religion, which is very much a part of its life.

13

THE ARMENIAN COMMUNITY

THE ARMENIANS TRACE THEIR ORIGIN TO 3,000 BC and at one time Armenia covered nearly the whole of Asia Minor. Armenia lies between the Black and Caspian Seas and is now one-tenth of what it used to be. The Armenians are Aryans by race, Christian by religion. In fact, they claim to be the first Christian nation in the world. They came to India in the sixteenth century as peaceful traders and here they found religious and secular freedom, property and peace and India became a second home to them. They settled down in Surat, Agra, Bombay, Madras and Bengal, which were important trading centres. Today, their community is a small one, countable in hundreds. They are deeply religious and their life centres round their church.

At Agra, the capital of the Mughal empire, their advance at the imperial court was rapid: the chief justice was an Armenian who adopted the name of Abdul Hai ('Hai' means Armenian); Domingo Pires, the chief interpreter was an Armenian with a Portuguese name; the doctor of the royal *harem* was also an Armenian, Lady Juliana; Akbar's Christian wife was Mariam Begum and he had adopted an Armenian son, Zul Quarnian whose real name was Alexander.

In Surat, as in other places, the Armenians traded in precious stones, silks and spices. Surat was an important trading centre in the sixteenth and seventeenth centuries and there was a large Armenian settlement there. The English had their factory and commercial house there and the Dutch and Portuguese traders also competed with the Armenians. The Armenians built a church there just as they built churches wherever they went and they also had their own large cemetery and some of its tombstones are works of art, now preserved by the Archaeological Department of the Government of India.

In the eighteenth century, when Surat's commercial importance began to wane, the Armenians moved to Bombay which became their greatest trading centre in Western India. Here they built a church, St. Peter's, in 1796, in Medows Street and lived mostly in the area around it. This church was pulled down after 160 years and a new one built in 1957. In front of this was erected the six-storey building 'Ararat' (after the Biblical Mount Ararat in Armenia). These two buildings reflect great credit on the small Armenian community in Bombay.

In Gwalior, there was a colourful Armenian figure, Jacob Petrus, who about the time of the decline of the Mughal empire, (later half of the eighteenth century) rose to be the commander of Scindia of Gwalior's army, holding this position for seventy years.

It is said that there were at least forty Armenian officers in Jacob's army, of whom several amassed fortunes.

In the seventeenth and eighteenth centuries there were Armenian settlements at Delhi and Lucknow and also at Lahore and Kabul. But little is known about them. In these places also they built churches and had cemeteries.

The first Armenian to arrive in Madras is said to have been Thomas Cana who is supposed to have landed on the Malabar coast in 780. There were Armenians in Madras as early as the sixteenth century and there was an Armenian settlement there in the seventeenth and eighteenth centuries. The Armenians here dealt mainly in textiles, spices and precious stones and amassed great fortunes. Among them was Petrus Woskan who became a member of the Madras East India Company's Council. When the Nawab of Arcot visited Madras, Woskan is said to have draped the main streets with rich silks and to have him entertained royally. When the Nawab asked Woskan what he would like as a favour in return, Woskan asked for the monopoly of the important trade in Madras and the hinterland. His request was granted and as a result he later became a millionaire. He built the Marmalong Bridge on the river Adayar which still stands and the flight of 160 stone steps to the crest of the hill on which St. Thomas's Church was erected, on the reputed site of the martyrdom of the apostle Thomas. The first Armenian Church in Madras was built in 1712 and a second in 1772 in Armenian Street. The Armenians have considerable church property, now managed by the Armenian Association in Calcutta.

In due course the main centre of Armenian activities in India became Bengal. The Armenians first settled down in Murshidabad (the then capital of Bengal), in the seventeenth century. In the time of Clive, there was among these Armenians a Petrus Arathoon, referred to by Clive as "the Armenian Petrus" who helped in the overthrow of Siraj-ud-Daula in favour of Mir Jaffar as the Nawab of Bengal, Bihar and Orissa. He was also involved in the overthrow of Mir Jaffar.

The Armenians were among the pioneers of the jute trade in Dacca in the last century, which was monopolised by the firm of M. David and Co. and M. Sarkies and Sons and some other Armenians. The former firm is a part of Jardine Henderson and Co. and later has been absorbed into James Finlay and Co.

There were Armenians in the coal industry also. There was an Apcar and Co. which owned ships (the Apcar Line) and collieries. One of the Apcars, (Sir) Apcar Alexander Apcar, was the president of the Bengal Club and the Bengal Chamber of Commerce, the only non-British person to hold these positions. The Apcar line has become the B.I. Line. Of other Armenians dealing in coal were the Crete family and C.L. Philips. P.J. Crete donated forty lakh rupees to the Roman Catholic Church in Rome and in return the pope made him Knight Commander of the Order of St. Gregory the Great. Phillips was known as the 'coal king'.

The Armenians were among the first to deal in shellac. They owned factories and exported shellac to all parts of the world. J.C. Galstaun who started out in shellac and then went into real estate, was the richest Calcutta Armenian in his time. He is said to have built over three hundred houses and to have owned over a hundred race horses.

A. Stephen built the Grand Hotel, Mount Everest Hotel, Stephen Mansions and Stephen House, which are no more in Armenian hands, and T.M. Thaddeus built and owned Park Mansions.

What the Armenians achieved, secured and consolidated, they gradually dissipated, probably because each built for himself and so when he went the business went with him. Many have begun to move out of India but there are a few hundreds left and there is considerable wealth in their churches.

14

JUDAISM AND THE JEWISH COMMUNITY

ACCORDING TO THE BIBLE, THE JEWS DESCENDED from the patriarch Abraham, Isaac and Jacob, who probably lived around 1,800 BC They were a clan of nomadic shepherds who originated in Mesopotamia (Iraq). Led by Abraham, they settled in Israel, originally called Canaan and later Palestine.

In 63 BC Palestine came under Rome rule and in AD 70. The Romans destroyed Jerusalem and exiled the Jews from the country which was renamed Palestine. From this time till 1948, when the state of Israel was established, the area came under a succession of conquests. From this time also began the *Diaspora* (Greek, "scattered"), a continuous process of dispersion when the Jews left Palestine in large numbers and were scattered all over the Roman empire.

In Europe the Jews were persecuted wherever they settled and were discriminated against in many ways. They were debarred from most professions and from the ownership of the land, were forced to pay arbitrary taxes and to wear a distinctive dress and a badge to show they were Jews. In some cities they had to live to ghettos and had to face death, a trend that ended with the extinction of over six million Jews in fascist (Nazi) Germany.

Their association with India predates the beginning of the Christian era. The oldest communities have been the Bene-Israel, whose home has been mainly the coastal areas of Maharashtra and the Jews of Cochin.

At one time there were thirty thousand Jews in India; in 1991 there were a little more than 5,000. A large number migrated to their homeland of Israel, which was established in 1948. The Jews in India comprise three main communities — the Bene-Israel, Kerala Jews and Baghdadi Jews.

Several hundred years after the advent of the Bene-Israel and the Jews of Cochin on the soil of India, a growing stream of Jews began to arrive and settle in this country. They came from the Middle East and established themselves mainly in Bombay, Calcutta, Pune and Surat, for commercial reasons and probably to escape the persecution they were suffering in the countries where they lived. As far back as the seventeenth century, small groups of Jewish businessmen also settled down in Madras. Then, with the arrival of David Sassoon in the early years of the nineteenth century, the foundation was laid in this country of the famous business house of Sassoons. At about the same time, Jews from the Middle East also converged upon Calcutta.

In the thirties of this century, the rise of Hitler and the persecution of the Jews in Germany sent them fleeing in all directions and some sought refuge in India.

With the passage of time, while adhering strictly to their religion, the Bene-Israel and other Jews began to integrate themselves increasingly with their surroundings, adopting the customs, dress, characteristics and day-to-day practice of the people among whom they lived and worked. Having made India their home, they also began to identify themselves with the towns and villages where they had their abode. This they did by deriving a family name from that of the relevant town of village. Thus from such places as Kehim, Navgaw, Pen, Cheul and Chinchol, such names emerged as Kehimkar, Navgawkar, Penkar, Cheulkar and Chincholkar. These are used as surnames, providing the Indian touch to such Jewish first and second names as Abraham, Jacob, David, Joseph, Elijah, Solomon, etc.

8

GLOSSARY

Acharya. A spiritual or religious teacher.

Adi Granth. The 'First Sacred Book' of the Sikhs, compiled by Guru Arjun in the sixteenth century, of the hymns and teachings of Guru Nanak and his successors as well as selections from Kabir and other *bhakti* and *Sufi* mystics.

Adyars. A group of Shaivite religious leaders and thinkers.

Agni. God of fire; many hymns are addressed to it in the *Rig Veda*; personification of three forms of fire, the sun, lightning and sacrificial fire.

Ahimsa. The doctrine of non-violence, or non-injury to animals or men. Of uncertain origin, it gained popularity in the sixth century BC among Jains and Buddhists and was later adopted into Hinduism.

Ahl-i-hadis. Originally the jurists who laid greater emphasis upon *hadis* (the traditions of the Prophet) than upon their own interpretation; in later days, in the sub-continent, the school which does not bind itself to any of the recognized schools of jurisprudence and believes in independent interpretation; the school is commonly called *ghair-muqallid*, "those who do not follow others".

Ahmadiyya. A nineteenth and twentieth century Muslim reform movement centering about the figures of Mirza Ghulam Ahmad; also referred to as the Qadiani movement.

Aiyar. A Brahman caste-cluster from Tamil Nadu worshipping Siva more than Vishnu.

Akali Dal. A Sikh party of the Punjab, founded before Independence, advocating a separate Punjabi speaking state that was established in 1966.

Aligarh Movement. A Muslim movement in the latter half of the nineteenth century encouraging Western education for Muslims and leading to the founding of the Anglo-Oriental College of Aligarh in 1875.

Amrit. Nectar.

Ambedkar, Bhimrao R. (1891-1956). Maharashtrian leader from a mahar (untouchable) caste, who opposed Gandhi by advocating separate electorates for untouchables, was chairman of the drafting committee for the new Indian constitution, first Minister of Law, who resigned after the failure of the Hindu Code Bill, publicly espoused Buddhism, and urged others to do likewise.

Amir Khusrow (c. 1254-1324). Muslim poet, musician, historian, and mystic who flourished during the Delhi Sultanate, studied Indian music, and introduced changes that made it acceptable to Muslim society.

Arhat. A Jain saint.

Arya Samaj. A religious movement founded by Swami Dayananda Saraswati in 1875, that tried to effect social and religious change through the elimination of caste, the denunciation of rituals and idols, and promotion of the Vedas as the ultimate source for religious authority.

Ashivins. Gods of healing.

Ashram Shalas. Hostels attached to ashrams.

Asoka (d. 232 BC). Mauryan emperor who came to power c. 269 BC and expanded the empire until after the conquest of the Kalinga, when he became deeply influenced by Buddhism and developed a policy of non-violence and tolerance.

Asuras. Denotes enemies of Gods.

Atharva Veda. The fourth and last of the Vedas compiled later than the other three and containing many non-Aryan elements such as spells and incantations employed in popular rather than ceremonial religion.

Aurangzeb or Alamgir (1618-1707). Mughal emperor and orthodox Muslim who began ruling India in 1658 after he had deposed his father Shah Jahan. He extended the empire to include Bijapur and Golkunda, yet his administration was unstable, partly because of his religious intolerance, and even before his death, the Mughal empire began to disintegrate.

Avarna. Casteless.

Baditeej. A rite celebrated on the third of *Bhadrapada* of the *Vikram Samvat* year when women pray for the longevity of their husbands.

Baniyas. Banians, Hindu traders.

Barat. Marriage Party.

Bhagavad Gita. Lit. Song of the Lord, regarded by Hindus as the very word of God, a philosophical interlude, forms part of the famous epic *Mahabharata*; completed sometime in the second century it received its present form in the third century. It is a dialogue between Arjuna and Lord Krishna on the eve of the battle of Kurukshetra. The central theme of the *Gita* is that one must do his duty in complete disregard of the consequences.

Bhakti. Fervent devotion to God.

Bhandaras. Store-keepers.

Brahmo Samaj. Society of the worshippers of God, a movement founded in 1828 by Rammohun Roy. The movement was eclectic in its religious outlook and style of worship, and it respected human reason. After the death of Rammohun Roy the movement broke into several factions.

Buddha-Gaya (Bodh-Gaya). The site in modern Bihar in which Siddhartha Gautama received enlightenment; a sacred pilgrimage center for Buddhists (not to be confused with neighbouring Gaya, a Hindu pilgrimage site especially important for final rites offered on behalf of deceased relatives).

Caliph (*Khalifa*). A representative or successor, the title adopted by the rulers of the Islamic community indicating, that as successors of Muhammad, they were both spiritual and temporal leaders. After the destruction of the Abbasid Caliphate in 1258, the title was held by various rulers, including the Ottoman sultans; the office is referred to as the Caliphate or Khilafat.

Chaitanya (1485-1533). A Bengali Vaishnava saint whose hymns and poems extol the love of Radha and Krishna. He preached that through love, song and dance, man could experience the personal presence of God and asserted that true religion transcends barriers of caste and sect.

Dasam Granth. (lit. Tenth Granth). It was written by the tenth and the last guru of the Sikhs Govind Singh (1666-1708). Guru Govind Singh knew Sanskrit,. Persian and Arabic and wrote inspiring poetry of great literary excellency in Punjabi.

Dayabhaga. One of the two principal divisions of Hindu Law, the other being *Mitakshara. Dayabhaga* by Jimutavahana (tenth century) is a commentary on the Srutis especially on Manu.

Dayananda Saraswati, Swami (1824-1883). Founder of the Arya Samaj in 1875 that claimed ultimate religious authority resided in the Vedas. Dayananda and his followers opposed idol worship, untouchability, child marriage, subjugation of women, and hereditary caste because they were not taught by the Vedas.

Dharma. Signifies code of conduct of the individual or group as found in the *Dharma Shastras,* Law scriptures.

Dharma Shastras. Ritual canon; whole body of scriptures dealing with the religious ceremonial and practice of Hinduism.

Dhammapada. (lit. meaning the Law Path), the best known of the Buddhist canonical texts. It is a collection of over four hundred aphoristic verses collected from the sayings of Buddha.

Din-i-Ilahi. 'Divine faith', an eclectic religion established by the Mughal emperor Akbar in 1582 that included elements of Hinduism (fire sacrifice ceremonies), Zoroastrianism (fire worship), Christian (baptism), as well as Islam. The cult, centering around Akbar himself and stressing a simple monasticism, rapidly faded away after Akbar's death.

Dravidian. A large language family.of the Indian subcontinent. Completely unrelated to Indo-Aryan, although there has been some mutual borrowing of sounds and vocabulary, it includes the four major languages: Tamil (Tamil Nadu), Telugu (Andhra Pradesh), Kannada (Mysore), and Malayalam (Kerala) as well as Toda and Kota (Nilgiri hills), Kondh or Kul (Orissa), and Brohui (Baluchistan). Dravidian languages are characterized by retroflex consonants and the lack of aspirate consonants. Telugu, Kannada and Malayalam have all been strongly influenced by Sanskrit vocabulary.

Durga Puja. A ten-day Bengali festival in October commemorating the ten-day battle and ultimate triumph of the goddess Durga over a demon.

Fa-hien (AD fourth-fifth century). Chinese Buddhist monk who travelled in India 401-411 during the reign of Chandra Gupta II in search of Buddhist scriptures. The diary of his travels gives much information about temples, monasteries, and Buddhist legends but little about social or political conditions.

Fiqh. Islamic jurisprudence, or the science of interpreting the *Shariat;* there are four orthodox schools: Hanafi, Hanbali, Maliki and Shafii. The sources of the Fiqh are the *Quran,* Hadis, Ijma and Quias.

Ganesa. Elephant-headed god (also known as Ganapati) identified as Siva's son who is 'Lord of Obstacles' and is worshipped at the beginning of ventures so that hindrances might be removed. Not attested before the fifth century.

Ganges (Ganga). A major river of North India considered especially sacred. Its alluvial plain is among the largest and most densely populated in the world and was the core site of Vedic and classical Indian civilization.

Garbhadhana. 'Womb-placing' in ancient times, a husband approached his wife ceremonially, massaging his body, chanting certain *mantras* praying for the birth of a child.

Ghazal. A lyrical ode, following a set pattern of rhyme, aa, ba, ca, da, ea, fa, etc. Usually a *ghazal* is a love poem, but occasionally, it has been utilized for other purposes as well.

Granth Saheb (Guru). It is the most holy book of the Sikhs. It is written in old Western Hindi, Marathi and in some parts in Persia. It is composed of the writings and sayings of the gurus as well as of other saints and reformers who lived before Guru Nanak.

Hadis. A tradition of the Prophet, a report about some saying or action of his, which, if recognized to be authentic, is considered to be a fundamental source of law; its authority, however, is subordinate to an injunction contained in the *Quran.*

Haj. The annual pilgrimage to Mecca on the 9th day of *Dhu-I-Hijja,* the month of the *Haj.* It is compulsory at least once in a life time for those who can afford it.

Hardwar (Haridvar). Hindu pilgrimage centre; located near the place where the river Ganges emerges from the Himalaya mountains.

Hijrah-hijra and hegira. The flight of the Prophet from Mecca to Medina, which is the beginning of the Hijrah era of the Muslims.

Hinayana. The lesser vehicle, the orthodox form of Buddhism.

Hindwi or Hindavi. The language of Hind, applied more particularly to the north dialect written in adapted Arabic script, the fore-runner of Urdu.

Huien Tsang (c. 600-664). Chinese Buddhist pilgrim who travelled to India AD 630-643 to collect Buddhist books, images and artefacts. The diary of his travels provides information about life in India at the time of Harsha.

Ijma. The consensus of the Islamic community as a source of law.

Ijtihad. The endeavour of human reason and knowledge to understand the application of a religious injunction to a particular situation, interpretation.

Imam. A leader of the Islamic community; among the Shias the descendants of Ali.

Isma'ilis. The followers of Isma'il, believers in his apostolic succession according to the Shi'ah theory of the imamate. They are also called the sect of the seven, because they believe in

Isma'il being the seventh imam and his being followed by cycles of seven imams in eternal succession.

Ithna'asharis. Believers in twelve imams. They reject the imamate of Isma'il. They form the larger wing of the Shi'ahs.

Japa. Prayer.

Jata. Caste.

Jihad. Literally: "the utmost endeavour", mainly used for taking up arms in a righteous cause, which is sometimes called *jihad bi's-saif,* "the utmost endeavour with the sword".

Jizyah. A poll-tax levied upon able-bodied *zimmis* who can afford to pay the tax after the satisfaction of their needs. Priests, hermits, servants of the state, cripples, women and children are exempt.

Ka'bah. The sacred shrine at Mecca.

Kabir (1440-1518). Bhakti mystic who attempted to synthesize Hinduism and Islam. He renounced rituals but spiritualized *yoga* and proclaimed this inner *yoga* to be the only way by which one might know God.

Kali. Goddess black in colour, wife of Siva, depicting one of the terror aspects of Sakti or divine energy. She wears a necklace of human skulls; holds a sword and dagger in her two hands, while in the other two are severed heads dripping blood.

Kalidasa (c. 400). Sanskrit writer of the Gupta period whose famous poem is the *Meghaduta* ('Cloud Messenger') and whose best known drama is *Sakuntala.*

Kama. The Hindu god of love whose bowstring is made of bees and whose arrows are flowers; frequently appearing in literature and legend, Kama is associated with an ancient spring festival.

Kama Sutra. A text on erotics (c. 300-500) attributed to the sage Vatsyayana, designed for the cultivated townsmen and courtesans as well as married couples of the Gupta period.

Kanyadan. Virgin-giving or formal gift of the daughter to the bridegroom.

Karma. Literally 'deed' or 'action'. The pan-Hindu law of moral causality that states that man's deeds in his present life have consequences and influence his life and status in this and subsequent lives.

Karma Yoga. One of the main forms of yoga which aims at salvation through deeds. There are many other forms of yoga such as *bhakti yoga*, salvation through faith, *gyan yoga*, through knowledge, *mantra yoga*, through mantras or spells, *hatha yoga*, through physical culture, *raja yoga*, through spiritual culture.

Karma Yogi. A person who strives to attain salvation through good deeds.

Karewa. Sanskrit: to offer, also to perform.

Karim. Benign, one of the names of God.

Kayastha. A caste-cluster of writers, village record keepers, and government officials. Known from the Gupta period (AD fourth-fifth century), they served the Mughals and other rulers in various parts of North and Central India.

Kevala. Trance.

Kevalin or Kaivalin. Those who have achieved a state of Kaivalya, i.e. realization of their own self.

Khan, Sir Syed Ahmed (1817-1898). Prominent Muslim leader who initiated the Aligarh movement and founded the Anglo Oriental College at Aligarh. He opposed Muslim participation in the Indian National Congress, favoured cooperating with the British, and urged that Western learning be introduced alongside traditional Islamic studies.

Khanqah. A hospice where the sufi Shaikh and his disciples live.

Khariji. A Muslim sect which does not believe in the canonical necessity of the *Khilafat.*

Khasi. An Austro-Asiatic language of the Mon-Khmer group spoken in Assam, not closely allied to the Mon-Khmer languages of Burma, Thailand, and Vietnam.

Khojah. An Isma'eli Shi'ah sect that migrated to Western India, especially Punjab and Sind, where they have become traders and merchants. The Aga Khan is the leader of their chief branch.

Khuda. God

Khwaja. A Persian title of respect. In the Sultanate it was used for the officer in each province who kept the revenue accounts.

Kolkali. A dance form developed by Moplahs in which 12 men with sticks and tiny cymbals attached dance in a circle.

Krishna. A heroic figure of Indian mythology, seen as an incarnation of Vishnu, with Mathura (Muttra) on the Yamuna river his alleged birthplace. Krishna's life is the subject of much literature and art in later medieval India (post-ninth-tenth century) including Krishna as child god, as pastoral divine lover, and as hero.

Kshatriya. A ruler of the ruling varna; the second of the four main ranks of traditional Hindu society. The function of Kshatriyas was military protection.

Kubera. The Hindu god of riches and treasure, guardian of the northern quarter, also well known in Buddhism and Jainism; usually dipicted as a dwarf.

Kuf. Adequate (companion for marriage); the doctrine which encourages marriages between groups which are compatible.

Kulin. Brahman 'noble', Brahaman subcaste.

Linga. Phallic symbol worshipped as representing the presence and power of the deity. *Lingas* date from the Harappan civilization; they are most commonly connected with Saivite cult practice.

Lingayat. An anti-brahman Saivite devotional (*bhakti*) sect following the teaching of Basava (twelfth century), whose members frequently wear a Siva *linga* as a sign of their affiliation. Lingayats are concentrated in Mysore, and much of their religious literature is in Kannada.

Madhyamika. A school of Mahayana sect founded by Nagarjuna (AD 100-200).

Madurai (Madura). An ancient temple city in Tamil Nadu located on the banks of the Vaigai river, once capital of the Pantiya dynasty, famed for its large temple to the goddess Minakshi.

Mahabodhi Temple. 'Temple of the Great Enlightenment'; located at Buddha-Gaya; originally early Tupta, restored many times by pious Buddhists.

Mahadeva. 'Great Lord'; an epithet describing one of the aspects of Siva.

Mahant. Head of a monastery or *math.*

Mahayana. The greater vehicle, that form of Buddhism which adopted beliefs and practices originally foreign to it.

Mahabharata. One of the two great epics of India, the other being *Ramayana.* It is world's longest epic. Its author is said to be the sage Vyasa who composed it in 24,000 verses; now it totals 1,10,000 couplets. The epic is woven around the great battle of Kurukshetra between Pandavas and Kurus which is ascribed to the period 850 BC and 650 BC.

Makar Sankranti. A new year festival celebrated on the first day of the solar month of *Magh* (between January 12th and 14th), a great mela is held at Prayaga (Allahabad) called *Magh Mela.*

Maliccha: also *Malishta.* An unclean outsider, used for non-Hindus.

Mahavira (c. 540-468 BC). 'The Great Hero', a title given to Vardhamana, the founder of Jainism. He renounced earthly life, begged for his food, wore no clothing, and through these methods became conqueror of his body and achieved *nirvana.*

Mama-pheras. A marriage custom when the maternal uncle takes the bride round the bridegroom four times.

Mandapa. The assembly hall in which worshippers gather in a Hindu temple. Originally, the hall was separate from the *sanctum sanctorum;* later it was connected by a vestibule.

Manjusri. The *bodhisattva* of meditation or Supreme Wisdom whose function is to stimulate understanding; portrayed in art with a sword to destroy error and a book to enlighten all men.

Mantra. 'Instrument of thought'; a general term for any sacred text or sound, syllable, word, or verse believed to have a spiritual or temporal effect when repeated; often used in meditation.

Mara. Destroyer, Evil One; according to Buddhist legend, the tempter and enemy of the Buddha and his religion who, by appealing to Siddhartha Gautama's sensual and material instincts, tried to dissuade him from renouncing the world.

Maruts. A group of Vedic gods who accompanied Indra across the sky in their chariots, singing martial songs, and epitomizing the recklessness of the storm.

Marwari. An inhabitant of the region of Marwar in Rajasthan. The term has come to designate the trading castes that spread from this area to urban centres throughout India.

Masnad. Literally "support"; a seat with a cushioned support used for a gubernatorial throne.

Matha (Mutt). A Hindu monastery; such monasteries began to flourish in the Middle Ages when they functioned as refuges for monks and learning institutions for the young.

Mathura (Muttra). A city and religious centre in north-central India on the Yamuna river; noted for being the birthplace of Krishna.

Maya. Creative power (of a god), magic, trick, illusion, etc. A key concept based on its earliest meaning, namely: creative power and activity of a god to manifest phenomenal reality. This is 'illusion' when not understood by normal men. Later philosophy particularly that of Shankara and his followers, used this term to denote the existential ('illusory') status of the phenomenal world.

Mecca. Holy city of the Muslims; scene of the Prophet Muhammad's first preaching; direction faced in prayer and pilgrimage goal of many Muslims throughout the world.

Medina. City in Arabia where Muhammad took up residence in AD 622, after he had fled his persecutors in Mecca.

Mimamsa. 'Enquiry, investigation'; probably the most conservative school of the six *darsanas*; an exegesis of the ritual portions of the Vedic literature.

Mirabai (b. 1550). A Rajput widow who, in spiritual life, became the bride of Krishna and left a legacy of devotional (*bhakti*) love poetry.

Mitakshara. One of the two main divisions of Hindu law; a commentary on Yajnavalkya written by Vijnanesvara (eleventh century).

Mleccha. Literally 'barbarian'; non-Aryan, or foreigner; any person who does not speak Sanskrit and does not conform to Hindu norms.

Moharram. 'That which is forbidden' (or sacred); the first month of the Muslim calendar; also the Muslim festival during the first 10 days of that month commemorating the martyrdom of Husain, grandson of Mohammad, observed primarily by *Shi'ahs*, but also by some *Sunnis.*

Mohed. A Zoroastrian priest.

Moksha. A 'letting go' or a 'release'; the ultimate goal of the Hindu religious life; release from the cycle of reincarnations and the consequences of causality.

Moplah (Moplpila). A group of Muslims living on the Malabar coast of India, whose uprising in 1921 seriously damaged national efforts at Hindu-Muslim cooperation.

Muhtasib. An officer under Muslim governments who prevented the committing of any public nuisance or flagrant and wilful breach of the moral code and law.

Mujahid. One who struggles against infidels on behalf of Islam, derived from the Arabic word 'to exert oneself vigorously against, to fight against'.

Mujahidin. Plural of Mujahid.

Mujtahid. One who is competent to undertake *ijtihad,* one who actually undertakes *ijtihad.*

Muni. Sage, seer, ascetic, first mentioned in the *Rig Veda,* as a class of non-brahman escetoris holy personages. Later *muni* came to be a general term for a holy man, often suffixed to the name of a revered author of a sacred Sanskrit work.

Murid. Disciple.

Muwwahhid. A monotheist. The Druz use it for one who has reached the highest stage in spiritual progress and attained freedom for exoteric as well as esoteric bonds of religion.

Naga. One of a group of tribes inhabiting hilly territory in extreme eastern India, originally head-hunters, later largely converted to

Christianity. Some Nagas have sought independence from India.

Nagaland. India's sixteenth State, a hilly territory in extreme eastern India on the Burmese border, populated by several tribal groups collectively known as Nagas, some of whom have sought independence from India.

Nagarjuna (AD second century). (Buddhist monk who founded the *Madhyamika* school of philosophy and developed the doctrine of Sunyata ('emptiness') as the school's central concept.

Naksatra. The series of 27 (or 28) constellations comprising the ancient Indian astronomical system and serving as a basis for astrological prediction.

Nalanda. Buddhist monastery and centre of learning in Bihar, founded in AD fifth century., offering training in both Buddhist and Vedic knowledge, and continuing till destroyed in 1197 by the Muslim invasions.

Namdev (fifteenth century). Maharashtrian *bhakti* saint, supposedly of low caste, who attempted to bring Hindus and Muslims closer together; also a poet who played a part in the development of early Urdu.

Naman. Caste mark of Vaishnavites. Three lines, one red perpendicular and two white at an incline meeting at the base and forming a sort of trident.

Narayana. Deity mentioned in Brahmana literature who come to be identified with Vishnu.

Nastika. A category describing non-orthodox Indian philosophical schools. The term...from *na-asti* meaning 'it is not'...refers to those schools that do not accept the authority of the Vedic-Upanishadic traditions and hence are not regarded as conveying true philosophic knowledge.

Natya Sastra An authoritative work on drama, dance and music, the authorship of which is attributed to Bharata; it was probably compiled in the early centuries of the Christian era.

Nayar (Nair). A caste-cluster in Kerala claiming Kshatriya status with a matrilineal family structure, unique in its absence of an institutionalized husband father role.

Nibbana. Extinction.

Nirvana. A 'blowing out'; in Buddhism it refers to final release from transmigration by extinction of desires and passions and the giving up of the illusion of selfhood. It refers to the state of bliss transcending all categories of existence.

Niyoga. Similar to system of levirate of ancient Jews legalized by many by which a man could have intercourse with his childless brother's widow or the wife of an impotant kinsman, in order to raise issue for the other's family without incurring any sin.

Om (Aum). Mystic monosyllable and sacred explanation, the object of profound religious meditation and reverence throughout Hindu India, taken to symbolize all sound and reality.

Padma. Lotus.

Padmasambhava (AD eighth century). An Indian prince, turned Buddhist monk and missionary who carried Buddhisnt to Tibet AD 750

Pali Canon. The collection of Buddhist scriptures consisting of three major divisions (baskets or *pitakas*) preserved by the Theravada school, according to the Sinhalese tradition committed to writing in Ceylon in AD first century.

Panchatantra. 'Five treatises', a collection of fables intended mainly for the instruction of kings and ministers in worldly affairs. The fables are prefaced by a king's concern over the ineptitude of his sons and his commissioning of a sage to instruct them.

Panchayat. A generally-recognized authority group within a caste or village or extending over several castes or villages that settles disputes, regulates moral conduct, and establishes standards for dowry, *jajmani* relations, etc. Although the term 'panchayat' suggests a council of five, the actual number of panchayat members varies widely depending on local circumstances and the particular case being reviewed.

Panda. A priest serving in a temple or at a pilgrimage site.

Panini (end of AD fourth century). One of the world's greatest grammarians, whose *Astadhyayi*, analysing and standardizing the

Sanskrit language in 4,000 succint rules, has provided a model for grammarians ever since.

Panth. 'Path'; a sect, custom, or religious order.

Parinirvana. 'Final blowing-out'; the death and entry into final bliss of a being who in his lifetime has attained perfection (*nirvana*). The term is used specifically to describe the death of the Buddha.

Pardah. 'Screen, curtain, veil', the seclusion of women, a custom observed by many Muslims and imitated by some higher caste Hindus.

Parvati (Uma). Wife of Siva, 'Daughter of the Mountain', so named because she is the daughter of Himalaya. Parvati tried to win the love of the ascetic Siva, succeeding only after she became an ascetic. Their son, the war-god Skand, rid the world of the evil demon Taraka.

Pasupati. 'Lord of Beasts'; an epithet of Siva signifying that he is the patron god of reproduction in animal life. In sculpture this is represented by a four-armed man in a posture of blessing, while from one of its hands a small deer springs.

Patanjali (second century BC). Grammarian, author of the *Mahabhasya*, who commented on both Panini and Katyayana in order to criticize and expand their grammars.

Phiran. Kashmiri dress.

Pinda. Rice cake.

Pir. The spiritual leader of a Sufi order; more generally an Islamic saint.

Pitha. A sacred place of pilgrimage.

Pongal. The festival of Pongal is celebrated in South India on the advent of the new year and coincides with Makar Sankranti of north India, i.e. first day of the solar month of *Magh* (between January 12th and 14th).

Prajapati. 'Lord of Creatures'; chief god of later Vedic mythology, regarded as the primeval person and protector of life, who was sacrificed and dismembered in the world's creation.

Prakrti. 'The original or natural form, primal substance'; in philosophical systems, especially *Sankhya*, 'nature' or the physical world as opposed to *purusa*, the realm of the spirit.

Prana. A term adopted for all vital airs but especially to the wind that has its seat in the heart and is also called *asu* breath.

Prithvi. Earth, goddess who in the *Rig Veda* is paired with Dyaus (heaven) and who as the mother of all existence symbolized fertility.

Preta. 'Spirit', i.e. of a dead person. Certain rites are performed to help the *preta* or spirit to become a *Pitri* or ancestor.

Pujari. One who conducts worship in a Hindu temple.

Purana. 'Ancient Story'; the 18 main Puranas are the sacred texts of popular Hinduism. Compendia of legends and religious instructions, they contain much ancient material but in their present form they date back to earlier than AD fourth century.

Puri Jagannath. A festival celebrated at Puri, Orissa in June/July, when the image of the god Jagannath, his brother, and his sister are paraded through the streets on a huge temple chariot.

Pururavas. Hero of an ancient Indian legend extending back to the *Rig Veda* (X, 95) and the *Satapatha Brahmana*, and retold by Kalidasa.

Purus(h) 'Person', in early Indian mythology it signified the Prima Man from which all other men sprang. In philosophical discourse it came to describe the essential soul (*purusa*) which is at rest as opposed to the existential world which evolves (*prakrti*).

Pushan. A god frequently referred to in the Vedas, worshipped by the Aryans; a nourisher of all created beings, shown as carrying an ox-goad and riding in a cart drawn by goats.

Qazi. A judge.

Qiyas. One of the sources of the *fiqh*; the principles of applying *hadis* to new situations by the use of analogy.

Prayas-Chitta. 'Penance', Ceremony of purification performed when a person does a thing regarded as taboo according to scriptures.

Quran. Holy book of the Muslims who believe it to be the very word of God; a revealed book sent down in Arabic through the Angel Gabriel to His Messenger the Prophet Muhammad, a person of about 20 years from about AD 610; the original key in Heaven as a well-guarded tablet. The record of Muhammad's inspired utterances, found not only in the memories of men but according to later traditions, written on shoulder blades, palm leaves and stores were collected after his death under the third Caliph Usman (644-655) and found into the authorised version of 114 Suras or chapters.

Radha. Divine love and consort of Krishna, whose longing for union with her lord exemplifies the *bhakti* ideal of the worshipper longing for union with God.

Rahim. Merciful, one of the names of God.

Rajput. A name given to the princely houses of Rajasthan as well as to members of a caste-cluster claiming descent from those houses. Rajputs typically claim to be of the Kshatriya *varna.*

Raksasa. One of the main characters in Visakadatta's Sanskrit drama 'The Signet Ring of Raksasa'.

Rama. Hero of the *Ramayana*; virtuous king of Ayodhya, who underwent voluntary exile to enable his father to keep a promise. He is regarded by Indians as the epitome of justice and virtue and is identified as the 7th incarnation of Vishnu.

Rama Lila. 'Rama's sport'; a dramatic festival occurring in villages and cities of North India during the latter part of September or early October, portraying events from the *Ramayana.*

Ramayana. One of the two great Epics of India, the other being *Mahabharata.* It is said to have been composed by the sage Valmiki. The oldest part of *Ramayana* dates back to 350 BC.

Ramakrishna Paramahansa, *Sri* (1836-1886). A Bengali saint and devotee of the goddess Kali, who through bhakti and austerities experienced union with various forms of God including non-Hindu forms. Swami Vivekananda, his most famous disciple, founded the Ramakrishna Mission Movement.

Rani. The consort of a raja, a ranee.

Ratri. The goddess of night to whom a hymn is addressed in the *Rig Veda.*

Ravana. The demon king and villain of the *Ramayana* epic, who abducted Sita and carried her to his kingdom in Sri Lanka. In the end of the epic, Ravana is destroyed by Rama.

Rig Veda. The first and most authoritative of the four Vedas which is ascribed to the period 1500 to 2000 BC, holy books of the Hindus, is composed of hymns and psalms of praise to the gods, recited by the sages, which was orally passed from generation to generation till finally it had a fixed test some 300 BC.

Rishi. A class of semi-legendary patriarchs and anonymous sages.

Rudra. A Vedic god who according to legend lived in the mountains, was an excellent bowman, and evoked fear among men who wished to avoid his arrows of disaster. After Vedic times he beeame less significant, but many of his aspects were assumed by Siva.

Sadhu. A Sanskrit term meaning 'good' 'virtuous', commonly used to refer to a saint or holy man especially one who has renounced the world.

Sadr-u's-sudur. The highest religious dignitary of the Muslims under Muslim governments in the subcontinent. He was the head of the department of religious affairs.

Sagotra. Of same gotra.

Saivite. A devotee of god Siva, the cult of the Siva worshippers dating from before the Christian era and representing aspects of popular religion from Kashmir to South India. In the latter region one of the most prominent sects of the Saivites, the Saiva Siddhanta, developed c. eleventh century.

Saiyid. A descendant of the Prophet.

Sakti. 'Energy or potency', a little ascribod to a god's wife — more specifically to the consort of Siva — who represents the energy and activity of god. In early medieval India her cult was popular.

Saktaism. The cults of goddess worshippers. In Hinduism they centre around the wife of Siva; in Buddhism, the cult centres around tantric groups that employ sexual symbolism and sexual practices as means of salvation.

Sakyamuni. A name designating Gautama the Buddha; Sakya was the tribe or clan over which Suddhodhana, Gautama's father, ruled. *Muni* means 'sage', hence Sakyamuni means the 'sage of the Sakyas'.

Sama Veda. Book of chants drawn largely from the hymns of the *Rig Veda* and employed by a special group of priests, the *udgatr.*

Samhita. A 'putting together', i.e., a compilation; or collection; specifically, the four collections of verses consisting of the respective Vedas.

Samsara. The cycle of transmigration in which the soul of any living thing continually dies and is reborn. Salvation in Hinduism involves release (*moksa*) from the cycle of transmigration.

Samskaras. Sanskrit term commonly translated as sacrament is applied to the rituals observed during any of the transitory phases in the life of a Hindu.

Samidheni. Special sacred chants.

Sanchi. Village located in Madhya Pradesh, site of a famous Buddhist stupa dating from the third century BC.

Sangha. The order or brotherhood of Buddhist monks, entrance into the order was achieved by shaving the head, donning the ascetic's robe, and accepting the precepts. Despite no central governing authority, the monastic rules of the *Vinaya Pitaka* kept a certain degree of uniformity within the Sangha.

Santour. A musical instrument.

Sanyasin (Sanayasi). The fourth *asrama* or stage of life in which a man completely renounces his ties with the world, becomes a homeless wanderer, and practises asceticism.

Saptapadi. Seven steps. Refers to Hindu custom of taking seven steps before the fire by the bride and groom together. Each step represents a particular blessing, namely food, strength, wealth, happiness, progeny, cattle, devotion.

Sastra. Treatise, instruction, code; a text containing materials of political, legal, and moral nature, sometimes an expansion and versification of an earlier *Sutra.*

Sayyid *(Syed).* A chief; also a name used by those who claim descent from Husain, the son of Mohammad's daughter, Fatima.

Samana. Social gatherings referred to in ancient society of pre-Aryan days when a sex goddess was worshipped. One of the main objectives on these occasions was the wooing of lovers for possible matrimony.

Shaikh. 'Old' man', a term used for a *Sufi* who guided disciples; also used to denote a caste or class among Indian Muslims.

Shankara (AD 788-820). A Brahman worshipper of Siva, a philosopher, and founder of the *Advaita Vedanta* school. He advocated a strict monism that allowed no second principle alongside the Absolute, *Brahman.*

Shar'a. Islamic Law.

Shariat (Sharia). The law of Islam, governing all the rules that govern life.

Shi'a. A Muslim sect which believes that the *Khilafat* should have been hereditary and limited to the House of 'Ali.

Siapa (Punjabi). Beating of breasts as a sign of mourning.

Sitala Devi. Sitala, 'Cool', goddess of small-pox propitiated in eastern, western and central India.

Sufism. The doctrines, principles, and practices of Islamic mystics (Sufis) stressing the immanence rather than the transcendence of God. The name is derived from the Arabic word for 'wool' characterising the garments these mystics wore in protest against many of the worldly ways of their fellow men. The Sufis were outstanding Muslim missionaries in India beginning c. twelfth century.

Suhrawardi. One of the orders of Sufi mystics, concentrated largely in the region of Sind.

Sunni. 'One of the path'; one of the two major sects of Islam, distinguished from the Shi'ahs in that the Sunnis recognise the

first four *Khalifas* (Caliphs) as the rightful successors of Mohammad.

Svetaketu. Son of the saint Uddalaha, authority on Vedic ritual;
author of a treatise on *Kama Sutra* mentioned in the epic *Mahabharata.*

Silsilah. Literally "chain", "continuation", used for a brotherhood
of Sufis following the same techniques of spiritual development.

Sunnah. The traditions of belief and action established by the
Prophet considered to embody tho interpretation of the revelation contained in the *Quran.*

Tali or *Mangalasutra.* A little golden or gold-coloured ornament on
a gold chain known as 'tali' tied around the bride's neck, a relic
of ancient *devadasi* rite.

Ta'ziyah. A model of the tomb of the martyred Husain, grandson
of the Prophet Muhammad, usually made of wood and paper
and carried in Muharram processions in India.

Tazkira. Literally "narration", often used for accounts of Sufis.

Tirathankaras. 'Ford finder' or ford makers, the title of Jain
patriarchs of the highest order because they show men the passage through the dark waters of life. There are supposed to be 24
tirathankaras.

Tirupati. A city and important Vaisnavite pilgrimage centre in
Andhra Pradesh.

Tukaram (1598-1649). A Sudra, *bhakti* poet-saint of Maharashtra
who used Islalmic as well as Hindu symbolism.

Tulsidas (1532-1623). Author of the popular Avadhi (Hindi
dialect) poetic version of the *Ramayana,* the *Ramachari-
tamanasa,* and several other works dealing with the Rama legend.

'*Ulama* (*Ulema*). 'Ulama is the plural of '*alim*', one who knows, a
learned man, applied more commonly to a doctor of Muslim
law and theology.

Tithe. According to Hindu system of reckoning a lunar year has
354 to 360 days, based on lunar months. A lunar day is called a
tithi or *tithe.*

Upanishad. A 'Sitting Near', referring to a student sitting near his teacher. The Upanishads are a series of 108 treatises, the approximately 15 oldest and most important of which were composed c. 600 — 300 BC. In them are first presented such central Hindu doctrines as transmigration and the unity of *Brahman* and *Atman*.

Valmiki. Ancient sage and reputed author of the *Ramayana*; legendarily a contemporary of Rama who gave refuge to Sita when she was banished from Ayodhya.

Varuna. A diety of Aryans; Prince of Oceans commanding white horses; ultimately received the worship of fishermen.

Vedanta. 'End of the Vedas', referring to the Upanishads, that represent the culmination of the Vedic scriptures. More specifically one of the six darsanas of Indian philosophy evolving c. seventh century and elaborating philosophical speculations begun in the Upanishads.

Vamamargi. A follower of the left-hand path, applied to those followers of Tantric Hinduism who indulge in sexual orgies as the highest form of worship.

Vidya Mandir. A temple of learning, applied to schools established under Gandhi's Wardha Scheme of education (*Vidya*-learning, *mandir* is a Hindu temple).

Vishnu. A Hindu diety worshipped as early as Vedic times and popularly conceived as the 'preservers' of the universe. He and his Avataras (incarnations), including Rama and Krishna, played an important part in *bhakti* (devotion) movement.

Vikramasila. Buddhist monastery and centre of learning in Bihar; one of the foremost *Vajrayana* monasteries from which missionaries carried *Vajrayana* Buddhism to Tibet in the eleventh century.

Visvadeva. A comprehensive term applied to a group of minor gods.

Visvamitra. One of the greatest *rishis* of the Hindu mythology; guru of Rama, in the epic *Ramayana*; also figures in the *Mahabharata*.

Vyana. *Vayu* or wind which moves all over the body, has its seat in the genitals, according to some.

Varatam. Religious prayer normally performed by ladies.

Wahhabi. A sect of Muslim puritan revivalists, founded in Arabia in the eighteenth century by Muhammad bin Abdul Wahhab. The Wahhabis emphasized the unity of Allah, the right of the individual to interpret the *Quran* and the *Hadith* and rejected the four orthodox law schools. The movement first came into India c. 1804 in Bengal.

Yajna. Sanskrit term commonly translated as sacrifice; one of the main pillars of the Vedic religious system.

Yoga. 'A Yoking'; one of the six *darsanas* that emphasized psychic training 'yoking' the soul to the divine as the chief means of salvation. The basic text of the *Yoga Darsana* is the *Yoga Sutra* of Patanjali. Any act of discipline — either mental or physical — whereby the soul of man is 'yoked' to the divine and is freed from earthly confinements.

Zakat. The Muslim poor rate, being 2½ of all wealth owned continuously for a year.

Zamindar (Zemindar). A landlord.

Zamindari. The rights of a zamindar in his land.

Zimmi. A non-Muslim living in the protection of Islam, a non-Muslim resident of a Muslim state whose authority he recognizes.

BIBLIOGRAPHY

Hinduism

Barth, A., *Religions of India*. Varanasi, Chowkhamba Sanskrit Series Office, 1963, xxiv, 309p.

Bloomfield, Maurice, *(The) Religion of the Veda*. Delhi, Indological Book House, 1972, ix, 300p.

Chatterjec, Satischandra, *Fundamentals of Hinduism*. Calcutta, Das Gupta, 1950, xiv, 177p.

Chattopadhyaya, Sudhakar, *Evolution of Hindu Sects*. New Delhi, Munshi Ram Manoharlal, 1970, xii, 216p.

Dandekar, R.N., *Some Aspects of the History of Hinduism*. Poona, the University, 1967, 142p.

Farquhar, J.N., *Outline of the Religious Literature of India*. Delhi, Motilal Banarsidass, 1966, xxviii, 451p.

Jacobs, Hans, *Western Psychotherapy and Hindu Sadhana*. London, George Allen & Unwin, 1961, 231 p.

Lajpat Rai, *(A) History of the Arya Samaj*. New Delhi, Oriental Longmans, 1967, vi, 217p.

Mascarenhas, H.O., *Quintessence of Hinduism: The Key to Indian Culture and Philosophy*, Bombay, Rev. Bento D'Souza, 1951, vii. 118p.

Malledevaru, H.P., *Essentials of Virasaivism.* Bombay, Bharatiya Vidya Bhavan, 1974, 136p.

Pandey, Raj Bali, *Hindu Sanskaras.* Benaras,Vikrama Publications, 1949, xxvii, 546p.

Radhakrishnan, S., *Hindu View of Life.* New York, George Allen & Unwin, 1957, 133p.

Ramakrishna Mission Institute of Culture, *Religions of the World.* Calcutta, 1938, 2 vols.

Ross, Floyd Hiatt, *(The) Meaning of Life in Hinduism and Buddhism.* London, Routledga & Kegan Paul, 1952, xi, 167p.

Shivapadasundaram, S., *Saiva School of Hinduism.* London, George Allen & Unwin, 1934, 189p.

Wilson, H.R., *Religious Sects of the Hindus.* Calcutta, Susil Gupta, 1958, viii, 221p.

Zachner, R.C., *Hinduism.* London, Oxford University Press, 1962, 272p.

Jainism

Jain, Champat Rai, *Fundamentals of Jainism.* Meerut, Veer Nirvan Bharti, 1974, 121p.

Jain, Kailash Chand, 1930, *Lord Mahavira and His Times.* Delhi, Motilal Banarsidass, 1974, xx, 406p.

Ramaswami Iyengar, M.S., *Studies in South Indian Jainism.* Madras, Hoe, 1922, xx, 327p.

Sen, Amubyachandra, *Schools and Sects in Jaina Literature.* Calcutta, Vishva Bharati Book Shop, 1931, vii, 47p.

Buddhism

Bapat, P.V. ed., *2500 Years of Buddhism.* New Delhi, Publications Division, 1959, xxiv, 499 p.

Conze, Edward, *Buddhism.* 2nd ed. Oxford, Bruns Cassirer, 1953, 212 p.

Coomaraswamy, A.K., *Living Thought of Gotama the Buddha.* London, Cassell, 1948, x, 224p.

Grimm, George, *Doctrine of the Buddha.* Berlin, Akademic-Verlag, 1958, vi, 413p.

Hamilton, Clarence, H., *Buddhism in India,* Ceylon, China and Japan: A Reading Guide. Chicago, 1931, viii, 107 p.

Herold, A.F., *Life of Buddha.* London, Charies E. Tuttle, 1961, xi, 286p.

Jacobson, Nolan Pliny, *Buddhism: The Religion of Analysis.* London, George Allen & Unwin, 1906, 202p.

Kern, H., *Manual of Indian Buddhism.* Varanasi, Indological Book House, 1968, 149p.

Lamotte, Etienne, *Spirit of Ancient Buddhism.* Venezia, Instituto Perla Colla-borrazione Culturale, 1961, 65p.

Malalsekera, G.P. ed., *Encyclopaedia of Buddhism.* Colombo, Government of Ceylon, 1961, 152p.

Rhys Davids, T.W., *Buddhism.* London, Society for Promoting Christian Knowledge, 1893, viii, 250p.

Shastri, Ajay Mitra. *(An) Outline of Early Buddhism.* Varanasi, Indological Book House, 1965, viii, 176p.

Thomas, Edward, J., *History of Buddhist Thought.* London, Routledge & Kegan Paul, 1951,xvi,316p.

Sikhism

Archar, John Clark, *(The) Sikhs in Relation to Hindus, Moslems, Christians and Ahmadiyyas.* Princeton, University Press, 1946, xi, 351p.

Doabia, Harbans Singh, *Introduction to the Philosophy of Sikh Religion. Based wholly on divine hymns; god, maya and death.* Chandigarh, Harbans Singh Doabia Satwant Kaur Charitable Trust, n.d. 184p.

Fauja Singh et. al., *Sikhism*. Patiala, Punjabi University, 1969, xvii, 161p.

Khushwant Singh, *The Sikhs*. London, George Allen & Unwin, 1953.

Macauliffe, Max Arthur, *(The) Sikh Religion: Its Gurus, Sacred Writings and Authors*. Delhi, S. Chand, 1963, 6 Vols.

Mcleod, W.H., *Guru Nanak and the Sikh Religion*. New Delhi, Oxford University Press, 1968, ix, 259p.

Teg Bahadur, 9th Guru of the Sikhs, 1621-1675, *Hymns of Guru Teg Bahadur: Songs of Nirvana*. Translation and commentary by Trilochan Singh. Delhi, Sikh Gurdwara Management Committee, 1975, xvi, 257p.

Islam

Ansari, Ghaus, *Muslim Caste in Uttar Pradesh: A Study in Cultural Contacts*. Lucknow, Folk Culture Society, 1960, 83p.

Azad, A.K., *Tarjumanul Quran*. Translated by Abdul Latif, Bombay, Asia, 1960, 92p.

Aziz Ahmad, *Islamic Modernism in India and Pakistan, 1857-1964*. London, Oxford, 1967, xi, 244p.

Aziz Ahmad, *Muslim Self Statement in India and Pakistan, 1851-1968,* edited by Aziz Ahmad & Von Grunebaum G.E. California, the University, 1970, 240p.

Fyzee, A.A.A., *A Modern Approach to Islam*. Bombay, Asia, 1963, viii, 127p.

Gibb, H.A.R., *Mohammedanism: A Historical Survey*. New York, Mentor, 1958, 206p.

Hollister, John, N., *The Shias of India*. London, Luzac, 1953, xiv, 440p.

Hughes, T.P., *Dictionary of Islam*. Delhi, Oriental Publishers, 1974. 758p.

Imtiaz Ahmed. ed., *Caste and Social Stratification Among the Muslims*. Delhi, Manohar Book Service, 1973. xxxiv, 256p.

Ivanow, W., *A Guide to Ismaili Literature*. London, Royal Asiatic Society, 1933. 138p.

Karandikahn, N.A., *Islam in India's Transition to Modernity*. Bombay, Orient Longmans, 1968. xviii, 414p.

Miller, Roland Eric, *Mappila Muslims of Kerala: A Study of Islamic Trend*. Delhi, Orient Longmans, 1976. xvi, 350p.

Misra, S.C., *Muslim Communities in Gujarat*. Bombay, Asia, 1964, xvi, 207p.

Mujeeb, M., *The Indian Muslims*. London, George Allen & Unwin, 1967, 590p.

Ram Gopal, *Indian Muslims: A Political History*. Bombay, Asia, 1959, x, 351p.

Smith, W.C., *Islam in Modern History*. London, Oxford University Press,1957, 317p.

Titus, Murray, T., *Islam in India and Pakistan*. Calcutta, YMCA Publishing House, 1959.

Walter, H.A., *The Ahmadiya Movement*. London, Oxford University Press, 1918. 185p.

Christianity

Brown, Lestie, W., *The Indian Christians of St. Thomas*. Cambridge, Cambridge University Press, 1956.

Church of South India, *(A) Brief Report of the Missionary Work of the Church of South India*. Madras, Church of South India Synod Board of Missions,1949, xii, 94p.

Dawe, Donald, G., *Paul Interpreted for India*. Patiala, Punjabi University, 1973. 135p.

Gandhi, M.K. *Christian Missions*. Ahmedabad, Navajivan Press, 1941.

Pickett, Jarre!l, W., *Christian Mass Movement of India*. New York, Abingdon Press, 1957.

Plattner, Felix, A., *Christian India*. New York, Vanguard Press, 1957.

Thomas, Paul., *Christians and Christianity in India and Pakistan.* London, Allen & Unwin, 1954.

Zoroastrianism

Balsara, Pestanji Phiroz Shah, *Highlights of Parsi History.* Bombay, K & J Cooper, 1964, 92p.

Bulsara, Jal Feeroso, 1899, *Social Reform Among the Parsis.* Delhi, Delhi School of Social Work, University of Delhi, 1968, 50p.

Dhalla, M.N., *History of Zoroastrianism.* New York, Oxford University Press, 1938, 525p.

Kulke, Eckehard, *(The) Parsees in India: A Minority as Agent of Social Change.* Delhi, Vikas Publishing House, 1974, 300p.

Modi, Jivanji, J., *(The) Religious Ceremonies and Customs of the Parsees.* Bombay, British India Press, 1922, 484p.

Nanavutty Piloo, 1914., *(The) Parsis.* New Delbi, National Book Trust, 1977, viii, 191p.

Taraporewala, I.J.S. ed., *Avesta Gatha, the Divine Songs of Zarathushtra.* Bombay, Taraporewala, 1957.

WOLVERHAMPTON
LIBRARIES

CONTRIBUTORS*

Chapter 1: Hinduism

Mahadevan, T. M. P.; Singh, Dr. Karan and R. G. K.

Chapter 2: Hindu Religious Orders and Movements

Chauduri, M. Singh; Hyder, Qurratulain; Nag, Jamuna; Narendra, K.; Ramanathan, K. N. and Sharma, J. M.

Chapters 3 to 6: Hindu Communities

Ali, S. Rifaquat; Anzar, Naosherwan; Azhicode, Sukumar; Banerji, Usha; Bond, Ruskin; Chettur, Usha; Chhabra, Lakshmi; Chopra, S. K.; Cox, Linda; Dayal, Chandravati; Desai, Bhishma; Deshpande, Gauri; Diggavi, R. C.; Doctor Geeta; Dutta, B.N.; Gandhi, Arun; Ganguly, Subal; Gowda, Annaiah; Gupta, Badlu Ram; Hiremath, Dr. R. C.; Jain, S.L.; Kaur, Jagdish; Kar, Subrata; Krishna, Prakash; Kuntia, D. C.; Kuttaiah, Ranee; Lakhotia, R. N.; Mellow, S. Melville de; Mookerjee, Ajit; Nag, Surabhi; Pandit, Avinash; Pant, Ila; Patil, Vimla; Rai, Amar Nath; Rajabhoj, P. N.; Raman, A.S.; Rao, H. K.; Rao, Padma; Sanyal, Shubi; Sarukkai, Saroj; Sen, Arati; Shetty, Rajshekar; Shroff, Hiro; Singh, Dr. Tajvir; Singh, Natwar; Singh,

---

*The various chapters in this book have been largely based on articles contributed by these authors to the *Illustrated Weekly of India*. In spite of our best efforts we could not trace the names of some of the contributors to whom we express our apologies. .

S. K.; Singh, Dr. Teg Vir; Sitaram, Uma; Srinivasachar, S.; Sundar, Pushpa; Suryavanshi, G. S.; Tungar, W. N.; Vohra, S.G.; Yadava, Dr. K. C. and Zelliot, Eleanor.

Chapter 7: Jainism

Doshi, Sarayu; Jain, Ashayakumar; Jain, S. C.; Kora, Kantilal D.; Rangoonwala, Firoze and Singh, Khushwant.

Cbapter 8: Buddhism

Krishna, R. Gopal and Sheth, Jyotsna.

Chapter 9: Sikhism

Dhillon, G. S.; Gargi, Balwant; Kalra, Inder Singh; Kalra, J. S.; Kohli, Mohindar Pal; Rehill, Gurdial Singh; Singh, Amarjit and Singh, Khushwant.

Chapter 10: Islam

Abdulla, V.; Ahmad, Syed Shahab; Ali, Hashim Amir; Bamzai, P. N. K.; Chopra, Hira Lal; Dasnavi, S. S.; Hyder, Qurratulain; Jamal, Shireen; Thedore, P. Wright Jr. and Zakaria, Rafiq.

Chapter 11: Christianity

Hyder, Qurratulain; J. B. C.; Mathai Samuel; Mellow, Melville de; Monterio, John; Rao, Elizabeth; Thomas, P. and Verghese, Jamila.

Chapter 12: Zoroastrianism

Karanjia, B. K.; Karkaria, Bachi J.; P. J. S. and Shroff, Phiroze J.

Chapter 13: The Armenian Community

Basil, Martin.

Chapter 14: Judaism and the Jewish Community

Japhett, M. D. and P.J.S.